EDGE OF MINISTRY...
THE CHAPLAIN STORY

Chaplain Ministry of the United Methodist Church: 1945-1980

JACK S. BOOZER

BOARD OF HIGHER
EDUCATION AND MINISTRY

NASHVILLE

Library of Congress Catalog Card Number
84-070728

COPYRIGHT 1984 BY BOARD OF HIGHER EDUCATION AND MINISTRY, THE UNITED
METHODIST CHURCH

ISBN 0-938162-02-0

MANUFACTURED BY PARTHENON PRESS AT
NASHVILLE, TENNESSEE, UNITED STATES OF AMERICA

Contents

Preface

Among the millions of bits of stock film footage universally used by film makers, few are as familiar or as compelling as the depiction of the explosion of a nuclear weapon. We flinch in horrified fascination at the blinding flash, the power of the shock waves smashing outward and the irresistible suction as air rushes into the vacuum created by the blast, then watch the upward blossoming of that monstrous signature of the atomic age, the towering mushroom cloud. We are shocked, fascinated, repelled.

Much more came to an end in 1945 with the introduction of nuclear weaponry than World War II. Gone also was the innocent belief that at the end of a war, life could again return to normal. Blasted away was the feeling of invulnerability provided by our oceanic isolation. Gone in a blinding flash were the simple verities by which we structured our individual lives and our personal relationships. Blown into dust were the certainties by which we ordered our lives as nations.

Now there was one undeniable truth with which to come to grips . . . the inevitability of change. Now there was a new characteristic required to be a successful human being . . . the ability to live tentatively, to be at home in a world of constant and often radical movement in every sphere of life. Leaders could no longer be identified by their list of certainties. Rather, we learned to prize those persons who could live comfortably and creatively in the midst of ambiguity and change.

The church and its approach to ministry was no less affected than our general society by the surging waves of change. The first unavoidable task was to probe the past for its values. The second task became to explore the future for its potential. Radical advances in communications made it impossible for the church to avoid knowledge of the rapid changes in our society, the problems

5

plaguing our communities and the communities of the world, and the impact which a now permanent involvement with the cultures of the world was making on our culture. Our identity, our sense of purpose, our operational style as the Church . . . all of these became subjects for scrutiny and possible change. Our world changed, and so did the Church!

It is this period of stress and change beginning with the end of the second world war and moving to the present time that this book seeks to explore. While a great deal has been written about ministry in the local church during this period, little if any attention has been given to those pastors of The United Methodist Church involved in ministry beyond the local church. Such ministries have as their aim to extend the body of Christ beyond the walls of the local church and into needy corners of the world. Neither these ministries nor their ministers need to be glorified. But, because they are a part of our total United Methodist heritage, they do need to be acknowledged and understood.

Several years ago, in preparation for the bicentennial of our denomination, a task force of pastors in appointments beyond the local church was assembled to discuss what a history of this special community ought to look like. Several ground rules were established. Neither a mere chronological account of events and persons nor a clustering together of anecdotal material about chaplain ministry would be acceptable.

What was needed, the task force decided, was a thoughtful and carefully researched manuscript which considered chaplain ministry not in isolation, but within the context of its total political, social, cultural and religious environments. The variety of chaplain ministries was to be faithfully represented through the direct involvement of persons involved in those ministries. In addition, the church was to be faithfully represented as it identified and supported these ministries, particularly through the Commission on Chaplains of the Methodist Church, later to become the Division of Chaplains and Related Ministries, the Board of Higher Education and Ministry of the United Methodist Church.

Primary data about chaplain ministry were gained through a systematic sampling of persons involved in the variety of extension ministries during the time period being considered. The responses gained were carefully tabulated and studied in terms of their specific information and general impressions about chaplaincy and in light of their historical context. In addition, chaplains were asked to identify their special problems and concerns and to deal with their relationships, positive and negative, with both their annual conferences and the Division of Chaplains and Related Ministries.

Finally, it seemed critical to the task force that a careful look be given the theological foundations which undergird all of Christian ministry and so, by definition, the work of chaplain ministries as well.

The result is a powerful examination of one of the most profoundly troubling and dynamic periods in American history, an exploration of the currents swirling about the Church and its ministries, and a thoughtful look at those persons who served our denomination and our Lord in appointments beyond the local church during that unique and difficult era. It is a history that helps us to look back with greater clarity in order that we may look ahead with greater wisdom.

The Division of Chaplains and Related Ministries is deeply indebted to the members of the History Task Force whose unselfish offering of time and advice over a period of several years helped insure the accuracy and completeness of this volume. We also appreciate the willing support and thoughtful information of the chaplains who shared in the survey process. Our greatest debt, however, is to Dr. Jack Boozer, Charles Howard Candler Professor of Religion, Department of Religion, Emory University, whose scholarship, persistence, intensity and love of chaplain ministry made this volume possible. With this book, Dr. Boozer has given the entire Christian community an invaluable instrument for measuring its life and ministry.

Division of Chaplains and Related Ministries
Nashville, Tennessee

Introduction

My own interest in writing this short history of the United States in the twenty-five years following World War II is to explore two questions. . . .

First, why did the United States, exactly as it became the most heavily armed and wealthiest society in the world, run into so much trouble with its own people?

And second, what are the possibilities, the visions, the beginnings, of fresh directions in this country?

(Howard Zinn, *Postwar America, 1945-1971*)

No understanding of American history is possible without a clear awareness of the religious forces that have continually molded American expectations and social structures. This relationship has not always been for the good. America has had its share of religious as well as political chauvinism. But the relationship has been there; the historical past with all its implications for creating a future correlation between religion and culture is available to us.

(Thomas M. McFadden, *America in Theological Perspective*)

Jaroslav Pelikan, Sterling Professor of History at Yale, was honored by the National Endowment of the Humanities with the invitation to deliver the twelfth annual Jefferson Lecture in the Humanities in the spring of 1983. For his overall theme he chose "The Vindication of Tradition." In discussing these lectures with a reporter he mentioned a passage from Goethe's *Faust.*

What you have as heritage,
Take now as task;
For thus you will make it your own.

As personal testimony, Pelikan said: "If anything is the motto of my life, that's it.[1]

In the pages that follow we will honor that theme in terms of

---

[1]*Chronicle of Higher Education,* Vol. XXVI, No. 10, May 4, 1983, p. 5.

citizenship in the United States, membership in the Christian church, and the relation between religion and the state in our critical and perplexing era. We will claim that recovery of the heritage is critical for America's future, but with equal conviction, will insist that the changes in human history in the last fifty years are so revolutionary that recovering that heritage must take account of our changed situation. That task of recovering, preserving, and renewing the heritage is shared by all sincere patriots as well as by all Christian believers.

For these reasons, this is one of the most stimulating and most perplexing times to be a citizen of the United States and to understand oneself as a Christian. We will see that most Americans did not realize at the time, that the end of World War II marked a decisive turning point for the United States and for the relations between membership in a religious community and citizenship in the state, and between religion and culture in the United States. Under the euphoria of ecstasy that attended the end of World War II, only a few visionaries sensed that the American people were passing unawares through a doorway into what Robert Bellah so aptly called the "third time of trial" of the American republic.[2] Having passed through that doorway, the American people found the door closed behind them. This meant that is was no longer possible to return to "life as usual;" to the pervasive confidence in America's purity, innocence, and "manifest destiny" to carry the cause of faith and civilization to the lesser nations of the earth. So, too, the door was closed against any return to the informal establishment of White Anglo-Saxon-Protestant Christianity which had prevailed for decades in spite of the existence of Jewish, Roman Catholic, liberal, humanistic, and scientific centers of influence and power in different places in the nation. The door was also closed against understanding America as God's Kingdom, as many religious people had done.

In the unbounded happiness of the people over the end of the war in 1945, any sense of criticism or awareness of flaws in American life was altogether obscured by pride in a magnificent

---

[2]Robert Bellah, *The Broken Covenant* (New York, 1975), p. 1. Cf. below p. 44ff for a discussion of the three times of trial.

accomplishment, the defeat of two formidable enemies who not only threatened the United States but also shook the foundations of Western culture. During the dark days of Hitler's threat to England, Sir Winston Churchill could not hide the urgency he felt when he made an impassioned appeal to President Franklin D. Roosevelt for help in saving civilization. He said as much again on March 23, 1944, in a speech to American forces in Great Britain.

"In these weeks that are passing so swiftly I see gathered here on English soil these soldiers of our American ally preparing themselves to strike a blow for a cause which is a greater cause than either of our two countries has ever fought for in by-gone days. . . . You have a great part to play. . . . Soon you will have the opportunity of testifying your faith in all those inspiring phrases of the American Constitution, and of striking a blow which, however it may leave the world, will, as we are determined, make it a better and broader world for all."

Having just "saved civilization" by defeating the most serious challenges to Western culture in the last millennium and, in the process, having sacrificed lives and wealth in that effort, the people of the United States were ready to point out flaws in other countries, but were largely oblivious to anything amiss in the United States. The facts were clear. American heroism had saved all nations from demonic monsters and had thereby won the privilege of setting the conditions for *pax Americana* throughout the world.

The wide disparity between the success of America and Britain, and the failure of other countries to stand against the menace, enabled Americans to bask in the light of righteous superiority and to locate evil altogether in nations other than the United States. Even the generous response of America to the needs of ravaged and destroyed nations contributed to this mood of justified and righteous superiority.

The struggle against Germany and Japan assumed a particularly religious dimension, as divine succor was sought for the loss of many lives, and as divine favor was sought for the cause of America. This was also seen as the cause of God and of the church. "The collapse of European order, the rise of Hitler, and other ideological challenges led Americans to a new concern for their national heritage, including its religious traditions."[3] Indeed, the total claims of Germany and Japan caused many in America to interpret the war in primarily religious terms (a war for God, a Holy War), and to interpret victory as God's vindication and preservation of America against godless "principalities and powers" in the world.

With the joy of victory and the end of the war, there was, then, not only thanksgiving to God, but a renewed sense of divine favor on the United States as a nation. Citizenship took new and special meaning in what Sidney Mead would later call "a nation with the soul of a church."[4] The clear implication was that although all citizens participated in the religious substance of American culture, those who attended worship and supported the churches were the most real and genuine patriots. With such a mood prevailing, it is no wonder that Americans exaggerated their righteousness as well as their knowledge, and began to offer American answers to all human problems.

Gradually, however, all of that began to change, at first imperceptibly, then finally in an undeniable and public way. Americans were stunned during the Korean campaign that any kind of propaganda or "brain-washing" could cause Americans in military service to lose confidence in their country. When many of our captured men died in enemy prisoner of war camps, apparently losing the will to resist ("give up itis," as it was called by some), and when some of our military personnel refused return to the United States in exchange of prisoners at Panmunjam,[5] there was a strong reaction, perhaps an over reaction. This reaction took the form of an extensive re-education program in citizenship through a "Code of Conduct" for all persons in military service.[6]

Increasingly, young people raised questions about the draft and required military service. Persons in minority groups who felt that they did not enjoy full citizenship in the United States began to raise questions as to why they should be expected to sacrifice

---

[3]Sydney E. Ahlstrom, *A Religious History of the American People* (New Haven, 1972), p. 950.
[4]Sidney E. Mead, *A Nation with the Soul of a Church* (New York, 1975).
[5]Cf. Virginia Pasley, *21 Stayed* (New York, 1955).
[6] In 1955 the President of the United States prescribed a Code of Conduct for every member of the armed forces of the United States who was in combat or in captivity.

themselves for the nation. That theme was picked up on college campuses throughout the country and gave added impetus to the civil rights movement. The nation that appeared as altogether righteous in 1945 seemed to the youth of the 1950's and 1960's to be unable to guarantee the elemental civil rights of the ballot, and equal access to education and health care.

With the Vietnam War, the right of the nation to ask any of its youth to risk their lives in "defense of America," and the right of the nation to ask anything of a person who did not enjoy full citizenship were questioned in such a powerfully combined way that the federal government lost much of its legitimacy in the eyes of many American youth. Later, revelations of official lying and calculated deception in connection with Vietnam and Watergate threatened to destroy the American people's confidence in the legitimacy of the claims to "righteousness" for the American Government.

A similar thing was happening in the religious life of the American people. The favor of God was accepted in its traditional forms, and efforts were made to tie religion more closely to the success of the nation. "Under God" was added to the Pledge of Allegiance so that a person pledged allegiance to the flag and to the nation for which it stands, "one nation, under God, with liberty and justice for all." Religious services were conducted in the White House and Will Herberg wrote of Protestantism, Catholicism, and Judaism as representing three different forms of devotion to the ultimacy of the American way of life.[7] President Eisenhower proclaimed: "Our government makes no sense unless it is founded on a deeply felt religious faith—and I don't care what it is."[8] Many Americans immediately sensed what he meant, and agreed.

Yet there were increasing numbers of people, who, for different reasons, expected more of their nation and of their religion than that. During the 1960's and 1970's, those expectations began to take tangible form under the generalized impression that the human life-world had changed in a fundamental way with the Holocaust and Hiroshima. This meant that not only was the door closed against a return to pre-World War II assumptions, but also

---

[7] Will Herberg, *Protestant-Catholic-Jew* (Garden City, 1955).

[8] Quoted by Dirk W. Jellma, *Christianity Today*, Vol. X, No. 16, May 8, 1961, p. 3.

that pre-war attitudes toward the nation and toward God were, for many, no longer legitimate because of Christian complicity in the Anti-Semitism that contributed to the Holocaust and because of the introduction of nuclear weapons in warfare by the United States.

The ecological movement was developing on the positive side at the same time, showing the physical interdependence of all life forms in an ecosphere. What ecology began to demonstrate in the physical environment, made vivid by poisoned land, streams, and air, others began to claim in the economic, psychological, moral, and religious environment of the life-world. The emergence of the "third world" of the European Economic Community and of the World Bank, indicated that the economic strength of each nation affected the welfare of other nations.

The Holocaust became the most tragic event of modern, if not all, human history because it showed a capacity for evil far beyond human imagining. It also demonstrated in stark horror what is possible if primal inter-human bonding is subordinated to religious, national, cultural, and ethnic affiliations. With the cost of religious and ethnic exclusiveness made so clear, the Post-Holocaust situation requires an explicit effort to cultivate the life and person affirming qualities of human interdependence among all religious, ethnic, and national groups. The attack upon the human dignity of anyone because of race, religion, or citizenship is indeed, an attack on the integrity of all groups. Martin Niemoller's sensitive confession about Nazi Germany suggests as much:

> "When they came after the trade unionists I did not protest, for I was not a trade unionist. When they came after the Jews I did not protest, for I was not a Jew. When they came after the Catholics I did not protest, for I was not a Catholic. Then, when they came after me, there was no one left to protest."

Robert Jay Lifton has called what happened at Hiroshima and in the Nazi death camps "psychic numbing," which he describes not as submission to the "death instinct" but primarily as a new cultural phenomenon of all-encompassing terror. This destroys all symbols and structures that relate persons to reality and to one another. In these situations, persons suffer "an absolute lose of the sense of human continuity," a destruction of all sense of relation "to the activities and moral standards of the life process."[9] The struggle for human meaning is decisively altered by the arrogant destruction of human solidarity in the Holocaust.

Hiroshima became a symbol of nuclear destructiveness so catastrophic that persons inside and outside religion began to abandon all forms of Just War theory and to seek other ways of resolving disputes between peoples and nations. At the time of the Hiroshima weapon in 1945, there was limited knowledge of the threat of radiation to the human environment. Since 1945, with the continued development of nuclear energy for both military and civilian use, many persons, including doctors, scientists, and military strategists have begun to question the nuclear development. This is not only because everyone is likely to lose a nuclear war, but also because of leaks, breakdowns, and after-the-fact discoveries of the destructive effects nuclear power plants have for civilian use.

In light of the Holocaust, Hiroshima, and a host of domestic and international crises since 1945, it can be argued that we have passed through a revolution as significant, cosmically, as the Copernican revolution (which saw the sun and not the earth at the center of the cosmos) and as significant, politically and religiously, as the American Revolution. The revolution through which we have been living during the last forty years has placed the survival of humanity in a habitable life-world as the one overriding moral, political, and religious issue which affects people of all nations, religions, and cultural groups. In the 1940's and 1950's only a few with peculiar insight recognized this new revolution. Although many had a sense that we must find new ways of acting politically in the United Nations, religiously in the ecumenical movement, and ethically in the human rights movement. During the last twenty years, however, the universal implication of population explosion, contamination, hunger, sexism, racism, poverty, and violence have forced most people to begin to think in terms of global interdependence.

The primary effect of this revolution in culture and consciousness

---

[9]Robert Jay Lifton, *Death in Life* (New York, 1967), pp. 501ff.

is the recogition of the solidarity of all persons in inter-human bonding, the interdependence of all national and racial/cultural groups, and the possibility of destroying civilization by destroying the "life-world" which sustains humanity. This means that whatever forms of racial, religious, or national identity continue to exist must be tempered by an enlightened responsibility of all groups for the common life-world. In such a situation, there is no meaningful victory of one group over another if the conditions for everyone's survival are destroyed.

The threat of nuclear war on the one hand, and the loss of all relation to human continuity and community on the other hand, present us with issues of such comprehensive magnitude that they transcend differences and barriers between nations, religions, or ethnic groups. Patriotism, competition, national and self-interest, as well as loyalty within a religious faith do not disappear in the new situation. Instead, they assume different forms when *evil* is primarily understood as destroying persons and the human life-world and *good* is primarily understood as preserving persons and the human life-world. Indeed, protecting the frontier of the human becomes a critical and essential aspect of protecting the borders of a nation or a group.

The early relation between religion and the state in the founding of the United States now becomes relevant in a new and different way within this revolution of human inter-dependence. Thomas McFadden affirms the continuing importance of that relation. "No understanding of American history is possible without a clear awareness of the religious forces that have continually molded American expectations and social structures."[10] But the relation must be understood within the new situation. We have suggested that a "loss of legitimacy" struck both the church and the state in the decades following World War II, largely because of abuses and over claims by both institutions. That does not mean that the need for the state or for a vigorous religious community has in any way diminished. On the contrary, there is a new urgency about the cultivation of the relation between faith and citizenship. An enlightened grasp of the significance of the American experiment

---

[10]Thomas M. Mcfadden, *America in Theological Perspective* (New York, 1976), p. vii.

to assure the rights of all persons is a needed corrective to the derogatory and exclusive claims of some religious groups.[11] A vital religious commitment to the reign of God that stands over the nation is an important factor against identifying one's nation with the reign of God.

The altogether new situation of human solidarity and interdependence presents both the nation and the church with an opportunity to regain credibility and legitimacy. This can be done by appealing to the deepest and most profound dimensions of patriotism and faith, and by setting the life of the nation and the church within the purpose of God for all people in all nations. Without implying that they grasped everything that was happening, we are impressed that the clergy who are the subjects of this study sensed both the flaws and the strengths in American culture and in the church. They show an awareness of flaws in the state by performing a Christian ministry among those who are crushed or made marginal by this culture, the so-called "throw-away people." They affirm confidence in the integrity of American citizenship by using the instruments of political, moral, and economic authority and accepting public responsibility for using these instruments in ministry to people.

They acknowledge flaws in the church by stepping outside the life of the "gathered church" to express the power and presence of God to the abused, the isolated, and the abandoned. They affirm confidence in the legitimacy of the church by basing their life and work on the church's confession of the holy and universal love of God. They, more than most, have affirmed the heritage, not by slavish devotion to words, but by applying the vision of the nation and of the church to the present plight of many people.

The persons in the study are chaplains, clergy who have given their lives to serve the institutions of American culture and also the people of the United States, especially those people who have known quite limited happiness in American culture. Neither the story of these people nor of their clergy has been adequately told. The purpose of this book, thus, is threefold: 1) to give a voice to

---

[11]News almost everyday carries word of another exclusive religious vigilante group identifying America's enemies variously as liberals, Jews, Blacks, Catholics, Homosexuals, etc.

many unknown clergy who convey worth and love upon persons in hospitals, jails, prisons, mental institutions, military service, homes for disturbed children, and, in some cases industry; 2) to relate the ministry of these persons (Chaplain-pastors) to the regular life of the main-line churches; and 3) to express an understanding of the theological foundation for Christian ministry and of patriotism in particular relation to acute challenges to human dignity in contemporary culture.

The primary focus of the study is a group of United Methodist clergy who served in some form of chaplain ministry between 1945 and 1980.[12] The research is based on a survey instrument sent to 1680 persons. Responses were received from 1309 (78 percent) of them. 1236 responses were coded, punched on cards, and entered into the computer.[13] The responses were divided into two categories, military chaplaincies and civilian chaplaincies. Army, Navy, Air Force, and Reserve Forces constitute the military category, while the civilian category includes chaplains in the Veterans Administration, non-military hospitals, confinement facilities, institutions, and industry.

Although the sample group is United Methodist, the tension between parish clergy and chaplain clergy as well as that between chaplains in military and civilian settings are issues in all denominations. Overriding these tensions is the critical issue of the continuing relation between church and state in the United States. It should be clear in all that follows that many supporters and critics of American culture today see the crisis in patriotism as directly related to the crisis of faith. As a consequence, the possibility of renewal and rebirth in the religious communities is important to the renewal and rebirth of citizenship as well as to the renewal of the church. The nurture of foundational convictions about human rights and about the ultimacy of God's love and righteousness is vital if the double heritage of America and of the church is to serve the cause of justice and happiness, of inter-human bonding, and of freedom for all people. The reaffirmation of confidence in

---

[12]The study was commissioned by the Division of Chaplains and Related Ministries, Board of Higher Education and Ministry of the United Methodist Church.

[13]See Appendix B for a copy of the research instrument.

principles and in people, accompanied by the restrained and wise use of power for the benefit of all, is as *crucial* for the life of the nation as it is *essential* to the understanding of the grace of God in the church.

Two movements in Christianity were early signs that a different future might be possible. Vatican II and Pope John XXIII sensed the "stuffiness" if not the "stiffness" of the church and initiated a shift in the understanding of Christian faith and of the church from triumphalism to servanthood. That move in its way followed a path heroically cut by Dietrich Bonhoeffer in his struggle with the Nazi government of Germany in the 1930's. Bonhoeffer appealed for a "relegitimation" of the church not so much in terms of power over and above history but as rooted primarily in the love of God among and within the suffering of people who were degraded by the principalities and powers of evil strident in the world.

Reservations about the legitimacy of any use of force in the name of Christianity surfaced, especially during the last three decades, in insistent requests that the military chaplaincy be replaced by a civilian chaplaincy, supported and sustained altogether by the resources of the church. The United Church of Christ, the Presbyterian Church in the United States, and the Episcopal Church made serious studies of the problem, and The United Methodist Church recently completed a reappraisal of its policy about chaplains to the military services.[14] The title of a book edited by Harvey Cox, *Military Chaplains: From a Religious Military to a Military Religion,* indicates the intensity of that discussion. All of these churches reaffirmed the religious legitimacy of the military chaplaincy, but they also vowed to stress the primacy of a Chaplain's obligation to God and the church rather than to the military service.

The study which follows is framed by a chapter describing the situation at the end of World War II and a concluding essay on Christian ministry. Because it is impossible to separate the struggle of the church from the turbulent events in American culture since the end of World War II, Chapter II examines at some length the Supreme Court Decision on Prayer in Public Schools, the Civil Rights

---

[14]See Chapter IV, pp. 141ff., for documentation and a fuller discussion of these actions.

Movement, Vietnam, Watergate, and the rapid growth of new religious movements.

In all of these events the voices of citizens and believers created an ambiguous maze for every young person to negotiate, largely on the basis of his or her own insight. In every instance, the advice of respected authorities in church and state was ambiguous. In Chapters III and IV, what chaplain pastors say about their ministry, what is Christian about it, and the tensions between their obligations to their employer and the church are rather fully reported. In those accounts the uniqueness of both the vulnerability and the privilege of those ministries is impressive.

In Chapter V, the problem all churches face of reconciling local church ministry with chaplain ministry is discussed in the specific context of United Methodist Church order. The wide variety of contexts within which chaplain pastors serve makes that problem more acute. Two conclusions emerge from that consideration: (1) the fundamental unity of worship and compassion in Christian ministry, and (2) the necessity for combining power, knowledge, understanding, and care in the church's supervision and support of ministry, especially in the diversified forms of chaplain ministry.

The constructive fruit of the entire study is contained in the final chapter on the theological foundations of Christian ministry for all clergy in all kinds of different contexts, a foundation quite as supportive of local church pastors as for chaplain pastors. That foundation gives rise to changed forms of Christian presence involving issues of salvation, love, human fulfillment, morality, and citizenship. Within that view, the tension, even the cleavage, between local church and chaplain pastors is seen as an unfortunate waste of power and love, a waste all the more regrettable in the face of extensive human need and suffering, especially among the outcast persons in the world today.

The study is published under the strong sense of the importance of renewal and rebirth in the church to the integrity of citizenship in the United States and in the universal cause of human rights. Sontag and Roth have emphasized the significance of American theology not only for the church but also for the political community.

"By interpreting the broad framework of existence into which God casts our lives; by stressing man's need for and God's relation to love, justice, and freedom; and by underscoring the theme that death, evil, and negation are not the final scenes in life's drama, American theology might open renewal, promise, and national rebirth." [15]

The ministry of chaplains reminds us of the urgency of the task and the vital meaning of a renewed understanding of Christian faith for the institutions which secure justice and offer happiness to people in a life-world which we all share. In a time of acute challenge and ambiguity, we have the opportunity to demonstrate that the American experiment will increasingly respond to peoples' aspirations for freedom and justice, and that the Christian faith is pertinent to the deepest hungers of the heart. Should that happen, the story of the chaplains may refresh us in the mission to be "stewards of reconciliation" to persons in a perplexing, broken, and often cruel world.

---

[15]Frederick Sontag and John K. Roth, *The American Religious Experience* (New York, 1972), p. 341.

I. *Between War and Peace*

"It was the biggest party in the history of the nation, a spontaneous eruption of emotion. It was New Year's at Time Square raised to the 10,000th, a generally pleasant form of mass hysteria, a Rose Bowl victory and a Super Bowl and World Series all rolled into one. It was an orgy of drinking and kissing and screaming, and occasionally praying, that swept the nation without need of confirmation by mass communications. Shipyards and aircraft plants locked their gates. Men threw away their lunch buckets, and women their shipyard coveralls. Servicemen fortunate enough to be within the country's boundaries were treated like conquering heroes for the last time. There were some incidents of pure rioting, of looting and vandalizing and rape, but they were scattered—most people simply wanted to have fun. It was the first time in four years they could do so without feeling guilty because of the men overseas, and the last time within our lifetimes, although none of us had any idea what life would be like within the confines of a superpower that was planning to save the world. How could we know that real social problems and invented personal problems would keep us so unhappy when we were not at war? How could we know that our nation was at its best when it was in all-out war? How could we know that plenty was never enough, and that happiness can be sold but never bought?" [1]

"At last the job is finished."

(See Winston Churchill)

"We know now that the basic proposition of the worth and dignity of man is not a sentimental aspiration or a vain hope or a piece of rhetoric. It is the strongest, most creative force now present in this world. Now let us use that force and all our resources and all our skills in the great cause of a just and lasting peace."

(President Harry Truman, August 1945).

Ordinary words cannot express the ecstatic and overwhelming sense of relief, joy, and thansgiving that seized the entire nation at the end of World War II. Sir Winston Churchill regarded that struggle

---

[1]Archie Satterfield, *The Home Front*, Playboy Press, 1981, p. 362.

as pivotal for the preservation of Western Civilization. Many in the United States shared his view. The Nazi challenge to the United States had never reached the point of a threatened invasion, as it had for England. The President of the United States did not have to urge the citizenry to fight house by house, block by block, town by town, and city by city to repel the invader. Yet the people of the United States understood themselves to be defending their homes, their families, and their homeland against the Nazi challenge. The Nazi threat to other cultural groups in the United States had not been as ominous as their threat to the Jews. There was, nevertheless, a strong suspicion that all cultural groups except the German *Volk* might be pronounced "subhuman" if the will of Hitler [2] should become the basis of law not only in Germany but also in England, France, and the United States.

An editorial on the "Week the War Ended" in a popular magazine proclaimed that week as conceivably being" . . . the most momentous week in human history."[3] Churchill could say at the same time: "At last the job is finished." These expressions seem on the surface to be excessive. But how else can one depict a crisis in which everything, literally everything, that the people cherish or own is threatened? That includes one's own life, the lives of every family member and friend, one's house, job, possessions, and every aspect of social and political stability. And most devasting of all, the crisis threatened one's confidence in a future of justice, human dignity, and peace for the human family. All of these are entailed in Churchill's claim that the future of Western civilization was at issue in World War II. Hitler and Hirohito had shaken the literal and symbolic foundations of human hopes that righteousness, justice, freedom, prosperity, and peace could be joined together in a "more perfect union."

It is no wonder, then, that strangely wild and poignantly meditative conduct attended the end of the war. That event made possible the preservation of all those things that people long for against the most demonic threat humanity had ever known. It is no

---

[2]Cf. the documentary film, "Triumph of the Will" which Hitler commissioned as a propaganda piece in 1934.

[3] *Life*, August 27, 1945, p. 29.

wonder that this victory was seen in profoundly religious and political terms, suggesting the sacral sense that, at root, the American vision holds the religious and the political as inseparably bound together. An editorial writer sees that relation clearly.

"The world is trembling on the brink of peace. At this hour, millions are bending almost breathless over their radios awaiting the word that will silence the guns. . . . With one accord, America and the Allied nations breathe a fervent 'Thank God!' To religious minds, these words will mean exactly what they say—a solemn gratitude to Almighty God that the scourge of war has passed. Even those of little faith, if they have any seriousness of spirit and any sense of the meaning of this event, can scarcely find other words in which to release the inexpressible emotion of the hour. . . . But even now, death is no longer raining from the sky. Thank God for that. The boys will be coming home. Thank God for that. There is a chance to guild a world of brotherhood and justice. Let us thank God for that, and pray that we may be humble, wise and patient as we go about it."[4]

With the exuberant celebration, however, came also a sense of foreboding about the complex and slow process of building the kind of peace which President Harry Truman hoped would be "just and lasting." In an address delivered at the University of Chicago, Robert M. Hutchins suggested what this might mean: "This is a day of Thanksgiving and prayer—thanks that we have been delivered from the bloodiest war in history, thanks to those brave men, living and dead, who have been the means of our deliverance; and prayer that we may show humility, humanity, and intelligence and charity in using the victory they have won for us."[5]

Sober foreboding about the complex work of "building peace" indicates that the people knew how complex and difficult that task would be. In the midst of the war, President Franklin D. Roosevelt had initiated the process of forming the United Nations. An organizing conference at San Francisco had already taken place. Despite an abundance of ideal statements about the aspirations and hopes of humanity focusing on the United Nations, people

---

[4]Editorial, *The Christian Century*, Vol LXII, No. 34, August 22, 1945, pp. 747, 749.

[5]Robert M. Hutchins, "In the Name of Our Dead." Published in *The Christian Century*, Vol. LXII, No. 21, May 23, 1945, P. 625.

nevertheless remembered President Woodrow Wilson's effort after World War I to establish the League of Nations. President Wilson sought an organization to make the world safe for democracy, a cause that never received the full support of the United States. Isolationist sentiments were strong. Many blamed meddling in foreign affairs for a war terribly costly in blood and dollars. If absolute isolation was not the answer to peace and security, some vehicle like the United Nations seemed to be essential if future armed conflict was to be avoided. Yet there were grave misgivings that the United Nations might not be allowed birth, or, coming to life, might be too fragile to guarantee peace.

Another fear arose in relation to the progress of science. Where is the science which produced the nuclear weapons used at Hiroshima and Nagasaki leading us? Clearly the science, technology, and productivity of the United States had made victory possible. Yet, uncertainty about our ability to control the power of science that produced the bomb tempered optimism about the future. A voice from the Vatican spoke of the bomb as casting "a sinister shadow . . . on the future of humanity." Science previously treated as an altogether life-conserving force, came to be seen as having a dark and negative side—mysterious, powerful, threatening, and, perhaps, fundamentally evil.

The end of the war in Europe also brought loud cries for revenge against the Nazis. The Nazis were perceived as so evil that it seemed to some a waste of time and money to give them formal trials. Others saw no reason "why courts, just like other agencies, should not be policy weapons."[6] Justice Robert H. Jackson, later appointed as chief prosecutor at the Nuremberg Trials, vigorously defended the principles of law and fair trials as essential to our way of life, even if some guilty persons might escape punishment through the court procedure. He saw no place in our society for courts organized only to convict, even if that was the way of Nazi courts. Jackson wrote eloquently of the importance of laws:

"To promote the idea of Law in Europe is more vital to us than killing Nazis. . . . Wherever we have a chance to promote this freedom and

---

[6]Editorial, *Life*, Vol. 18, No.22, May 28., 1945, p. 34.

law, as in Europe now, it is to America's self-interest to do it. . . . It is far, far better that some guilty men escape than that the idea of law be endangered. In the long run the idea of law is our best defense against Nazism in all its forms."

The trials of war criminals at Nuremberg following the war did much to resolve the tension between justice and revenge, but they hardly put an end to the debate.

The pressures of the war accentuated prejudice, causing one writer of a book on the American people, 1939-1945,[7] to entitle a chapter, "The Civil Liberties Disaster." There is general agreement that the most flagrant violation of civil liberties in the United States involved the evacuation of 70,000 Americans of Japanese ancestry from the Pacific coast to be interned against their will in inland camps called "relocation centers." Conditions in these centers approximated those in most American prisons. All were required to take an oath of loyalty to the United States. In 1943 that requirement was intensified and every internee was forced to swear loyalty to the United States and to repudiate Japan.[8] The seven thousand who refused to take the new oath were segregated in a maximum security camp at Tule Lake, California. Although conditions for the internees became better as the United States began to experience successes in the war with the Japanese in the Pacific, this action remains an unhealed sore in the conscience of America.

But there were also other violations of human rights. Anti-Semitism was widespread, along with prejudice against all conscientious objectors. Suspicion of aliens entering the country was so great that America refused to raise its immigration quota for Europeans, even to provide an escape for Jews in Germany and the occupied countries who were being brutally and systematically killed by the Germans. Strangely, the worst treatment went to the Jehovah's Witnesses, a religious group whose members constituted most of the conscientious objectors who were imprisoned. Many draft boards simply ordered them inducted into the Army. There they were quickly court-martialed for refusing to salute the flag. Some

---

[7]Geoffrey Parrett, *Days of Sadness, Years of Triumph,* (New York, 1973), pp. 357-367.
[8] *Ibid.,*p. 364.

were sentenced to life imprisonment and were held in solitary confinement for months at Fort Leavenworth, Kansas. Although there was a reversal of these actions later, the record of the United States on Civil Liberties during this time was not a proud one. When detailed news and pictures of the Nazi death camps reached the United States after the end of the war, the sense of horror at what others had done called up considerable shame about our own actions. Making peace with the evil of the Nazis and with our own evil proved to be as difficult a task as ending the war. It is a task still not completed.

One of the most pressing problems America faced at the war's end was the disruption of people and the destruction of property throughout Europe. Tens of millions of displaced persons at the point of starvation in cities throughout Europe that had been reduced to piles of rubble by bombing, created serious problems in sanitation, health, transportation, and public order. The war on tyranny that began in 1941 became a war on famine in 1945. The story of the effort of the American people to assist in rebuilding life and order in Europe, especially Greece, Germany, Italy, and France through the Marshall Plan and the Agency for International Development is well known. A story less well known is that of 34 conscientious objectors who volunteered for "hunger tests" at the University of Minnesota. These men were subjected to systematic starvation to help the United States find the best way to "rehabilitate the hunger-wasted millions of Europe."[9]

Taken together, these problems made vivid the sober recognition that the task of rebuilding the western world could prove to be an even more difficult task than winning the war. There is a sense in which the war was won by the sheer magnitude of American arms in the hands of determined and self-sacrificing soldiers, sailors, and airmen. Cities could be destroyed in one day, thousands of persons could be incinerated or vaporized by one bomb. Destruction was immediate, irrestible, and comprehensive. But the process of rebuilding, healing, restructuring, and reconciling is always gradual and painfully slow. The war was ended with an unprecedented bang. Peace, true peace, would come only

---

[9] *Life*, July 30, 1945, p. 13.

gradually, "like sunrise, like spring." With almost universal determination, the American people pledged themselves to the building of a "just and durable peace." Few could have realized at that time, however, the difficulty of such a task. Nor could they foresee the peacetime problems that would raise questions not only about external forms of civil order but also about the inner character and purpose of the American people.

Three factors countered the noble intention of using the time after the war to make peace: 1) the determination of persons returning from the war to make up for lost time in education, vocation, and family relations; 2) questions raised by other nations and cultures about the altruism of America's proposals for solving their problems (pax Americana); and 3) the persistent sense of American righteousness in saving the world, a sense so pervasive that it obscured problems in American identity and character, problems that cried for attention. Energies which might have been devoted to self-understanding and to solving the problems of race, justice, education, and economic opportunity where spent in "getting ahead" and in exporting American answers to human problems. William Shirer noted that people in other countries were becoming distrustful of us, partly because we seemed frightened and unwilling to admit and deal with the "great popular forces which this war has unleashed."[10] A French critic was most caustic. "America will believe it her duty to concern herself with the rest of the world, but she will not do this without being paid for it. . . . If she intervenes in the affairs of the world it will be to impose her ideas and she will consider her intervention a blessing for lost and suffering humanity."[11]

Without agreeing completely with either Shirer or Raoul de Russy de Sales, we acknowledge that there was considerable vagueness about America's character and destiny in the 1950's, 60's, and 70's as well as confusion as to how the problem of the turbulent years, 1945-1980, should be faced.[12]

In 1959, that vagueness and confusion were identified by Professor Clyde Kluckhohn, a Harvard anthropologist, who pro-

---

[10] Time, September 13, 1943.

[11] Raoul de Russy de Sales, The Making of Yesterday, entry for July 7, 1942.

[12] See Chapter II below.

posed a series of publications and television programs "which might help us as a people to become more aware of the values which motivate us."[13] Huston Smith edited the major publication of the project, *The Search for America*.[14] Writers of essays in that volume identified fifteen critical problems facing the nation, but with considerably more conviction that the problems *must* be faced rather than *how* they were to be faced. Reinhold Neibuhr, for example, spoke of the general nature of our dilemma. "We have been so deluded by the image of our innocence that we are ill prepared for the moral ambiguities that our rise to power has forced upon us." Niebuhr regarded the temptation to control ourselves and the world as fraught not only with a false innocence but with a dangerously naive attitude toward the use of power.

> "The irony of the American present is that we have become powerful, yet find our scope of action contracted; that we have achieved an unprecedented standard of comfort, yet happiness eludes us; that we have accumulated a great and useful compendium of scientific knowledge, only to run into larger problems of human destiny. Our very success has hastened the exposure of our limitations. Bewildered by historical impasses and deflated in our pretensions to purity, our minds today have become touched with self-pity. We feel that history has tricked us—that it has played some kind of crude joke on us to leave us, often such an auspicious beginning, precisely where man has always been: neither masters of our fate nor pawns relieved of the burden of responsibility. There is danger that our frustration may prompt us to a final desperate attempt to bring history under our control, the political name for such an attempt being 'preventive war.' "[15]

A few years before the Search for America Project began, a similar project arose among the churches, a search for the true meaning of Christianity, suggesting again that political confusion about American character and identity is closely related to religious confusion over the same issues. H. Richard Niebuhr was appointed director of a project, assisted by Daniel Day Williams and James M. Gustafson. Their purpose was *The Study of*

---

[13]Huston Smith (ed.), *The Search for America* (Englewood Cliffs, N.J., 1959), p. vii.
[14]Ibid.
[15]Reinhold Niebuhr, "From Progress to Perplexity." Huston Smith, *op. cit.*, pp. 144, 145.

Theological Education in the United States and Canada. Somewhat similar studies had been made of *Higher Education for American Democracy* by a Commission appointed by President Truman. The faculty of Harvard University had also appointed a committee on college teaching with instructions to concentrate on the *Objectives of a General Education in a Free Society.*

The first of two volumes written by H. Richard Niebuhr and his associates was entitled *The Purpose of the Church and its Ministry.*[16] Obviously disturbed by a facile identification of God's purposes with a denomination or a nation, Niebuhr sought a foundational understanding of Christian answers to the "ultimate questions with which religion and theology are concerned."[17] With surprising simplicity, Niebuhr identified the goal or purpose of the Christian church as, "the *increase among men of the love of God and neighbor.*"[18] Upon that base he analyzed the superficiality and the creative substance of Christianity in the 50's, illuminating the mission of the church in a time between war and peace.

"Our schools, like our churches and our ministers, have no clear conception of what they are doing but are carrying on traditional actions, making separate responses to various pressures exerted by churches and society, continuing uneasy compromises among many values, engaged in little quarrels symptomatic of undefined issues, trying to improve their work by adjusting minor parts of the academic machine or by changing the specifications of the raw material to be treated." [19]

"Alongside conventionality, which is sometimes downright antiquarian, one encounters vitality, freshness, eagerness and devotedness among these teachers and students. Alongside perplexed preparation for manifold tasks one finds present in many of these men a drive toward knowledge of the fundamental issues of life. Alongside tepid birthright loyalties to denominations and schools of thought, one encounters in faculty and students the fervent convictions of new converts about the greatness of the common Christian cause." [20]

---

[16]H. Richard Niebuhr, *The Purpose of the Church and its Ministry* (New York, 1956).
[17]H. Richard Niebuhr, *op. cit.*, p. IX.
[18]*Ibid.,* p. 31.
[19]*Ibid.,* p. 101.
[20]*Ibid.,.,* p. 102.

It seems, then, that the situation between war and peace in the republic is paralleled by that in the church between unfaith and faith. The nation, properly proud of her effort to silence the guns, was unsurely engaged in the more difficult effort to build a "just and lasting peace." The church, properly committed to the ultimacy of the love of God in Christ Jesus, was halting, even pedantic, about venturing that bold claim within the radically new problems the post war world presented. The silencing of the guns was not without staggering cost, and the use of the time to build a genuine peace was unlikely without a realistic and persistent hope. Understanding the post war decades requires a fair account of both that cost and that hope.

A. Counting the Cost: Looking to the Past

World War II was the most costly war in human lives, money, and general destruction in the history of humanity. That really astounding fact should convince us of the importance of the causes for which it was fought and, more importantly, incline us to accept the sacrifices of millions of persons as an inescapable obligation to learn well the lessons the war can teach us.

Mainland USA was the only national territory not invaded, bombed, or sacked among all the combatant nations in World War II. It was necessary to keep that fact in mind in post war discussions with the British, French, Russians, Italians, and others, especially when the topic was resources to save the starving and to rebuild Europe. Further, as we will see, American casualties, devastating as they were, were small compared to those of other countries. Even so, more than ten million Americans had gone overseas and for the first time in American history, the United States suffered more than a million casualties, with over 405,000 military deaths.

Russia suffered far more casualties than any nation, about twenty million, a fact which influenced Russia's attitude toward Germany in the post war period. Germany and Austria suffered a total of nearly six and one-half million civilian and military casualties, many of whom (about 400,000) were Jews exterminated by Germany and Austria. There is both irony and pathos in the statement made by General Jodl to General Smith after signing the articles of capitulation for the armed forces of Germany in May of 1945. After speaking in English, "I want to say a word," he continued in German.

"General, with this signature the German people and the German armed forces are, for better or worse, delivered into the victor's hands. In this war, which has lasted more than five years, both have achieved and suffered more than perhaps any other people in the world. In this hour I can only express the hope that the victor will treat them with generosity."

The fact that General Jodl could make such an appeal in the face of a war begun by Germany, a war which saw the killing of over forty million people and which cost an estimated four trillion dollars, indicates the importance of the Nuremberg Trials and of the Denazification Program in Germany, in spite of serious faults in both of them. The further fact that Germany had calculatedly and systematically killed six million Jews in addition to millions of other persons for political and racial reasons, more persons than the non-Jewish, German and Austrian casualties in the entire war, makes Jodl's appeal for "generosity" a specious and unrealistic one.

The special danger of chaplain ministry in military service is obvious when chaplain casualties are considered in relation to total casualties. Total military casualties of the United States in World War II were 1,102,112.[21] Total chaplain casualties were 210, of whom 105 were killed. This total though fewer proportionately than of chaplain casualties in the Civil War, still provides impressive evidence of the shared danger that inevitably accompanies military chaplain ministry.[22] There are dangers in all forms of chaplain ministry. The sharpest contrast, however, may be drawn between the ministry of military chaplains and that of local church pastors. Casualties among local church clergy during World War II were unknown simply because their ministry was within the security of our national borders. Casualties among military chaplains were both inevitable and understandable as they accepted the risk and

---

[21]Baldwin Hanson, *Battles Lost and Won.* (New York, 1966), p. 519.
[22]cf. Chapter III, pp. 120ff. below.

shared the dangers with those in combat around the world. Christian ministry to persons in military service requires being with those at risk and in danger.

We are not allowed to minimize the astounding sacrifices made in life and blood to gain for us the opportunities and challenges of peace. But in addition to the tragic loss of life, there was another heavy casualty of the war in the temptations and challenges it presented to the character of the American people. That casualty was the loss of national innocence, the end of the myth of America as the Garden of Eden, a myth made possible and supported by our simple, happy, and righteous isolation from the forces of evil which dominated the profane and pagan world "out there." The rise of neo-conservative isolationism and the strident battle of Senator Joseph McCarthy seem, in retrospect, to be forced efforts to hide America's loss of innocence beneath an avalanche of accusations against the evils of Russia and Communism. Whether the people of the United States desired it or deserved it, the period of happy isolation was over. America had arisen to the status of a preeminent world power with the capacity and the moral will to do something about the hunger, poverty, disease, and destruction in the world.

> "Emerging thus into the world scene, the United States came to know both failure and success, to understand the onerous responsibilities of leadership, and to realize that not all problems could be solved or all questions answered. In learning to live with such international ambiguities, Americans discovered and experienced a state of being that contradicted everything in their problem solving, pragmatic tradition."[23]

For better or for worse, as a loss or as a gain, the innocence was gone. Americans suddenly found themselves in a situation in which they had power and could not escape using it. The price of prevailing in the war and the price of the power that victory thrust upon us was to distinguish good from evil in the exercise of power and accepting responsibility within complex and ambiguous

---

[23]Eisinger, Chester E., The 1940's: Profile of a Nation in Crisis. (New York, 1969), p. 453.

situations for the moral exercise of that power toward a just and lasting peace.

For the nation, this responsibility entailed the reaffirmation of the Washington-Jefferson-Lincoln tradition of citizenship, but acted out within a volatile, newly complex, and interdependent group of nations. For the church, this responsibility meant the reaffirmation of what H. Richard Niebuhr termed "the sense of the great tradition of the Church," a responsibility experienced in the context of tempting superficialities and trivial denominationalisms which obscured the depth of the challenges and opportunities that the post war would offered. There was, then, gain in the loss, hope with the cost, and that gain and hope merit attention.

B. Discerning the Hope: Looking to the Future

On September 9, 1945, General Douglas MacArthur spoke to Lieutenant General Robert L. Eichelberger, Commander of the United States Eighth Army in Tokyo: "General Eichelberger, have our country's flag unfurled and in Tokyo's sun let it wave in its full glory as a symbol of hope for the oppressed and as a harbinger of victory for the right."[24] And so, according to Henry Steele Commager, "the most devastating of all wars came to an end." Commager boldly attributes the failure of the Nazis to their denial of human values and human faith and their use of violence and terror, although he admits that they came very close to succeeding.

"Civilized men everywhere had hoped that World War I would be the war to end all wars. In this hope they were typically disappointed. After twenty troubled years evil and ambitious men had ventured once more to gain their ends through violence and terror. They had almost succeeded . . . But the fundamental reason for their failure is clear enough. They failed because they repudiated human values and human faith . . . In the end it was those who had faith in the virtues and dignity of man who triumphed. Against wickedness and terror and hatred, the free peoples of the world fought back." [25]

---

24 *The New York Times*, Sept. 8, 1945.
25Henry Steele Commager, *A Short History of the Second World War.* (Boston, 1945), pp. 565, 566.

Commager is correct in describing the American people as seeing the war not only in political or military terms but explicitly as a struggle between the forces of good and evil, as a moral and religious crusade against demonic "principalities and powers" which threatened humanity. Subsequent revelations about the death camps and the calculated official policy of genocide against Jews and others gave support to Commager's view of the real meaning of the war. For many, that moral justification of the war persisted, influencing Americans to accept the obligation to use the peace for the same moral ends. Before his death on April 12, 1945, President Roosevelt spoke eloquently for most of America when he outlined a commitment and a hope for peace.

> "Today we seek a moral basis for peace. It cannot be a real peace if it fails to recognize brotherhood. It cannot be a lasting peace if the fruit of it is oppression or starvation, or cruelty, or human life dominated by armed camps. It cannot be a sound peace if small nations must live in fear of powerful neighbors. It cannot be a moral peace if freedom from invasion is sold for tribute. It cannot be an intelligent peace if it denies free passage to that knowledge of those ideals which permit men to find common ground. It cannot be a righteous peace if worship of God is denied."[26]

This prevailing mood of moral hope and determination was soon put under severe stress by three events: the emergence of Russia as a strident adversary; the gradual realization that the nuclear age was indeed a new age; and the call from among our own people for a continuation of the American Revolution until it accomplished liberty and justice for all. Each of these challenged the foundation of America's moral hope, and each performed a role in transforming the postwar world.

The challenge of Russia was grossly underestimated in the euphoria following the victory in which Russia and the United States were allies. Herbert Agar reports a conversation with Harry Hopkins, chief adviser to President Roosevelt, revealing that almost unbounded optimism.

---

[26]Quoted in Commager, *op. cit.*, p. 566.

"We really believed in our hearts that this was the dawn of the new day we had all been praying for and talking about for so many years. We were absolutely certain that we had won the first great victory of the peace—and, by "we," I mean *all* of us, the whole civilized human race. The Russians had proved that they could be reasonable and far-seeing and there wasn't any doubt in the minds of the President or any of us that we could live with them and get along with them peacefully for as far into the future as any of us could imagine." [27]

Churchill had never been so hopeful, and a succession of presidents—Truman, Eisenhower, Kennedy, Nixon, Ford, Carter, and Reagan—have had to fashion American foreign policy in the sober recognition of the sharp differences between the policies and goals of the Soviet Union and the United States. The tensions of continuous cold war and the constant possibility of a hot war provided the environment which influenced most postwar decisions. Two new world powers became, in effect, super powers—powers that could not agree on major issues yet powers who could not survive an absolute showdown with one another.

At times it seemed quite enough for an American to be anti-Russian. Certainly many political rewards came to those who could clearly outdistance others in this hatred of the Russians. But cooler heads have generally prevailed against both excessive hope and excessive despair concerning relations with the Russians. Gradually the Russians came to be seen neither as *incognito* lovers of peace and freedom nor as committed agents of the "Evil Empire." As the stereotype softened it became possible to see the Russians as persons facing human problems common to us all in a life-world that is shared. Real and profound differences continue while awareness of elements of our common humanity increase. A writer for the *New York Post* put the issue correctly. "The simple, corny and rather sordid question which each of us faces today is whether he is for democracy or just afraid of Russia. It makes a difference . . . If one is only afraid of Russia, one is on the defensive, and we learned a few years ago that defense will not win the war."[28]

---

[27]Herbert, Agar, *The Price of Power* (Chicago, 1957), pp. 10, 11.

[28]Samuel Grafton, "I'd Rather Be Right," *The New York Post*, December 4, 1947. Quoted in Hanson Baldwin, *The Price of Power*. (New York, 1947), p. 327.

For most Americans, hope for the future rests on the firm conviction that principles of human freedom and dignity, of self-government, and of international cooperation are fundamentally true for all people. Hope is neither make believe nor wishful thinking. Real denials of these principles can readily be found not only in Russia but in other countries with whom we have friendly and supportive relations. But the chastened and restrained hope of the American people in the postwar world holds fast to the positive conviction that the American Revolution claimed universal principles for all people, however much these principles may be violated or denied by our own or other governments. This hope must embrace force to neutralize the power of those who deny these fundamental principles, just as force became necessary against Hitler in World War II. But the hope is always positive, a confidence that the hunger of the heart for freedom, dignity, and justice cannot be suppressed forever by guns and tanks.

The confrontation with Russia is, of course, related to the second event that dramatically changed the life-world upon which all of us are dependent: the beginning of the nuclear age. Americans in general supported the use of the nuclear weapon at Hiroshima. It was seen as the only immediate way to end the war, prevent still greater loss of life for both Japan and the United States, and avoid further destruction of the Japanese homeland. Fewer Americans supported the dropping of the second weapon on Nagasaki. Hardly anyone imagined at the time that with the end of the war there was also an altogether "new age" in the history of humanity, the "nuclear age."

Limited realization about the nature of the "new age" prevailed for years in the military, in industry, and among the American people at large. The military began to experiment with different sizes of nuclear weapons, the different effects of underground, surface, and air bursts, the effects of radiation, the kinds of clothing and shelter that offer the most protection, and the most reliable ways of predicting casualties at different distances from different sized weapons. Civilian industry made heavy investments in the control and use of nuclear energy. The possibility that nuclear power would provide a cheap and clean source of electricity was especially attractive as an alternative to fossil fuel. Americans tended to regard the mastery of nuclear energy as another achievement in a long line of accomplishments of American ingenuity. Some went even further and claimed the splitting of the atom as a gift of God to the American people. We are, after all, they claimed, God's chosen people to bring God's Kingdom to all the dark places of the earth. Overall, there developed an exuberant confidence that the American ingenuity which had produced the "nuclear age" could certainly solve whatever problems nuclear weapons or nuclear energy might produce.

Few people could fully realize that America had ushered the entire world into a "new age." With the new age came new and immensely troubling problems—health care in crisis situations, the changing meaning of national sovereignty, the possibility of a "just" nuclear war capable of being won, problems of garbage and waste disposal, the depletion of non-renewable natural resources, and radical dimensions of human interdependence among them—problems far greater than our accepted positions of an earlier day could manage.

Further nuclear development led to still further problems: disposal of contaminated waste, unavoidable accidents and malfunctions, and the immense possibilities of uncontrollable radiation and pollution. The time had come to reflect seriously upon the impact of our actions on present and future humanity and on the life-world upon which we were all dependent. Dead fish, polluted lakes and streams, acid rain, deformed babies, and dying plants and forests forced us to consider the possibility that in the nuclear age, human beings may have the power to destroy the earth and its people. Stunned by the thought of that possibility, sensitive persons began to seek alternatives to this vision of death.

Henry L. Stimson, twice Secretary of War and once Secretary of State, spoke for many in 1947.

"War in the twentieth century has grown steadily more barbarous, more destructive, more debased in all its aspects. Now, with the release of atomic energy, man's ability to destroy himself is very nearly complete. The bombs dropped on Hiroshima and Nagasaki ended a war. They also made it wholly clear that we must never have another war. This is the lesson men and leaders everywhere must learn, and I believe that when they learn it they will find a way to lasting peace. There is no other choice."[29]

What was clear at the end of the war became even more clear in the subsequent decades: there was no consensus about the meaning of hope for the future of America. For many, hope for the future was altogether in terms of prewar conditions: winning wars, a winnable peace, the sovereignty of nation states, America secure and supreme in the world, and unbounded confidence in American ingenuity and enterprise to solve both the problems of the world and the small flaws in America. For rapidly increasing numbers of others, however, the words of Henry L. Stimson were prophetic and true. As they became increasingly aware of the terror of nuclear war, Americans began to seek a less destructive way to resolve differences. Even Teilhard de Chardin was able to maintain his confidence in the future because he was sure that the bombs on Hiroshima and Nagasaki would turn humanity toward a total renunciation of nuclear weapons.

Hope of the American people in 1945, then, took quite different forms. For many it remained a simple hope in America's inevitable and continuing success and supremacy. For others, it became a chastened hope which, while not renouncing the nuclear age, entered it with a heightened sense of its terrifying power to enrich or to destroy life. Those in the second category began spiritedly to seek ways to promote understanding across national and cultural boundaries, including work with the United Nations. Their hope found expression in a struggle to live together at peace in a shared life-world, a cause in which all could win, as an alternative to a war in which all would lose.

Probably, the most serious challenge to the moral hope of Americans after World War II came, unexpectedly, from among the people of America.[30] President Truman's bold action in integrating the Armed Forces was tacit recognition of a moral issue

---

[29]Henry L. Stimson, "The Decision to Use the Atomic Bomb," *Harpers Magazine* (CXCIV, February 1947), p. 107.

[30]See Chapter II, below, for an account of some of these conflicts and how they created acute dilemmas for the youth of America who wished to honor both their nation and the moral and religious qualities which they claimed for themselves and for America.

that could no longer be ignored. The struggle for equality in citizenship would nearly tear America apart in the decades following. The Supreme Court decision banning prayer in the public schools appeared to many to be a flagrant insult to the God who had "blessed America" and a betrayal of the religious foundation of morality, righteousness, and hope. Beyond these, the Vietnam War and the Watergate Affair troubled the soul of America and raised serious questions about the integrity of such basic American institutions as law, government, education, economics, and religion. No longer could Americans accurately describe their nation as "the land of the free and the home of the brave." No longer could Americans speak with certainty of "liberty and justice" for all.

These questions, not explicit in 1945, were nevertheless inescapably present. Those who continued to exaggerate America's righteousness within a "manifest destiny" under God continued to hope for America, but that hope rested on controlling these new problems and wishing that they would go away. Desperate to maintain the *status quo,* some went so far as to brand such persons as Martin Luther King, Jr., as subversives, giving aid and comfort to America's enemies. Others remained hopeful for America in quite another way, acknowledging the flaws, and seeking, without perfectionist pretentions, to build a more reasonable, fair, and just America.

Taken together, these challenges from Russia, from the "nuclear age," and from groups within America clamoring for more full human rights, justice, and opportunity created a crisis in the postwar period that could not be met by conventional patriotism or conventional religion, nor even by sophisticated political or religious efforts alone. Discerning the signs of the true hope for America's future, therefore, required a careful and critical search for new foundations for patriotism and for a valid religious support for morality. Reclaiming the great tradition of American honor and citizenship, as well as the great tradition of religious faith within the radically new challenges of the postwar world, became a vocation for all thoughtful Americans.

How the American people understood religious faith and the living of their faith in the Institutional church became critically important to the success of this vocation in the 1950's, 60's, and 70's. In the eighteenth century, Dean Swift said: "We have just enough religion to make us hate but not enough to make us love."[31] Swift's words suggest that true religion (probably he meant true Christianity) is primarily concerned with love, not hate. Christian conviction about the ultimacy of God's love for all persons and about human responsibility to preserve the world God created became peculiarly important in the postwar world. This Christian conviction included a vision of a universal human community in which persons of all nations can be loved (even when opposed), in which our interdependence in a common life-world can be acknowledged, and in which we can affirm the cries for human rights, justice, and opportunity as altogether consistent with the great traditions of citizenship and religion in the United States.

In the turbulence of the postwar decades, a time Robert Bellah correctly identifies as the third great crisis for the United States, the churches are challenged to increase love and to manifest that love by including all citizens in the American dream and by championing the cause of those marginal to or excluded from that dream: the poor, the disenfranchised, the unemployed, the sick, the imprisoned, women, and minority groups.

In addition, the churches have recognized for years their responsibility to extend the love and ministry of Christ to those special communities of persons who are unable to participate in the congregational life of local churches. The largest of these communities is that of the armed forces and their families. Serving on widely dispersed and often geographically and culturally isolated military installations around the world, these persons are offered Christian ministry by military chaplains. Because they share the problems and risks with others, and because they have responsibility as clergy within the military organization, chaplains are able to offer the love of God and the power of faith and hope to individuals, while at the same time influencing the military institutions toward the moral control of the use of power and authority.

During the postwar years, many other "specialist ministries"

---

[31]Quoted by Herbert Agar, *op. cit.,* p. 8.

emerged in response to newly recognized human needs. The following chapters give an account of those specialist ministries, showing how they are a part of the "great tradition" of religion in America, and how they are rooted in firm theological ground for comprehensive, critical, and compassionate Christian ministry in a radically new and turbulent age.

In his statement about peace quoted earlier, President Roosevelt also said: "It is for this generation to make sure that a moral peace, a lasting peace, and a righteous peace is achieved." The churches embrace that political/moral obligation and include it within a profoundly religious commitment to the presence of God among us to preserve the creation and to promote redemption and fulfillment of all human life. The postwar decades give cause for discouragement *and* for hope. The church continues to live in hope in spite of tragedy, disappointments, and frustrating perplexities. For the church, hope is a form of love, and both entail a firm confidence that righteousness, justice, and peace are essential for human happiness. Being loyal to that hope and love proved to be acutely challenging to the church in the postwar decades. Issues which faced the nation and the church shook them to their foundations. Tracing those challenges in some detail will help us understand how Christian pastors ministered to people in a badly divided nation and church.

II. The Turbulent Years, 1945-1980: From Triumph to Vertigo

"For here we are in the twentieth century, at once the most religious and the most secular of Western nations . . . We do much evil in order to do good." [1]

(Reinhold Neibuhr)

"We live at present in a third time of trial at least as severe as those of the Revolution and the Civil War." [2]

(Robert Bellah)

A. The Identity and Purpose of America

There are, to be sure, eternal truths in Christian faith which are as valid at one time as another. Yet these truths are also related to the processes of history, the ebb and flow of events, the peculiar confidences, doubts, and crises of particular periods and epochs. This means that if one intends to understand and be engaged in Christian ministry, one must understand the "marks" of the time, the context within which the struggle for human meaning and integrity, the struggle for faith and hope and love, takes place. Because of the peculiar turbulence of the years since 1945, real understanding is especially difficult.

Persons who have studied the post World War II period find it difficult to describe the extraordinary changes and challenges of the time. Robert Bellah, for example, describes the situation faced by Americans in the last half century as the "third time of trial" in the

---

[1] Reinhold Neibuhr, *Pious and Secular America* (New York, 1958), pp. 1, 4.
[2] Robert Bellah, *The Broken Covenant* (New York, 1975), p. 1.

44

history of the United States.[3] He sees the first decisive trial as the struggle for independence in the 1770's and 1780's. That trial entailed both a revolutionary vision of a "people" with inalienable rights to life, liberty, and the pursuit of happiness, governed by the consent of the people, and the securing of that vision in battle and in the writing and adopting of a constitution. The immensity of that achievement is suggested by the fact that the Constitution of the United States is the oldest written constitution still in effect. The first trial, indeed, the first revolution, accomplished the independence and self-government of a group of colonies which became the United States. That step of throwing off the *yoke of an external enemy* was decisive for subsequent history. With the gaining of independence, however, the other many problems of the new nation were far from solved.

The second critical time of trial dealt with an internal, not an external, enemy and centered on the meaning of citizenship. The focal issue was slavery, whether the rights of American citizens included the right to own slaves, to possess persons. The implications of that issue were quite broad, entailing all of the aspects of "human rights," the entitlements of citizenship and the relation of the powers of government to the rights of the governed. That struggle was bitter and tragic, placing person against person, family against family, church against church, state against state, parents against children, and brothers and sisters against one another. Abraham Lincoln described the internal issue as consisting of the question "whether this nation can endure half-slave and half-free." The formal conflict ended in principle in 1865 with the abolition of slavery and the subsequent ratification of the 13th (1865), 14th (1868), and 15th (1870) amendments.

In the first great trial an outside power was the dominant enemy. In the second great trial the focus shifted to the question of internal assent and order, subordinating for a time but not removing all external challenges. That suggests a pattern in which the trials of the nation are cumulative because the issues of independence,

---

[3]Robert N. Bellah, "Civil Religion in America." *Daedalus,* Winter 1967, pp. 1-21, especially pp. 16-19. (Reprinted in Donald B. Jones and Russell E. Richey (ed) *American Civil Religion* (New York, 1974), pp. 21-44, especially pp. 37-38.

internal order, and consent are really inseparable. Their interrela-
tionship itself becomes critical in the third great time of trial, the
period after World War II. In the years since 1945, there is both an
erosion of confidence in America's foreign policy and the raising of
serious questions about citizenship, what rights and obligations the
citizenry have under the Constitutional form of union.

The third great time of trial is, then, the most critical, for in it,
radical challenges are raised both internally and externally at the
same time, and raised so sharply that the solutions found in the era
of the Revolution and in the 1860's cannot simply be recovered and
reapplied. In the first and second times of trial there was a
consensus and a confidence in the rightness of the cause which
provided the energy, the justification, and the unity of the effort.
Overriding the issues at stake, even that of slavery, was a
commitment to the task of building a people and a nation.

By contrast, the third time of trial is altogether different in that the
nation at the end of World War II was soundly built, strong, secure,
recently victorious over the most demonic threat to human culture
in the whole of history, confident, "righteous," perhaps even
self-righteous, and ready to bless and set the example for the world
with *Pax Americana.* But in the ensuing decades, that victorious
euphoria turns to strife and self-doubt as flaws and corruptions in
our foreign policy and in all of the institutions of our society are
gradually and inescapably exposed. Vietnam became a symbol
of our loss of innocence as a nation in foreign policy. Watergate
became a symbol of the internal abuse of power that shook
confidence in the legitimacy of the institutions of government, law
and justice, the economy, education, the press, and religion.

Sidney Ahlstrom speaks of the "sixties" as marking a fundamental
turning point in national history as well as in the history of Western
culture.

"The decade of the sixties seems in many ways to have marked a new
stage in the long development of Amerian religious history. Not only did
this intense and fiercely lived span of years have a character of its own,
but it may even have ended a distinct quadricentennium—a unified four
hundred year period—in the Anglo-American experience. A great
Puritan Epoch can be seen as beginning in 1558 with the death of Mary

Tudor, the last monarch to rule over an officially Roman Catholic England, and as ending in 1960 with the election of John Fitzgerald Kennedy, the first Roman Catholic president of the United States. . . Histories of the rise of organized Puritanism begin their accounts with the decisive first decade of the reign of Queen Elizabeth; and the terms "post-Puritan" and post-Protestant" are first popularly applied to America in the 1960's."[4]

Ahlstrom is certainly not suggesting that there were no other religious and cultural traditions in the United States. Nor is he in any way implying that the "turbulent sixties," as he calls them, were, indeed, turbulent because of the election of a Roman Catholic as President of the United States. He is claiming that the settlement and civilization of the new colonies and the United States "were profoundly shaped by the Reformed and Puritan impulse, and that this impulse, through its successive transmutations, remained the dominant factor in the ideology of the Protestant Establishment."[5] This meant that all of the other religious and cultural traditions had, in one way or another, to accommodate themselves to the Protestant Establishment until the 1960's. The Protestant Establishment was not replaced by another, but by the loss of any fundamental agreement and consent about the cause, the value, and the rightness of the United States. Before the 1950's or 1960's, the people of the United States were foundationally united in spite of differences, even those of the Civil War. After the 1950's and 1960's the people of the United States were foundationally divided in spite of different kinds of agreements here and there.

> "The decade *did* experience a fundamental shift in American moral and religious attitudes. The decade of the sixties was a time, in short, when the old foundations of national confidence, patriotic idealism, moral traditionalism, and even of historic Judaeo-Christian theism, were awash. Presuppositions that had held firm for centuries—even millen-iums—were being widely questioned. Some sensational manipulations came and went (as fads and fashions will), but the existence of a basic

---

[4] Sidney E. Ahlstrom, *A Religious History of the American People* (New Haven and London, 1972), p. 1079.
[5] *Ibid.*, p. 1079.

shift of mood rooted in deep social and institutional dislocations was anything but ephemeral."[6]

Ahlstrom summons an impressive list of events to support his claim about the sixties. A popular Roman Catholic president of the United States was assassinated. Pope John XXIII was leading a radical reappraisal of the relation of the church to the world. Israel's Six-Day War intensified Jewish self-consciousness and heightened Jewish-Christian and Jewish-Arab tensions. The Supreme Court handed down two revolutionary decisions in 1962 and 1963, the first establishing the one-person-one-vote principle and the second pronouncing required prayer and religious exercises in the public schools unconstitutional. The Watts riot in Los Angeles; the demonstration in Selma and the march to Montgomery, Alabama; the arrest and jailing of Martin Luther King, Jr. in Birmingham;[7] and the James Meredith march from Memphis, Tennessee to Jackson, Mississippi; all of these indicate the agony and intensity of the Civil Rights struggle.

President Lyndon Johnson signed the Civil Rights Act in 1965, and in the same year authorized the bombing of North Vietnam. Between 1965 and 1969 American troop strength in Vietnam had increased from 200,000 to over 500,000. By the end of the 1960's America was engaged in the longest war in its history and the unity of the United States was the lowest it had ever been, with the possible exception of 1861-1865.

"The full significance of these several compound events will not be knowable until the end of time, but it was perfectly clear to any reasonably observant American that the postwar revival of the Eisenhower years had competely sputtered out, and that the nation was experiencing a *crise de conscience* of unprecedented depth. The decade thus seemed to beg remembrance for having performed a great tutelary role in the education of America, for having committed a kind of maturing violence upon the innocence of a whole people, for having called an arrogant and complacent nation to time, as it were, and for reminding it that even Mother Nature is capable of dealing harshly with her children when they desecrate and pollute her beauty.

---

[6] *Ibid.,* p. 1080.

[7] For the full text of the statement by Clergy, April 13, 1963, see Appendix A.

There are good reasons for believing that the decade of the sixties, even at the profoundest ethical and religious levels, will take a distinctive place in American history."[8]

While Ahlstrom's analysis identifies the sixties as manifesting the center of the storm, the focus of the turbulence, the qualities which marked the "radical turn" in a more general way characterized the entire post World War II period from 1945 until 1980. Robert Bellah agrees with Ahlstrom's appraisal of the 1960's and of the post-war period.

"Never before had so many aspects of our history and our culture been critically examined and found wanting. From our traditional sexual and marital mores to our treatment of minorities, from our impact on the national environment to our military posture in the world, we stood condemned . . . And it was indeed the case that there was profound failure of nerve at the top, an uncertainty as to the meaning and value of our institutions and an inability to move resolutely to meet our problems. And it was also the case that an important segment of our student and youth population opted out of established society, adopted strange oriental religions, developed alternative life styles that seemed to threaten both our sex ethic and our work ethic. Major ethnic groups, blacks, Spanish-speaking Americans, Indians, for the first time on a large scale publicly questioned the American consensus and demanded different sorts of solutions from what ethnic groups had ever demanded before. What may yet prove to be the most profoundly disturbing force of all, the women's movement, was reborn in the 1960's and has led to the questioning of every aspect of our emotional, familial and occupational life." [9]

Conrad Cherry in *God's New Israel: Religious Interpretations of American Destiny* [10] agrees with Ahlstrom and Bellah about the

---

[8] Ahlstrom ibid., p. 1081. Cf also Ahlstrom, "The Radical Turn in Theology and Ethics: Why it Occurred in the 1960's." *The Annals of the American Academy of Political and Social Science*, Volume 387, January 1970, pp. 1-13, and "Requiem for Patriotic Piety," *Worldview*, Vol. 15, No. 8 (August 1972), pp. 9-11, and "The National Faith: Where Did It Go? How Can We Find It in 1973?" *Yale Alumni Magazine* (January 1973), pp. 8-9.

[9] Robert N. Bellah, "American Civil Religion in the 1970's" in Russell E. Richey and Donald G. Jones (ed.) *American Civil Religion* (New York, Hagerston, San Francisco, London, 1974), pp. 264-265.

[10] Conrad Cherry, *God's New Israel: Religious Interpretations of American Destiny* (Englewood Cliffs, N. J., 1971).

crisis, labeling it a "crisis in self-understanding" or a crisis about "National Destiny." "Since the middle of the twentieth century America has been undergoing a crisis in self-understanding. Disturbing events both within and beyond her boundaries have been forcing her to an agonizing reassessment of her identity and mission."[11] But Cherry's way of putting the crisis unites the internal and external aspects impressively. His discussion of "destiny" illuminates unresolved problems about the nature of the New Nation in relation to other nations which come to explicit expression in the Vietnam War. And his way of identifying the crisis in terms of doubts that the national destiny can really include "all these citizens who have been driven or excluded from the mainstream of society by the repeated blows of poverty and prejudice"[12] illuminates unresolved problems about the meaning of citizenship for all Americans (the problem of the 1860's) which came to inescapable expression in the conflicts over racial and civil rights.

Cherry affirms that the notion of "providential calling" was the motivating and unifying vision and power during the entire history of the United States until after World War II. That calling was understood as coming from God and compared to God's deliverance of Israel from Egyptian bondage from the very beginning. In the writings of John Winthrop and other founding fathers, Cherry finds the theme of the New Israel repeated frequently.

In the introduction to the book he edited, *Nationalism and Religion in America,* Winthrop S. Hudson describes the situation tersely and briefly.

> "The American continent and the American people became blended in a universally accepted myth of great symbolic signifiance. The continent was the Promised Land. The people were Israel, escaping from Egyptian bondage, crossing a forbidding sea, living a wilderness life, until, by God's grace and their own faithfulness, the wilderness became a new Canaan. Their pilgrimage was part and parcel of God's scheme of redemption for the whole human race.[13]

---

[11] Conrad Cherry, *op. cit.,* p. 309.
[12] Conrad Cherry, *Ibid.*
[13] Winthrop S. Hudson (ed.), *op. cit.,* pp. xxxii-xxxiii.

Hudson, then, sees the American revolution and the founding of the United States as a "religious revival" which, in the words of Perry Miller, had "the astounding good fortune to suceed."[14]

This strong identification of righteousness and divine sponsorship was sorely tested during the 1860's. Two parties within the nation were moving with righteous zeal against one another. In his Second Inaugural Address in 1865, Lincoln expresses the pathos of the situation in which both parties read the same Bible and prayed to the same God; one party invoking God's help to "make war rather than let the nation survive," the other invoking God's help to "accept war rather than let it perish." But the woe of the war, the purpose of God in relation to slavery, and the anguished division of the "city upon a hill" are vivid in the repentant, contrite, resigned, and compassionate words of Lincoln.

> "The Almighty has his own purposes. 'Woe unto the world because of offenses, for it must needs be that offenses come; but woe to that man by whom the offense cometh.' (Matthew 18:2) If we shall suppose that American slavery is one of those offenses which, in the providence of through his appointed time, he now wills to remove and that he gives to both North and South this terrible war as the woe due to those by whom the offense came, shall we discern therein any departure from those divine attributes which the believers in a living God always ascribe to him. Fondly do we hope, fervently do we pray, that this mighty scourge of war may speedily pass away. Yet, if God wills that it continue until all the wealth piled up by the bondsmen's two hundred and fifty years of unrequited toil shall be sunk and until every drop of blood drawn with the lash shall be paid by another drawn with the sword, as was said three thousand years ago so still it must be said: 'The judgments of the Lord are true and righteous altogether.' " (Psalm 19:9)

> "With malice toward none, with charity for all, with firmness in the right as God gives us to see the right, let us strive on to finish the work we are in, to bind up the nation's wounds, to care for him who shall have borne the battle, and for his widow, and his orphan—to do all which may achieve a just and a lasting peace, among ourselves and with all nations." [15]

---

[14] Perry Miller, "From the Covenant to Revival," in James W. Smith and A. Leland Jamison (eds.) Religion in American Life (Princeton, 1961), Vol. I, pp. 350-353. Quoted in Winthrop S. Hudson, op. cit., p. xxxiii.

[15] Abraham Lincoln, "Second Inaugural Address," March 4, 1865. Quoted in Winthrop R. Hudson (ed.), op. cit., pp. 85-86. Cf also Inaugural Addresses of the Presidents of the United States (Washington, D.C. 1965), pp. 3, 127-128.

Although Lincoln's sensitive spirit and eloquent words provided a way for citizens to separate their claim to righteousness within a kind of "manifest destiny" from God's calling the people to be his people, it is clear that the majority of the American people refused Lincoln's insight and continued to interpret the security, success, prosperity, and expansion of the United States as God's gift to a just and righteous nation. The critical flaw of the evil and sin of slavery was not allowed to penetrate the union of "righteousness" with "divine favor." Before the war was over, George S. Phillips showed the way for what became an elaborate and unrepentant view of the apocalyptic destiny of the United States.

> "Our mission . . . should only be accomplished when the last despot should be dethroned, and last chains of oppression broken, the dignity and equality of redeemed humanity everywhere acknowledged, republican government everywhere established, and the American flag . . . should wave over every land and encircle the world with its majestic folds. Then, and not till then, should the nation have accomplished the purpose for which it was established by the God of heaven." [16]

The first World War, the great depression, and the severe challenge to Great Britain and the United States during World War II made it difficult to boast of the United States as a New Canaan, flowing with milk and honey, the Kingdom of God. Shortly after the war, however, President Dwight Eisenhower wove many of the threads of religion in America together in a public and explicit fabric of "God and Country" that was the most public and far-reaching in American history. Indeed, through the interpretation of the victory of the United States in the 1860's, in World War I and World War II, President Eisenhower came so close to identifying the cause of God with that of the United States that it became almost impossible to raise questions about evil within and of the United States.

To question God was to question the United States, and to question the United States was to question God. It was both unpatriotic and atheistic to raise serious questions about God or

---

[16] John Howard Pugh, *The Success and Promise of the American Union* (Philadelphia, 1865), pp. 171-173. Quoted in Winthrop S. Hudson, *op. cit.*, p. 74.

about the United States. Given that view, it was particularly difficult to claim the "Will of God" as the basis of any serious question about social, economic, and political conditions in the United States. "There seemed to be consensus that personal religious faith was an essential element in proper patriotic commitment.[17]

While he was President of Columbia University, Eisenhower said: "Democracy is the political expression of a deeply felt religion."[18] Whatever profundity that statement might possibly contain was soon obscured by another declaration in 1954. "Our government makes no sense unless it is founded on a deeply felt religious faith—and I don't care what it is."[19] Under his leadership, religion was almost "established," as prayer breakfasts became regular at the White House, "under God" was added to the Pledge of Allegiance (1954), and, in 1956, there was a special ceremony celebrating the issuance of a new postage stamp with the motto, "In God We Trust," raising that statement to the level of national motto. President Eisenhower became, in the view of Sidney Ahlstrom, "a prestigious symbol of generalized religiosity and America's self-satisfied patriotic moralism."[20]

Through his own utterances and the interpretation given to the struggle by his Secretary of State, John Foster Dulles, the stage was set for the turn to piety to be identified with the national strategy of the United States. In an address in 1956, Dulles could say: "This nation was conceived with a sense of mission and dedicated to the extension of freedom throughout the world" and conclude that address on "Freedom's New Task" with a statement by Benjamin Franklin in 1777.

> "It is a common observation here that our cause is the cause of all mankind, and that we are fighting for their liberty in defending our own. It is a glorious task assigned us by Providence: which has, I trust, given us spirit and virtue equal to it, and will at last crown it with success." [21]

[17] Sidney E. Ahlstrom, *op. cit.,* p. 954.

[18] Cf. Martin Gustafson, "The Religion of a President." *Christian Century,* April 30, 1969, pp. 610-13.

[19] *Christian Century* 71 (1954). Quoted in Ahlstrom, op. cit., p. 954.

[20] Sidney E. Ahlstrom, *op. cit.,* p. 954.

[21] John Foster Dulles, "Freedom's New Task," delivered to the Philadelphia Bulletin Forum, February 26, 1956. *Vital Speeches of the Day,* March 15, 1956, pp. 329-31. Quoted in Conrad Cherry, *op. cit.,* pp. 320-27. Cf. especially p. 327.

Given that kind of sentiment among the leaders and the people it is not surprising that close league developed between religion and the anti-communist foreign policy of the nation. The contrast between the "religious principles of democracy": and "godless communism" became customary even if many people did not finally agree with the slander and extremism of Senator Joseph McCarthy's hunt for communists throughout the land. Such a clear and neat view of the situation; light against darkness, freedom against slavery, righteousness against evil, God against Satan, hardly encouraged the American people to attend to the unfinished business of their own revolution. It is quite understandable, then, that protests of the counter culture and the civil rights movement appeared at the outset to be subversive explosions caused by witting or unwitting agents of the communist enemy.

In his incisive analysis of the Nixon Second Inaugural Address, Robert Bellah points out that except for the final sentences, Nixon is more intent on renewing confidence in ourselves and in America than he is in placing our present existence under the judgment of God. He confesses no errors or sins in relation to human rights, poverty, racism, sexism, or Vietnam. On the contrary, he points accusingly at those who have exposed the flaws in American culture and worked to remove them. God is invoked as the one to whom we shall answer for the present (1973) and for the future. Nothing in Nixon's words reflects the tragic realism of Lincoln's Second Inaugural with its awareness of the offense of war and the judgment of God upon a nation. On the contrary, Nixon sees nothing about America for God to judge negatively as he boldly proclaims America's unparalleled righteousness. Bellah sees Nixon as proclaiming "an American innocence that is awe-inspiring, stupefying, in its simplicity."[22]

In his First Inaugural Address Nixon had said: "I know America. I know the heart of America is good . . . . When we listen to 'the better angels of our nature,' we find that they celebrate the simple things, and the basic things—such as goodness, decency, love, kindness."[23] With the disclosures of the White House tapes to the

---

[22]R. Bellah, "American Civil Religion in the 1970's" in Richey and Jones, *op. cit.*, pp. 255-272. Cf. especially pp. 259-262.

[23]Quoted in Charles P. Henderson, Jr., *The Nixon Theology* (New York, 1972), p. 6.

Select Committee of Congress and the House Judiciary Committee in 1973-1974 and the humiliation of his resignation from the presidency, all of his words about "no selfish advantage," "peace with honor," "goodness, decency, love, kindness" seem hollow indeed.

However deeply one may regret the tragic simplicity of Mr. Nixon's understanding of religion, there is hardly more in the common life of the churches and the religious leaders in the United States to be encouraged about. Charles Henderson finds Nixon able to appropriate the vocabulary necessary to stimulate the confidence of Americans in themselves and in their nation, without placing the lives of the people and their nation before the power and righteousness of the transcendent God. "... Lacking a transcendent God, he seems to make patriotism his religion, the American dream his deity. Far from returning to the 'spiritual sources' that made this nation great, he accomplishes a macabre reversal of those traditions, selling the mirror image as an original."[24]

Perhaps it was to neutralize the churches, to muffle any discordant voices that might raise questions about American righteousness and chosenness, that Nixon instituted White House worship services. Even the voice of God through God's spokespersons could be made subject to White House invitation lists and protocol! In the White House worship service following Nixon's Second Inaugural, Rabbi Edgar F. Magnin outdid the Reverend Dr. Billy Graham in offering the resources of religion to support Nixon's version of the national self-interest. He spoke of Nixon as "Our great leader" and "a beautiful human being," just as Nixon together with Dr. Graham had so often evoked the perfect harmony between faith in God and faith in the nation, identifying the will of God with the welfare of the state.[25]

The totality of the capitulation of religion to the state was partially averted by the sensitive and strong words of Archbishop Joseph L. Bernardin at a service on January 21, 1973, reviving the spirit of Nathan's speech to King David: "Thou art the man," as well as the spirit of Lincoln's Second Inaugural.

---

[24]Charles P. Henderson, *op. cit.*, p. 193.
[25]Charles P. Henderson, *op. cit.*, p. 13.

"For our purposes this morning, I would simply emphasize then the need to keep alive in our society the profound sense of compassion for the poor, the suffering and the oppressed and to cultivate a firm and continuing commitment to the cause of world justice and peace.

"After the example of the Lord himself, as portrayed in the Gospel, we should be appalled at the sight of degrading poverty, racial, discrimination and all of the other forms of alienation and oppression which are still sometimes present in our affluent society.

"We must have, as did the Lord, compassion on our less fortunate brothers and sisters and more than that, we must pray for the moral courage to make whatever personal sacrifices and to adopt whatever public measures may be required to enable them to exercise their God given rights."[26]

The cumulative effect of the momentum toward unifying patriotism and religion during these critical years was to isolate the authority of justice and righteousness. The traditional association of justice with law and order was put to the test and, in instance after instance, the institutions of law and order were found lacking in justice and were challenged in the name of a higher law. Although the motivation of persons in the counter culture and the civil rights movement were varied, altogether they claimed a justice and a righteousness over against the prevailing laws and customs of mainline culture. At the same time, unprecedented duplicity and evils were becoming known in the most revered institutions of this society: government, law, education, military, family, business, medicine, labor and religion. The massive delegitimation of the unifying institutions of the culture created a situation characterized not only by vertigo and rootlessness but by a deep cleavage between the old and the young.

On May 9, 1970, President Nixon left the White House before dawn and went to the Washington monument where thousands of young persons were assembled in protest of Nixon's policies in Vietnam and Cambodia and the Kent State tragedy. In that tense and critical time, the effort to communicate with the youth ended as a tragic mismeeting. The president and many of the youth of the

---

[26]Quoted in Robert Bellah, "American Civil Religion in the 1970's" p. 263. Archbishop Bernardin was elevated to the Sacred College of Cardinals on February 2, 1983.

country find no common ground for moderating their opposition to one another. Nixon was confident of his rightness on the basis of knowledge, law, and order. The youth were confident of their rightness on the basis of justice and righteousness. A member of the Cabinet wrote a personal letter to Nixon about the matter: "I believe this Administration finds itself, today, embracing a philosophy which appears to lack appropriate concern for the attitude of a great mass of Americans—our young people."

A few days before the shooting of our students at Kent State, the governor of a western state who later won a high position in the United States government said in regard to campus demonstrations: "If it takes a bloodbath, let's get it over with." The country was so polarized that John D. Rockefeller, III wrote an article deploring our failure to know and understand our own children.[27] To many, it was impossible to be loyal to conscience and loyal to the nation as well. In that situation, many chose the costly risk of honoring a higher law, hoping that the political community would understand. The task of discerning the issues and the courage to act accordingly was difficult for all thoughtful people during those years, in spite of the limited support some received from a rather monolithic peer group.

Confusion over the relation of justice and righteousness to law and order points to tensions in the understanding of the religious calling and destiny of the United States. It is not possible to understand the American experience without regard for the religious foundations and motivations of American life. Contrary to most other modern states, the United States as a nation was founded on religious claims to deliverance from European exile and to the calling to be a people based on inalienable rights and obligations established by God. Yet there never has been general agreement about what that religious foundation means.

Conrad Cherry claims that Americans have been rather sharply divided for a long time over the meaning of the national mission, one group regarding America as called to be a "light to the

---

[27] John D. Rockefeller, III, "In Praise of Young Revolutionaries," *Saturday Review,* December 14, 1968, pp. 18-20. "Reconciling Youth and the Establishment," *Saturday Review,* January 23, 1971, pp. 27-29, 92.

nations," showing by example and persuasion the attractiveness of freedom in America; another group understanding Americans as a "chosen people" with an obligation "actively to win others to American principles and to safeguard those principles around the world,"[27a]

Cherry follows Clinton Rossiter in regarding the first understanding as the "true American Mission" the "finest expression of American nationalism," dominant during the Revolutionary and Constitutional periods, and he quotes Rossiter as follows:

> "It assumes that God at the proper stage in the march of history, called forth hardy souls from the old and privilege-ridden nations; that He carried these precious few to a new world and presented them and their descendents with an environment ideally suited to the development of a free society; and that in bestowing His grace He also bestowed a peculiar responsibility for the success of popular institutions. Were the Americans to fail in this experiment in self-government, they would fail not only themselves, but all men wanting or deserving to be free." [28]

Rossiter and Cherry admit that this understanding of the mission of America might be used to support a policy of isolationism and the refusal of responsibility for human welfare outside the United States. At the same time, they do not regard isolationism as necessary to the view, and rather read it as implying "a healthy attitude of international cooperation."[29]

The case is strikingly different with the second view of the national mission. Here Americans understand themselves as being called beyond being an example, to accepting the responsibility to assure in all nations the rights, freedom, justice and righteousness God has given America. Such a view motivated the foreign mission efforts of the American churches, especially in the 19th and 20th centuries, as well as the military obligation of the United States to defend and protect victims of totalitarian aggression in two World Wars, Korea, and Vietnam.

What may have been a legitimate and compassionate concern

[27a]Conrad Cherry, *op. cit.,* p. 22.

[28]Clinton Rossiter, "The American Mission," *The American Scholar,* 20 (1950-51), pp. 19-20. Quoted in Cherry, *op. cit.,* p. 22.

[29]Clinton Rossiter, *op. cit.,* p. 27.

for the plight of others in this view, developed into a fusing of the political and the religious missions, and the assumption of the role of savior of the world with self-justifying force. The conflict between an attitude of international cooperation with its openness and mutuality tended to be obscured by a sense of chosenness and destiny that justified and bestowed authority over other nations and cultures.

Cherry sees this second interpretation of American destiny as giving rise to a destructive and arrogant self-righteousness.

> "It has been all too easy for Americans to convince themselves they have been chosen to be free and powerful people not because God or the circumstance of history choose in mysterious ways, but because they *deserve* election. The blessing of success, wealth, and power are readily taken as signs of their having merited a special place in history." [30]

The whole experience which had the "good fortune to succeed" became questionable during the last thirty-five years. This was due partly to the uncritical fusion of national vocation and success which made it impossible for most citizens to understand the successive challenges to the legitimacy of America provided by the civil rights movement; protests against the war in Vietnam, the Supreme Court decision against prayer in public schools; the sexual revolution; increasing racism; and the loss of confidence in public order accompanied by outbreaks of violence in the streets.

B. Major Crises in American Society Since 1945

The vertigo of the last few decades and the identity crises in the church and in the chaplaincy are directly related to changes in American life and culture, many of which have happened at the same time, creating a generalized sense of confusion, fear, being lost (anomie) and even of terror. Had there been some ideas or institutions which retained their power, changes in other areas might have been contained and controlled. Had the churches and synagogues, the courts of law, or the educational institutions retained their dependability, for example, American society would

---

[30]Cherry, *op. cit.*, pp. 23-24.

have remained more steady, and changes in human rights, political and economic expectations, statute law, sexual relations, the family, and so forth might well have been handled with moderation and poise. But that was not to be. No institution was innocent or stable during this period. The luxury of reforming one institution at a time was not possible. All institutions and all conventions were in the cross fire of criticism, rejection, and reformation at the same time that individuals were searching for a dependable base for a successful human existence, a base that would not hold firm in the face of present and impending changes and assaults.

Around 1850, Herman Melville spoke of Americans as a peculiar, chosen people, who "bear the ark of the liberties of the world."

> "God has predestined . . . great things from our race; and great things we feel in our souls. . . . Long enough have we been skeptics with regard to ourselves, and doubted whether, indeed, the political Messiah has come. But he has come in us, if we would but give utterance to his promptings." [31]

That kind of assurance about America along with an unquestioning confidence in wealth and power as signs of the fulfillment of the promise of America were no longer present in American culture after the early 1950's. Ambassador Warren Austin could speak to the United Nations at the outset of President Truman's commitment of American armed forces to defend South Korea, claiming the generous and self-sacrificing nature of that action with no self-serving interest by the United States. In that speech there was resonance with Melville's claim a century earlier that with America, almost for the first time in the history of earth, national selfishness is unbounded philanthropy; for we cannot do a good to America, but we give alms to the wolrd. [32] But even as Ambassador Austin was claiming American righteousness before the world, there were increasing signs that the causes of native Americans, Blacks,

---

[31]Ernest Lee Tuveson, *Redeemer Nation* (Chicago 1968), p. 157. Quoted in Robert Bellah, *The Broken Covenant*, pp. 38-39.

[32]Ernest Lee Tuveson, *op. cit.*, p. 157. Quoted in Robert Bellah, *The Broken Covenant*, p. 39. Melville later changed his mind, Cf. Clorel, published in 1876.

minorities, women, and the poor would erupt and put in question all claims to "manifest destiny" and the "New Israel."

The most shattering crises to the internal stability of the United States were: 1) the Supreme Court Decision about Prayer in Public Schools; 2) the Civil and Human Rights Movement; 3) the Vietnam War; and 4) Watergate. One of the most tangible indications of how many people responded to these crises as well as to the religion of the main line churches is suggested by the growth of the new religious movements.

1. Prayer in the Public Schools

With the rulings of the Supreme Court in *Engle vs. Vitale* in 1962 and in *Abingdon School District vs. Schempp* in 1963, the long-standing practice of prayer and devotions in public schools became illegal. Tremors from these decisions shook the nation at volatile and foundational levels causing shocked citizens and officeholders to appeal to the people to disobey the decisions and to press Congress to pass a law reversing the decisions.

In June 1962, the Supreme Court ruled in *Engle vs. Vitale* against the use of a required prayer presented by the Regents in New York. The long dissenting opinion was written by Justice Stewart who saw free exercise of religion rather than establishment of religion as the overriding issue. Elements of Justice Douglas' concurring opinion,[33] as well as the decision of the Court itself, gave the American people pause about the precedent this decision set for future decisions. In his analysis of this decision, Paul Ramsey spoke alarmingly of the radical shift in both American and western culture which these decisions represented; "The prayer decisions signal the final end of the Constantinian era, and Christianity (or religion) has likely been conducted to its exit from determinative influence upon the institutions of society at the point where it entered."[34]

For Ramsey and for many others, these prayer decisions went further than ruling against the establishment of religion and constricted the "free exercise" of religion in schools so completely,

---

[33]*Engle v. Vitale*, 370 U.S. 421 (1962).
[34]Paul Ramsey, "How Shall We Sing the Lord's Song in a Pluralistic Land?" *Journal of Public Law*, Volume 13, No. 2, 1964, p. 360.

that, in effect, secularism or secular humanism became established. Ramsey saw the decisions as setting the precedent for
removing "In God We Trust" from our coins, "under God" from the
Pledge of Allegiance to the Flag, chaplains from the military
services, prayer from the floor of Congress and every other vestige
of the acknowledgement of God from the public life of America.
He acknowledged the increasing pluralism of religion in American
life, particularly the role of Roman Catholicism and Judaism in
taking the place of a dominant Protestant culture, but feared a
new movement in culture.

> "There is . . . a sub-pagan culture gaining the dominance in post-
> Protestant America, as there is a sub-pagan world culture gaining
> world-wide dominance in this post-Christian and also post-religious age.
> In neither case is the civilization of the future likely to be based on a
> humane or humanistic culture congenial to any of these pluralistic
> religious communities."[35]

The general response of the public to these decisions confirmed
the widespread notion that a foundation stone of American life
had been tampered with, that opposition to religious activities in
the public schools was, in effect, opposition to religion and to God.
Senator Talmadge (Democrat, Georgia) described the decision
as "unconscionable . . . an outrageous edict . . . .[36] Congressman
Williams (Democrat, Mississippi) regarded the decision as "a
deliberately and carefully planned conspiracy to substitute
materialism for spiritual values and thus to communize America."[37]
Senator Robertson (Democrat, Virginia) said that this was the most
extreme ruling the Supreme Court had ever made in favor of
atheists and agnostics.[38]

Representative Rivers (Democrat, South Carolina) charged the
Supreme Court with having "now officially stated its disbelief in
God Almighty."[39] Even Senator Eugene McCarthy (Democrat,

---

[35]Paul Ramsey, op. cit., p. 363.
[36]108 Cong. Rec. 11675 (1962).
[37]108 Cong. Rec. 11734 (1962).
[38]108 Cong. Rec. 11708 (1962).
[39]Quoted by Leo Pfeffer in Information Bulletin No. 6 Commission on Law and Social Actions of
the American Jewish Congress, August 15, 1962, p. 2.

Minnesota) joined those who denounced the decision saying that it will lead to "not only a secularized government but to a secularized society."[40] Congressman Andrews (Democrat, Alabama) was quoted as saying of the Court: "They put the Negroes into the schools and now they have driven God out of them."[41]

The decision on *Abingdon School District vs. Schempp*, handed down on June 17, 1963, aroused much less opposition than the *Engel* decision. A Gallup Poll showed seventy percent opposed to the decision, twenty-four percent approving and six percent having no opinion. The formal religious communities were more moderate in this case than in the *Engel* case, but political opposition, perhaps related to popular opinion, became deep and determined. Governor Wallace of Alabama, copying his adversaries in the school desegration decision of 1954, called for a "pray-in." If the court rules "that we cannot read the Bible in some school I'm going to that school and read it myself," he said.[42] Governor Ross Barnett of Mississippi declared his intention "to tell every teacher in Mississippi to conduct prayers and Bible reading despite what the Supreme Court says."[43] One member of the Kentucky State Board of Education said, after its meeting was opened with a Bible reading, sermon, and a prayer: "If the procedure is illegal, I move to violate the Constitution.[44]

Following the *Schempp* decision there were 113 constitutional amendments introduced in the House and twenty-seven in the Senate to reverse the Supreme Court Decision, almost twice the number introduced after the Regents Prayer case.

The effort to counter the Supreme Court was led by Gerald K. Smith and Dr. Carl McIntyre's International Christian Youth and its "Project American." The "Jew" Emmanuel Celler was designated as the demon of the piece, but a wide spectrum of persons were branded as enemies of God, religion, and America. An article in McIntyre's *Christian Beacon* was hardly short of venomous in its

---

[40]108 Cong. Rec. 11844 (1962).

[41]Cf. *Journal of Public Law*, note 15, p. 478.

[42]*New York Times*, Aug. 6, 1963, p. 17, col. 3, Quoted in Beaney and Beiser, *op. cit.*, p. 486.

[43]*New Orleans Times Picayune*, June 20, 1963, p. 6. Quoted in Beaney and Beiser, *op. cit.*, p. 487.

[44]*Louisville Courier Journal*, June 27, 1963.

appeal. "It is going to be up to the great rank and file of the Christian people of the United States to stand against this coalition of modernists, Jews, infidels, Unitarians and Atheists in their determination to keep the Bible out of the schools."[45]

The argument for Bible reading in the public schools became increasingly uniform and shrill, and has persisted in similar form even into the 1980's. Beaney and Beiser describe the argument: "The people favor such practices; the Court's decisions are an attack on God and on religion; this country was founded on a belief in God, and cannot exist without it; majorities have rights, and they need not always bow to the will of an 'atheistic' minority."[46]

Under the impact of growing opposition from a broad based religious coalition and serious and unanswered questions posed by astute and scholarly opponents, all of which received wide press coverage, support for the Becker Amendment began to dissolve and it became politically "safe" for Congressmen to take positions against the amendment. It was clear that sharp differences divided the people of the United States as to the meaning of religion in relation to government and public education. Some thoughtful and patriotic persons of faith maintained that required prayer in public schools would violate the Constitution. Others, equally thoughtful and patriotic persons of faith, strongly maintained that the republic would be destroyed without it.

2. The Civil and Human Rights Movement

At the burning center of the turbulent changes within the United States in the post World War II years were two issues. One involved foreign relations, especially the relations with the Soviet Union which entailed several strategies to "contain" communist influence and which eventually split the nation morally and politically over the Vietnam War. The other issue was an internal one, that of full rights and citizenship for all the people of the United States, especially the blacks who had been brought to this country against their will, bought and sold as goods or possessions, and segregated from the dominant culture in housing, employment,

---

[45]"Fighting the Bible" in *Christian Beacon,* November 21, 1963.
[46]William M. Beaney and Edward N. Beiser, *op. cit.,* p. 499.

voting, eating, medical care, education, recreation, and religion. Reflecting on their equal sacrifice during the war, their equal taxation, their equal stake in the future of the United States, and strongly motivated by moral outrage at justice deferred and postponed, many blacks in many places took to the streets to put their case before the American people. No issue since 1865 had divided and aroused the people about the meaning of citizenship as this one did. Again, as was the case with the issue about prayer in the public schools, the voice of religion was ambiguous as contenders on all sides claimed divine sanctions for their positions. Before looking at the Vietnam War, we must reconsider the Civil Rights movement.

Mr. Thurgood Marshall, legal director of the National Association for the Advancement of Colored People (NAACP), pleaded the case before the Supreme Court known as *Brown vs. Board of Education*. On principle, he won the case handsomely, for Chief Justice Earl Warren wrote of the decision: " . . . In the field of public education the doctrine of 'separate but equal' has no place." In practice, however, the victory was only partial because of the absence of enforcement provisions. The southern states pleaded for a gradual enforcement.

A "Southern Manifesto" signed by nineteen senators and twenty-seven representatives from eleven southern states called for "massive resistance" to the Supreme Court's decision. Alabama declared "*Brown* 'null, void and of no effect' and defied a court order to admit a black woman to the state university. In response to Alabama's action the federal government did nothing."[47] Because of what appeared to be indifference in the federal government, many southern whites joined the Ku Klux Klan or organized "citizens councils" to resist implementation by punishing anyone, clergy-person or farmer, who was inclined toward compliance. The *Brown* decision had made southern whites more fearful, more angry, more resourceful and more violent than before, But it had also made blacks hungrier than ever for equality.[48]

---

[47]Milton Viorst, *Fire in the Streets: America in the 1960's.* (New York, 1978), p. 27. I am indebted to Viorst's work at a number of points.

[48]Viorst, *op. cit.,* p. 27.

On December 1, 1955, Rosa L. Parks was arrested for violating the Alabama segregation law, was taken off a bus by policemen, and driven to the jail where she was formally charged. Her offense was that she refused to give up her seat on the bus as whites were filling the bus from the front. On December 3, many black leaders met at the Dexter Avenue Baptist Church and decided to start a bus boycott on December 5. Soon the blacks formed an organization, the Montgomery Improvement Association (MIA), through which it was possible to focus their challenge to the power of the white majority. E. D. Nixon was elected treasurer and Martin Luther King, Jr. was elected president. Nixon saw the struggle as predominantly economic and possibly violent. King saw it as predominantly moral/religious and absolutely non-violent. In a tense moment after King's house was bombed he said to the gathered crowd:

"If you have weapons take them home. If you do not have them, please do not seek to get them. We cannot solve this problem through retaliatory violence . . . Jesus still cries out in words that echo across the centuries: 'Love your enemies; bless them that curse you; pray for them that despitefully use you.' This is what we must live by. We must meet hate with love."[49]

Looking back on it, the three conditions which the MIA set for ending the boycott seem surprisingly modest: 1) courteous treatment of blacks by bus drivers; 2) seating on a first-come first-served basis, blacks back to front, whites front to back; and 3) employment of black operators on routes through predominantly black neighborhoods. With these demands, modest or not, what was to be known as the Movement had begun.

Just when it seemed that the wealth and power of the white power structures would win against the bus boycott, the MIA gave up on getting the Rosa Parks case through the appeal process in Alabama to the Supreme Court and decided to file a civil suit directly in federal court on behalf of several persons who swore that they had been mistreated on the buses. Three federal judges heard the case and on June 4, 1956, ruled in favor of the MIA, two to one,

---

[49]Martin Luther King, Jr., *Stride Toward Freedom* (New York 1964), p. 117.

and declared the Montgomery bus segregation ordinance unconstitutional.

The City of Montgomery appealed the case. The Supreme Court sustained the decision of the lower court in favor of MIA on November 13, 1956, but the decision did not arrive in Montgomery until December 20. The city commission insisted that it "will not yield one inch, but will do all in its power to oppose the integration of the Negro race with the white race in Montgomery, and will forever stand like a rock against social equality, inter-marriage, and mixing of the races under God's creation and plan."[50] White citizens Councils and the Ku Klux Klan escalated the threats of terror and predicted violence and bloodshed. King and other MIA leaders urged the black community to stay together and to "move from protest to reconciliation," and many of the leaders actually rode the buses for the first few days after the boycott to reduce provocation and to encourage Blacks to keep to the strategy of non-violence.

This marked the end of an era of segregation and the beginning of the Civil Rights Movement, not so much in the actual achievements in Montgomery, but in the new confidence among the blacks, supported by many whites, that the cause was right and just and that it could be won through the combined strategy of challenging the law and arranging carefully chosen demonstrations and protests. And, although it would be severely tested later in the Movement, King's leadership in Montgomery had established the convictional and tactical importance of non-violence.

"It was that nonviolence was not a strategy of weakness, passivity and cowardice, as many had once believed. Nonviolence was not valuable merely in demonstrating the moral superiority of the oppressed over the oppressors. The experience had shown that it was a positive strategy to which blacks could adapt, which the south could not ignore, and which the world would applaud. The challenge would now be to apply it to other situations, for more grandiose ends."[51]

The more grandiose ends were, indeed, the reversing of two

[50]Martin Luther King, Jr., op. cit., p. 147.
[51]Viorst. op. cit., p. 50.

centuries of denial of freedom, injustice, and the vote to the Negro. The Movement had begun, the most visible part of which was the demonstrations. But, the not so visible aspects of the Movement were nonetheless important—registering voters, organizing committees, taking legal actions, and developing organization at the local and national levels. The Movement had begun because people had broken out of voluntary submission to the inevitability of the structures that had prevailed in the past. They began to sense new possibilities and caught fire, which meant that they were singing and hopeful, confident that their actions could open the doors to a new and different kind of future. As Martin Luther King, Jr., put it: "The once dormant and quiescent Negro community was now fully awake."[52]

The black church was not only the rallying place for the movement, but the keeper and formative influence of what W.E.B. DuBois called "the souls of black folk,"[53] a soul with the courage to undergo severe trial for the sake of justice and a soul with such love that there was care even for the enemy, a love expressed in a disciplined strategy of non-violence.

The Little Rock school desegregation battle came in 1957, a battle in which the powers of the federal government through the Arkansas National Guard confronted the powers of Governor Orvill Faubus of Arkansas. The Supreme Court ordered that nine black students be admitted to Central High School of Little Rock. The state defied the order and federal troops were sent in to enforce it. All of the elements of crisis that were to be repeated many times were present: the black students, the white students, school officials, local police, federal troops, angry parents, and others assembled outside the school. There were skirmishes, insults, accusations—but Central High School was no longer, and probably would never again be, a segregated high school.

On February 1, 1960, the "sit ins" began when four freshmen from the all-black North Carolina Agricultural and Technical College in Greensboro, North Carolina sat at the lunch counter at Woolworth's and ordered coffee. They were refused, but sat at the counter until

---

[52]Martin Luther King, Jr., *Stride Toward Freedom* (New York 1964). p. 40.
[53]W. E. Burghardt DuBois, *The Souls of Black Folk* (New York 1967).

the store closed for the day. Twenty other students joined the four the next day. Soon there were hundreds of others, black and white. All remained non-violent; but with anger rising, the officials at Woolworth's decided to close the store. Quickly the idea of a sit-in spread to other towns and campuses, including Raleigh, Durham, and Charlotte, North Carolina and Hampton, Virginia.

In Nashville, there were months of preparation under the poised leadership of John Lewis, a theology student, and James M. Lawson, Jr. who was convinced of the power of "New Testament pacifism," and who enrolled in the School of Theology at Vanderbilt University. Lawson became the real teacher of non-violence, conducting workshops and training sessions continuously. On February 18, twelve days after the almost spontaneous event in Greensboro, a well rehearsed, carefully planned sit-in effort started in Nashville which has been called the "largest, best-disciplined and most influential" of all the sit-ins of the early 1960's.[54]

The sit-in in Nashville began peacefully, with the students well-dressed and polite, and the clerks at the lunch counters and city officials more bewildered than angry. There were no arrests and no attacks on the blacks by vigilante groups. But toward the end of February the situation changed and on February 27, seventy-seven blacks and five white students were arrested and charged with disorderly conduct. The police did not restrain the white militants who were anxious to handle the black's protest in their own way.

The mood among the demonstrators was more of confidence in the rightness of the cause for all of America than fear of what the local power structure might do to them. For many of them, that was the first time to be arrested, and parents and friends were upset because they had always thought of arrests in relation to *immorality,* not to *morality.* John Lewis described what it was like being on the other side of the law.

"It was the first time in my life I had ever been arrested. This cop came up and said, 'You're under arrest,' and hundreds, maybe thousands of

---

[54]Viorst, *op. cit.,* p. 107.

angry whites who were standing on the streets applauded when they took us away. I had a certain amount of fear, because growing up in rural Alabama had instilled in me that you don't get in trouble with the law . . . Yet in a strange way I found it was also a good feeling. I felt at the time it was like a crusade. All of us then believed that we were in a holy war. Back on the campuses, the students heard we had been arrested and, after an hour or so, there were about five hundred more students occupying our places."[55]

Many of the persons arrested were convicted of disorderly conduct and chose jail and/or a workhouse to paying the fine of fifty dollars. It was a matter of principle for them not to cooperate with the system by paying the fine. When they stated their position, many of those who had been released rejoined those in jail.

In the negotiations with the officials of Nashville, made possible by a bi-racial committee appointed by Mayor Ben West, the name of the Reverend James Lawson became public for the first time, and he was arrested. In a meeting with Mayor West on March 1, James Lawson became conspicuous among the black clergy present when he told the mayor of Nashville "that the local segregation ordinance was a 'gimmick to manipulate the Negro.'"[56]

Shortly thereafter, Lawson held a press conference in response to the new interest in him. The white community was surprised to learn that Lawson had been training workshop groups in non-violent protests for over a year, instilling self-esteem and confidence in the morality and rightness of the cause at the same time. They were also surprised that Lawson was a doctoral student in Theology at Vanderbilt University. In spite of strong support from the faculty of the Divinity School, Lawson was quickly expelled from Vanderbilt because of his involvement in unlawful acts.

The blacks became restive toward the end of March and began again to exert pressure through boycotts, prayer vigils, and appearances at local white churches. Even so, the bi-racial committee had reached no substantive agreement. That truce was

---

[55]*The Nashville Tennessean.* Sunday, February 28, 1960, p. 1 under heading: "75 Students Arrested Here."

[56]Viorst, *op. cit.,* p. 109.

dramatically broken on April 19, however, when a bomb exploded at the house of City Councilman Z. A Looby, a highly respected citizen, leader in the NAACP, and legal counsel to those protesting segregation in Nashville. The house was almost demolished, two other houses nearby were damaged, and over a hundred windows broken in the Meharry Medical College across from the Looby house.

Things in Nashville took a new direction immediately. The Central Committee sent a telegram to Mayor West announcing a non-violent march from the campus of Tennessee State University to the City Hall. A crowd estimated by the *Nashville Tennessean* to have been "3000 demonstrating Negroes" and by John Lewis as nearly "6000 blacks and whites" confronted the Mayor at City Hall. Mayor West announced that he favored opening the restaurants of Nashville to all persons and he made an appeal. "I appeal to all citizens to end discrimination, to have no bigotry, no bias, no hatred."[57]

On the day after the march to City Hall, Martin Luther King, Jr. came to Nashville to join the victory celebration. The Fisk gymnasium was filled with white and blacks who heard King say: "I came to Nashville not to bring inspiration, but to gain inspiration from the greatest movement that has taken place in this community." The sit-ins in Nashville had raised the Movement beyond the effort by blacks for local change.

The Movement had become a call for justice overall for the blacks and it had become the cause of massive numbers of Americans, black and white, in all regions. The strategy developed in Nashville was to be followed in place after place. The students also became a self-conscious group and emphasized their peculiar place in the struggle by organizing the Student Non-Violent Coordinating Committee. They championed "participatory democracy," but found it difficult to hold to the conviction and strategy of non-violence.

In 1961 the Congress of Racial Equality sponsored the Freedom Rides. James Farmer was the strategist for the rides. He was convinced that the bigots of the south would be outraged by the

---

[57]Viorst, *op. cit.*, p. 116.

rides and would react violently, forcing the federal government to take action to *protect* the constitutional rights of black Americans. The rides succeeded and the world learned through these media events what segregation was in the United States and what some people would do to their fellow citizens, fellow Christians, and fellow human beings in order to perpetuate segregation.

There was brutality in Anniston and Birmingham, Alabama, and in other cities. The nation was aroused and President Kennedy and the Attorney General dispatched federal marshalls to protect the riders until the governors of the states ordered National Guardsmen to control the situation. The tenseness of the situation was told to Viorst by James Farmer.

> "I had seen fear in the eyes of some of the kids as they climbed the steps of the bus. But there was also something there that transcended fear. On the bus I noticed some of the students writing notes, boys writing notes and putting them in their pockets, and girls putting them in their brassieres. I went across the aisle to find out what it was. They were writing names and addresses of next of kin. They really had not expected to live beyond that trip. But it was something they had to do, and they were determined to go."[58]

The Freedom Rides brought an end to segregation in interstate commerce on November 1, 1961. Beyond that, however, they had forced the United States government to take sides on the issue. The federal government became a significant ally of the Movement to protect the civil rights of all persons.

By 1963, Birmingham, Alabama, had become a place of repeated confrontations between determined blacks and equally determined officials of the white power structure. Demonstrators were met with fire hoses, beatings, cattle-prods, and arrests. Many feared the explosive destructiveness of a riot. Joining one of the demonstrations, Martin Luther King, Jr., was arrested with others, and his well known "Letter From Birmingham Jail" was written, April 16, 1963, in response to a statement published by eight fellow clergy from Alabama. The published statement, in essence, asked the blacks to be patient, claiming that progress was being made

---

[58]Viorst, *op. cit.*, pp. 156-157.

and that the new mayor of Birmingham (Albert Boutwell) should be given a chance. Anxiety was expressed about the breaking of laws, and the Police Department of Birmingham was commended for keeping order and preventing violence.[59] The split within the church over the Civil Rights Movement, especially in the south, is precisely expressed in Martin Luther King's letter.

My Dear Fellow Clergymen:
While confined here in the Birmingham city jail, I came across your recent statement calling my present activities "unwise and untimely." . . . .

I think I should indicate why I am here in Birmingham, since you have been influenced by the view which argues against "outsiders coming in." I have the honor of serving as President of the Southern Christian Leadership Conference, an organization operating in every southern state, with headquarters in Atlanta, Georgia . . . . Several months ago the affiliate here in Birmingham asked us to be on call to engage in a non-violent direct-action program if such were deemed necessary. We readily consented, and when the hour came we lived up to our promise. So I, along with several members of my staff, am here because I have organizational ties here. . . .

Though I was initially disappointed at being categorized as an extremist, as I continued to think about the matter, I gradually gained a measure of satisfaction from the label. Was not Jesus an extremist for love: "Love your enemies, bless them that curse you, do good to them that hate you, and pray for them which despitefully use you, and persecute you." Was not Amos an extremist for justice: "Let justice roll down like waters and righteousness like an ever-flowing stream." Was not Martin Luther an extremist: "Here I stand, I cannot do otherwise, so help me God." And John Bunyan: "I will stay in jail to the end of my days before I make a butchery of my conscience." Abraham Lincoln: "This nation cannot survive half slave and half free." And Thomas Jefferson: "We hold these truths to be self-evident, that all men are created equal . . ." So the question is not whether we will be extremists, but what kind of extremists we will be. Will we be extremists for hate or for love? Will we be extremists for the preservation of injustice or for the extension of justice?

I wish you had commended the Negro sit-inners and demonstrators of

---

[59]See Appendix A for the full text of the letter from the Birmingham clergy and the names of the clergy who signed it.

Birmingham for their sublime courage, their willingness to suffer and their amazing discipline in the midst of great provocation. One day the south will recognize the real heroes. . . . They will be the young high school and college students, the young ministers of the gospel and a host of their elders, courageously and non-violently sitting in at lunch counters and willingly going to jail for conscience' sake. One day the south will know that when these disinherited children of God sat down at lunch counters, they were in reality standing up for what is best in the American dream and for the most sacred values in our Judaeo-Christian heritage.

I hope this letter finds you strong in the faith. I also hope that circumstances will soon make it possible for me to meet each of you, not as an integrationist or a civil-rights leader but as a fellow clergyman and a Christian brother. Let us all hope that the dark clouds of racial prejudice will soon pass away and the deep fog of misunderstanding will be lifted from our fear-drenched communities, and in some not too distant tomorrow the radiant stars of love and brotherhood will shine over our great nation with all their scintillating beauty.

Yours for the cause of Peace and Brotherhood,

Martin Luther King, Jr.[60]

In 1962 many students focused their protest in the organization of Students for a Democratic Society (SDS) and in the writing of "Port Huron Statement" which gathered together many aspects of resentment against the establishment and stated the case for an option of the "New Left." "Participatory democracy" and "let the people decide" were chanted repeatedly. All sorts of malaise about contemporary life were mobilized against business, government, the military, and the educational system as institutions repressive of human needs and values. Hence a strategy of militancy was legitimized by the elitist claim that these and these only were the ones who would save society.

From its opening words, "We are the people of this generation, bred in at least modest comfort, housed now in universities, looking uncomfortably to the world we inherit," opposed "the depersonalization that reduces human beings to the status of things," and, in general, enfranchised and elevated discontent which could be focused on many different issues as the occasion arose, and

---

[60]Martin Luther King, Jr., "Letter From Birmingham City Jail."

justified the effort by a vague, implicit if not explicit, utopian expectation that all the problems besetting humanity could be solved if we only make the right moves.

On August 28, 1963, there was the march on Washington and King's electrifying speech, "I Have a Dream" That was the largest demonstration for human rights ever: a movement of almost ecstatic vision of the possibilities of different cultural groups working and living together as a human family in peace and justice. A. Philip Randolph, the tireless pioneer in the struggle for Negro rights, and Bayard Rustin, who had envisioned a march on Washington since 1941, worked out details of a plan for between 100,000 and 250,000 persons to come into Washington early in the morning and leave late in the afternoon. The prospects of success were boosted considerably when on July 17, President Kennedy announced his support of the march. He saw the march as a "peaceful assembly for the redress of grievances. They are going to express their strong views. I think it's in the great tradition. I look forward to being there."[61] White clergy—Catholic, Protestant, Jewish—joined in sponsoring the march. The event was by all estimates a unique one in American history. To be sure, it provoked Strom Thurmond and it set the stage for the passage of President Kennedy's Civil Rights Bill in 1964.

As the warm memory faded before the hard facts of unemployment, underemployment, and the problems in the centers of the cities, new strains developed on the strategy of non-violence as they had previously sharpened in Birmingham. Black Power became a slogan and the vision of racial harmony within love was pushed back until the genuineness of the love and equality of the black were assured.

Black separatism took many forms—black religion, black theology, black business, black education, black caucuses, black community—all expressing that the secret of the birth of a new America lies with the blacks, not with the whites. As Stokely Carmichael was to say: "For racism to die, a totally different America must be born."[62]

---

[61]Quoted in Viorst, op. cit., p. 225.

[62]Stokely Carmichael, "What We Want," New York Review of Books, Vol. 7, No. 4 (Sept. 22, 1966), p. 6. Quoted in Vincent Harding, "The Religion of Black Power," Donald R. Cutter (ed.), The Religious Situation, (Boston, 1968), p. 27.

Black Power came to represent a challenge to the strategy of non-violence which was fundamental to Martin Luther King, Jr. In a chapter on "Black Power" in *Where Do We Go From Here?*, King identifies the issue.

"There is nothing essentially wrong with power. The problem is that in America power is unequally distributed. This has led the Negro Americans in the past to seek their goals through love and moral suasion devoid of power and white Americans to seek their goals through power devoid of love and conscience. It is leading a few extremists today to advocate for Negroes the same destructive and conscienceless power that they have justly abhorred in whites. It is precisely this collision of immoral power with powerless morality which constitutes the major crisis of our times."[63]

Black Power became significant precisely because "love and moral suasion" seemed to be a "powerless morality" with limited results, and, more importantly, because the achievement of justice for the blacks would otherwise depend on the whites to surrender power. King had a dream of reconciliation but to some he seemed not to be realistic enough about entrenched forces of evil in society and the reluctance of persons with power to surrender it voluntarily. Black Power, on the other side, was quite realistic about confronting entrenched power even if bloodshed were necessary, but seemed to have no dream of reconciliation. Vincent Harding, who has been identified with Black Power, recognized the need of these two perspectives for each other, "for the mutual sharing and the possible mutual growth which may well be the nation's only visible hope in the racial crisis."

In a passage reminiscent of Reinhold Niebuhr and Paul Tillich, Harding expresses a hope for the future in religious terms, with each position purged of its "love without power" and its "power without love" and motivated to serve the purposes of God's kingdom, a kingdom beyond full identification with either side of this struggle.

"Perhaps there is still a Beloved Community ahead. But if it is, it must be seen as the Kingdom whose realization does not depend upon whether

---

[63]Martin Luther King, Jr., *Where Do We Go From Here?* (New York, Bantam, 1968), p. 43.

whites (or anyone else around) really wants it or not. If it comes, it may come only for those who seek it for its own sake and for the sake of its Lord, recognizing that even if he is black, the final glory is not the glory of blackness, but a setting straight of all the broken men and communities of the earth. In some strange ways Black Power must be headed in that way, but it probably needs some new and stripped-down coming of Martin King's most fervent hopes to accompany its path."[64]

In 1954 there was the decision to desegregate the public schools. This was followed by the Civil Rights Bill in 1964 and the Voting Rights Act in 1965. Each of these steps brought about limited changes accompanied by an appalling amount of resistance and refusal. The union was preserved, but, overall, this Movement represented the shaking of the foundations of American society, leaving the meaning of citizenship, patriotism, and morality very confused, and the role of religion so ambiguous that every thoughtful person was forced to reassess all of the elements of the "received tradition" and to decide within the complex cauldron of events where the interests of the Kingdom of God most clearly lay.

3. The Vietnam War

There is wide agreement that the war in Vietnam was the most divisive foreign policy issue in the United States in the twentieth century and perhaps for the entire history of the country. The extent of the polarization is suggested by the sharply contrasting appraisals of Vietnam by President Johnson, by Telford Taylor, who had been U.S. Chief Counsel at Nuremberg following World War II, and by a leading military strategist during that war, General William C. Westmoreland.

"We are in Vietnam to fulfill one of the most solemn pledges of the American nation. Three Presidents—President Eisenhower, President Kennedy, and your present President—over eleven years have committed themselves and have promised to help defend this small and valiant nation." (President Johnson, July 28, 1965).

"One may well echo the acrid French epigram, and say that all this 'is worse than a crime, it is a blunder'—the most costly and tragic national

---

[64]Vincent Harding, "The Religion of Black Power," *op. cit.*, p. 37.

blunder in American history . . . None there will ever thank us; few elsewhere that do not now see our America as a sort of Steinbeckian 'Lennie' (John Steinbeck, *Of Mice and Men*), gigantic and powerful, but prone to shatter what we try to save. Somehow we failed ourselves to learn the lessons we undertook to teach at Nuremberg, and that failure is today's American tragedy."[65](Taylor)

"On the other hand, history may judge that American aid to South Vietnam constituted one of man's most noble crusades, one that has less to do with the domino theory and a strategic interest for the United States than with the simple equation of a strong nation helping an aspiring nation to reach a point where it had some reasonable chance to achieve and keep a degree of freedom and human dignity. Even though American resolve fell short in the end, it remains a fact that few countries have ever engaged in such idealistic magnanimity; and no gain or attempted gain for human freedom can be discounted."[66] (Westmoreland)

How could it be that such different interpretations of the involvement of the United States in Vietnam could arise? An exemplary and rare instance of "idealistic magnanimity" or "the most costly and tragic blunder in American history." Careful, if abbreviated, attention must be given to that question for the ambiguities and confusions which allows these radically contradictory interpretations of the involvement in Vietnam also characterized the context within which the church, young persons of draft age, persons within the military service, and chaplains generally, but especially in the Armed Forces, had to discern their duty to God, to humanity, to their country and to themselves.

Although heavy American involvement in Vietnam began in 1965, the pattern and rationale for that was set considerably earlier. By the end of World War II the whole of Vietnam was sympathetic to communism, partly as a reaction to the colonial policy of France. The communism espoused by Ho Chi Minh was a form of national liberation and self-determination. With the resignation of Bao Dai in August, 1945, the last vestige of power of an hereditary Emperor turned in favor of Ho Chi Minh. The Provisional Executive Committee

---

[65] Tedford Taylor, *Nuremburg and Vietnam: An American Tragedy.* (New York, 1971), p. 207.
[66] William C. Westmoreland, *A Soldier Reports,* (Garden City, 1976), p. 422.

for the South (Saigon) also acted in that same month to operate under the authority of Ho Chi Minh and Hanoi.

That situation was changed when the French decided to reestablish colonial rule and French troops attacked the new administration in Saigon hardly a month after the decision by the Provisional Executive Committee of the South. When five months of military effort to establish authority over Vietnam brought no success, the French made an agreement with Ho Chi Minh in March 1946. That agreement recognized the government of Ho Chi Minh while at the same time claiming Vietnam as a "free state" within the French Union. The agreement also stipulated that there would be elections in the south for the reunification of Vietnam and that France would withdraw from Vietnam within five years.

Because the French had persuaded Chiang Kai-shek to remove China's occupation forces from Vietnam, Ho Chi Minh agreed to allow France to place fifteen thousand troops in parts of Vietnam under communist control. France reneged on the agreement, announcing that only force would restore French rule over Indochina. The French suspended plans for the election in the south, and on June 1, 1946, proclaimed South Vietnam (Cochin-china), a separate, French controlled state. In the face of military efforts to seize control over all of Vietnam, Ho Chi Minh was able to appeal to all Vietnamese to resist the French as a patriotic act of national independence.

President Truman and Secretary of State Dean Acheson were apparently convinced that the French cause in Vietnam was a war against Communist aggression. Acheson even stated in June 1952 that because of American support of the French, "Communist aggression has been checked."[67] Increasingly, the United States saw the effort of the French not as a colonial war, but as help for the free peope of Indochina to resist the imposition of Communism. President Truman's words were clear. "The Communist assault in Indochina has been checked by the free peple of Indochina with the help of the French."[68]

---

[67] Secretary of State Dean Acheson, Press Conference on June 18, 1952. He also said: "Once again the policy of meeting aggression with force is paying off."

[68] Gabriel Kolko, "The American Goals in Vietnam," *Pentagon Papers* (Gravel ed.), Volume V, (Boston, 1972), p. 3.

By 1954, the United States had given three and one-half billion dollars to help France in the war in Indochina.[69] But in spite of an army of up to 391,000 men, the French military effort was to fail. Dien Bien Phu in May, 1954, marked the end of the French presence.

In July 1954, the French signed the Geneva Agreements ending the war. The agreement provided that Vietnam would be temporarily divided into two military zones, and elections were set for July, 1956, on the basis of which the country might be reunified. The United States did not oppose the agreement although it clearly represented a victory for Ho Chi Minh and the Communists. Even so, the United States chose to intepret the agreement as establishing not two military zones, but two separate states with borders at the seventeenth parallel. Further, the United States disregarded the part of the agreement which entailed elections and the reunification of the country. The United States also disavowed any colonial claims as it set about to assist the South Vietnamese to establish a free, democratic, and prosperous state as a buffer against the expansion of Communism.

Ngo Dinh Diem became the leader of South Vietnam in June 1954, and President in October 1955. By 1959, however, it was clear that his regime had become a repressive and brutal dictatorship. President Diem was assassinated on November 2, 1963. Many Americans, including President Kennedy, spoke at that time as if the end of the war was in sight, and that the number of American military advisers could be reduced. President Kennedy suggested that the 16,500 advisers could soon be reduced to 1,000. The number was actually increased to 23,000 during 1964.

After President Kennedy's assassination on November 22, 1963, the Vietnam War became President Johnson's war, and he made the decisions to bomb North Vietnam in February and to send U.S. Marines to South Vietnam in March of 1965. The justification was again to defeat external Communist aggression against a small and weak, freedom-loving country. This new American presence in Vietnam was to be the determinative factor in winning the war.

But things did not work out that way, and there was an appeal for

---

[69] May 1971, Quoted in Joseph Buttinger, *Vietnam, the Unforgettable Tragedy*, (New York, 1979), p. 28.

more troops, more artillery, more planes and more bombs, each time with the assurance that this additional amount of help by the United States would turn the tide and end the war. That was the pattern between 1965 and 1969 when there were 541,000 American troops stationed in Vietnam. During this time the American people were beginning to realize the cost of the war in the lives of their sons and in dollars. The destruction of the land and the people we were commited to saving, showed little convincing evidence that we could actually win the war in Vietnam.

The overall cost of the war has been estimated at 160 billion dollars, Americans killed at 56,000, Americans wounded at 303,000. Although it is extremely difficult to be accurate, estimates are that over 183,000 South Vietnamese were killed, 499,000 wounded, 924,000 Vietcong and North Vietnamese killed, and the number of Vietcong and North Vietnamese wounded is unknown. With the tide of American opinion turning against the war, President Nixon adopted a strategy of "Vietnamization," gradually reducing the number of American troops in Vietnam and assuring the American people that our effort there had been so successful that the Vietnamese were now able to defend themselves, needing only the continued presence of American air power.

In October of 1972, Henry Kissinger and President Nixon proclaimed that peace was finally at hand. But President Thieu of South Vietnam balked at signing the agreement because it provided for the participation of South Vietnamese Communists in the governing of the country. Even so, the cease-fire agreement was signed on January 27, 1973. This agreement was basically a political resolution requiring the removal of all American troops in sixty days and leaving the balance of power clearly in the hands of the Communists and North Vietnamese. President Thieu refused to implement the "political solution" of the agreement and resigned April 21, 1975. By that time the possibility of a political solution had passed and Saigon was ready for the taking. The state of moral and political disintegration in the army of South Vietnam was such that in spite of a three-to-one advantage in personnel and a five-to-one advantage in equipment, the city collapsed in ignominy between March 10 and April 30, 1975.[70]

---

[70] Cf. Dennis Troute, "Last Days in Saigon", *Harpers Magazine*, July 1975, pp. 45-60.

I have gone into this much detail about our twenty year commitment to Vietnam, ten years with American armed forces, in order to suggest something of the complexity and ambiguity of that commitment from the beginning to the end. Several things are especially important in the picture.

1. American leaders were so fearful of the ideology of Communism that they seemed to lose all discriminating judgment about different forms of anti-Communism. The fundamental question about the war was the "justness" or the "rightness" of the war from the outset. Some say we misunderstood the nationalist nature of Ho Chi Minh's communism which was distrustful of alignment with either Russia or China, and that by entering the war, we turned a civil war into a war between the self-interest of the Vietnamese and the encroachments of other nations on their sovereignty. The failure of the United States to learn from the French experience and the undercutting by the United States of the Geneva Agreements in 1954 obviated any legitimate claims of the United States to a "just cause" in Vietnam. Most of the protest against the war in Vietnam probably rested on this claim. The issue became poignant for many when the cost of a draft of the country's youth and the price in lives and dollars were put alongside serious questions about the legitimacy of the effort.

Others say that we entered the war to protect a small and weak but free people from the armed imposition of Communism. Some even claimed that the justification of the effort was to save civilization. A careful analysis of the history of Vietnam from 1945 to the present would certainly lead to serious questions about the vital interests of the United States that were at stake and the justification of this effort to save the Vietnamese people or to save civilization. Excessive claims about the rightness of the cause by four presidents of the United States made it difficult for anyone to provide documentation to the contrary, even when people had suspicions that there were serious gaps and weaknesses in the claim.

2. A second fact that strikes one about Vietnam is that the stated intention of preventing South Vietnam from falling to Communism became so shrill that little attention was given to the ways in which people might be persuaded to choose freedom and democracy over Communism on their own terms. The strange irony of the

situation is that the United States offended and alienated the people we were there to help and win over to the cause of freedom. Finally, by the military strategy of destroying the land and killing the people, and the political strategy of supporting autocratic and repressive dictatorial regimes in Saigon, we lost contact with the Vietnamese people and the indigenous residuum for a life of self-determination and peace. We seemed to learn nothing from the fact that it was taking more and more involvement to protect South Vietnam. More importantly, we did not learn that the brutality of our destructiveness was not only against our nature, but it was making any answer to their problem look more desirable to them than that offered by the United States. It is as if the conviction about the rightness of our cause made us not only oblivious to data to the contrary, but that the conviction gave us license to fabricate, to deceive, and to lie, not only to other people but to our citizens as well. Perhaps Joseph B. Teamster does not overstate the case when he said that "what doomed the American venture in Vietnam was an addiction to lies and deception."[71]

3. All of these things make inevitable the tragic dilemma Vietnam presented to all morally sensitive Americans, especially the young who were subject to the draft, service persons who were ordered to Vietnam, and chaplains in the Armed Forces. The government ordered its military servicemen to risk their lives in Vietnam in a cause claimed to be of "vital interest to the United States." On the ground in Vietnam, however, it was difficult to distinguish friend from enemy and to detect any strength of a free and stable government in South Vietnam which had the support of the people. Beyond that, the mission of the American armed forces was increasingly subject to political decisions. These political decisions became more and more confusing and the American serviceman was left in an untenable position, his life threatened on all sides by the lack of clear battle lines and dependable indigenous forces in Vietnam and growing confusion about America's "cause" and support for those sent there.

Ordinarily persons wanted to serve the honor of their nation but were confronted with contradictory signals about the desires and

---

[71] Joseph B. Teamster, "The Fraud of Vietnamization, "*Harpers Magazine,* July 1975. Cf. also Hannah Arendt, *Crises of the Republic,* (New York, 1969), especially pp. 1-47.

possibility of self-determination by the South Vietnamese. Religious persons sought a moral base to justify and to limit killing to that necessary to establish freedom, law, and order. All of these wished to protect themselves and survive the war. Although they were prepared to die if that became necessary for the cause of justice and freedom, all of them were at the same time in unusual and critical jeopardy. They were apparently appalled by the lack of support from the United States and unappreciated by the South Vietnamese, whose freedom they were risking their lives to secure. Maintaining their own self-confidence and personal meaning became extremely difficult, especially for those who deliberately and consciously wanted to be patriotic citizens and faithful Christians at the same time.

Some chaplains sensed the conflict deeply and could not continue in the military service. But there was no "out" for the ordinary serviceman except to apply for non-combatant status or discharge as a conscientious objector. Hence, many chaplains who themselves may have come to doubt the honor of the cause, stayed on to share the danger and ambiguity with those who had little or no choice, and to honor and dignify their struggle of conscience to make moral sense out of their lives in that situation.

There were astounding acts of evil by servicemen in Vietnam, the events of My Lai being the most publicized. But overall the more grievious fault lay with those who required our servicemen to undertake the task in Vietnam as one of vital interest to the security of the United States. The future confidence of the youth of America in the claims of vital self-interest of the United States that justify military service will without doubt be affected by the way in which the physical, psychological, and moral wounds of the servicemen in Vietnam are regarded by the American people. Trust by the American people in their political leaders was thoroughly shaken by American involvement in the Vietnam War. In his introduction to the Pentagon Papers, Senator Mike Gravel sadly acknowledges the tragedy.

"We now find policies on the most fundamental of issues, war and peace, adopted without the support or understanding of the people affected by them. As a result of these practices, especially with respect to our involvement in Southeast Asia, our youth have virtually abandoned hope in the ability of their government to represent them, much less to stand for the ideals for which the republic once stood. The trust between leaders and their people, without which a democracy cannot function, has been dangerously eroded, and we all fear the result."[72]

As was the case in the Supreme Court decision on prayer in the public schools and in the Civil Rights Movement, the counsels of religion were divided and no institution in America gave clear and reliable advice to young persons as to where the priority interests of the Kingdom of God lay. The weakened and compromised authority of the church, courts, Selective Service System, military services, and educational institutions, meant that the burden of final moral discernment lay on the individual person, a burden sharply accentuated when this entailed questioning the judgment of the President of the United States about the vital national interest. While resenting that situation, many young people felt a moral and patriotic obligation to protest the war, to join the counter culture, and in some instances, to give up citizenship in the United States.

4. The Watergate Affair

If Senator Mike Gravel was correct about the importance of peoples' trust in their leaders in a democracy and in his assessment of the severe erosion of that trust because of Vietnam, it is a wonder that the government and people of the United States could sustain their poise during the successive revelations of improprieties, crimes, and "cover-ups" which came to be known as Watergate. And few if any were prepared for the final, undeniable evidence that the President of the United States had used the privileges of his office to cover up those crimes. The evidence was so compelling that Pat Buchanan, trusted and loyal friend of the Nixons, counseled Julie Nixon Eisenhower and Tricia Nixon Cox on the morning of August 3, 1973: "They had only one choice: either their father would be the first President of the United States to resign or he

---

[72] Mike Gravel, *The Pentagon Papers* (Gravel ed.), (Boston, 1971), Introduction," pp. ix-x.

would be the first president to be impeached and convicted."[73] Elizabeth Drew portrays the effect of the unprecedented event.

"In the years 1973 and 1974, this country lived through the most extraordinary political events in our history. For many of us it was both a national experience and a personal one. We went through things we had never gone through before and had never imagined we would go through. We struggled with questions that had never previously occurred to us and with anxieties that it would have been impossible to anticipate. More major political events took place than we had ever believed could happen in such a brief period. Even now, looking back, we have some difficulty believing that it happened, that it was real." [74]

Between July 27 and 30 the House Judiciary Committee voted to recommend impeachment of the president on three charges: obstruction of justice, abuse of power, and defiance of committee subpoenas.

On July 23, after many charges and counter charges, Representative Lawrence Hogan (Maryland) announced that after going over the evidence again and again, he had concluded beyond a reasonable doubt that Nixon had committed impeachable offenses and should be removed from office. His statement of charges against the president tersely described the issue before the people, the courts, and the Congress of the United States.

"The evidence convinces me that my president has lied repeatedly, deceiving public officials and the American people. He has withheld information necessary for our system of justice to work. Instead of cooperating with prosecutors and investigators, as he said publicly, he concealed and covered up evidence, and coached witnesses so that their testimony would show things that really were not true. He tried to use the CIA to impede the investigation of Watergate by the FBI. He approved the payment of what he knew to be blackmail to buy the silence of important Wategate witnesses. He praised and rewarded those whom he knew had committed perjury. He personally helped to orchestrate a scenario of events, facts, and testimony to cover up wrong-doing in the Watergate scandal and throw investigators and

---

[73] Theodore H. White, *Breach of Faith, The Fall of Richard Nixon.* (New York, 1975), p. 17.
[74] Elizabeth Drew, *Washington Journal, the Events of 1973-1974,* (New York, 1974), p. xi.

prosecutors off the track. He actively participated in an extended and extensive conspiracy to obstruct justice." [75]

On the following day the Supreme Court rendered a decision sustaining Judge Sirica's ruling that required Nixon to produce taped recordings of the "President's private conversations which might contain evidence of crime."[76] Among those recordings, was the tape of the voice of Nixon "directing the CIA to halt an FBI investigation which would be politically embarrassing to his reelection—an obstruction of justice."[77] The long ordeal was over and the case against Nixon was clean and tight. Gradually, even those most loyal to the president came to agree with Pat Buchanan's words to Nixon's daughters: the choice was now simple, either impeachment or resignation.

On the evening of August 7, 1974, President Nixon decided to resign. While he was in the throes of that decision Haldeman and Erlichman tried unsuccessfully to get messages to the president, asking him to grant them pardons.[78] A national television appearance was scheduled for 9:00 P.M. (eastern time), Thursday, August 8. The President of the United States was speaking: ". . . In the past few days . . . it has become evident to me that I no longer have a strong enough political base in the Congress to justify continuing the effort. . . . Therefore, I shall resign the presidency effective at noon tomorrow."[79] And so, on Friday, August 9, 1974, power passed from Richard M. Nixon to Gerald Ford as Nixon was flying over Illinois or Missouri on the way to the Western White House.

It was a tragic day, not only for the Nixons, but for all the people of the United States, especially for the young who must have had a premonition, even as they felt mournful and betrayed by the loss of honor in high places, that there is no future for the real America unless the people, at all levels of life, are honorable and just as well as free.

As distressing and astounding as the duplicity was of Nixon

---

[75] Quoted in Clark R. Mullenhoff, *Game Plan for Disaster*, (New York, 1976), pp. 349-350.
[76] Theodore H. White, *op. cit.*, p. 5.
[77] Theodore H. White, *op. cit.*, p. 29.
[78] Theodore H. White, *op. cit.*, p. 29.
[79] Quoted in Theodore H. White, *op. cit.*, p. 32. The full text of the statement is given as Appendix B, pp. 349-352.

boasting of the moral greatness of America in his Second Inaugural while at the same time committing "high crimes and misdemeanors," the greater tragedy was that Nixon betrayed the long heritage of America and of her presidents by not acknowledging the righteousness of God and the absolute moral law and his violation of both of them. He missed the opportunity for a profundity that characterized President Lincoln and for a dignity if not a measure of greatness in his fall by acknowledging only errors of judgment and never admitting or confessing before God and before the American people that he had done evil and had betrayed them.

Much damage had been done in the minds of the people generally. "If there is no moral law by which the president is judged, perhaps there is no moral law by which I am judged. Why, then, should I not seek what I want in money, position, and power without regard to the rights and needs of others? If, at some point, I am caught in a violation of the law, I will admit to an 'error in judgment' and pay what is required." Many persons may have reasoned that way after Watergate! That is why Hannah Arendt speaks of lying and deception as constituting a "crisis in the Republic," whether that entails President Johnson and Vietnam or President Nixon and Watergate.[80] In any case, all of us are the losers, because these events increase skepticism if not cynicism about morality and patriotism.

5. The Appeal of the New Religious Movements

In addition to the specific crises discussed earlier, there are many other developments and events in the last few decades that affect the way people see themselves and their world. The bomb and the mushroom cloud, for example, invade the consciousness of many, resurrecting images of the "last days" and undermining confidence in a human future. Suddenly the problems of overpopulation, world hunger, and the ecological crisis also become pressing in such a way that we can neither avoid them nor solve them.

---

[80] Speaking of the Pentagon Papers, she writes, "The crucial point here is not merely that the policy of lying was hardly ever aimed at the enemy, . . . but was destined chiefly, if not exclusively, for domestic consumption, for propaganda at home, and especially for the purpose of deceiving Congress." Hannah Arendt, *Crisis of the Republic* (New York, 1969), p. 14. Cf. pp. 3-47.

Altogether, these suggest that a more radical change in human life is necessary than "gradualism" and "tinkering" with aspects of our institutions. Suddenly, the problems came to be generalized and overwhelming. That being the case, many opted out of the "establishment" and sought a simpler, purer, less destructive, and less competitive life-style in some form of the counter culture. Many also found the evil of the culture and the difficulties of reform or renewal to be so far beyond their power to "cope" that they sought sedation in alcohol and drugs. Unexpectedly, and too late, some discovered that these alternatives were devastatingly destructive.

There were also break-throughs in medical research. The pill and other contraceptives along with the discovery of antibiotics, changed the sexual options for many and the "sexual revolution" joined the parade of revolutions. Bio-medical technology, together with better understanding of nutrition, not only made organ transplants possible but increased the possibility of life for defective newborns and extended life for the old and dying beyond the point where many wished to live, changing that profound issue from "death by chance" to "death by choice" as one writer put it.[81]

Further, there was the emergence of the "Third World" and the revolution in expectations for justice and health and economic development among all the peoples of the world. Religion played a prominent role in that revolution as "liberation theology" became a significant part of education in most colleges, universities, and schools of theology. People began to look differently at various kinds of limits and deprivations. These appeared increasingly not to be "necessary" or as the will of God, but within the realm of things that can be changed. That shift threw a new light on many issues of social, political, and economic morality. Rather than seeing God as a comfort within an "acceptance of things that cannot be changed," people everywhere came to understand God as a resource and sanction for "changing those things that can and ought to be changed."[82]

---

[81] Daniel Maguire, *Death by Choice* (New York, 1925).

[82] The full text of the prayer of Reinhold Neibuhr: "God, give us grace to accept with serenity the things that cannot be changed, courage to change that which should be changed, and the wisdom to distinguish the one from the other" (1943).

When one considers the overall effect of these different crises and revolutions, it is easy to understand how many persons concluded that there is something fundamentally wrong with our culture, and that the various "new" religious movements confirm and feed the deep human hungers while avoiding the "wrongs" in "establishment" culture. Why people turn to these movements and what they find in them are important indications of what has happened in culture and religion in the United States in recent years.

Theodore Roszak's book, *The Making of a Counter Culture*,[83] published in 1969, focused attention on the widespread and generalized discontent among the youth of America over the prospect of continued movement toward a technological utopia. Although he acknowledges that his interpretation was not accurate for all youth, Roszak makes positive and general claims for the counter culture as having "that healthy instinct which refuses both at the personal and political level to practice such a cold-blooded rape of our human sensibilities" as that of the fact and of "the total *ethos* of the bomb."[84]

In 1970 Jacob Needleman published *The New Religions*[85] as a "portrait" of the "spiritual explosion" in which hundreds of thousands of Americans were turning "toward the religions of the east and toward the mystical core of all religion."[86]. His partial list of those religions included Zen Buddhism, Meher Baba, Subud, Krishmamurti, Transcendental Meditation, Yoga, Sufism, Tibetan, Buddhism, Vedanta, and Humanistic Mysticism. A more complete list would include the Hare Krishnas, the Unification Church, Process, the Children of God, Scientology, The People's Temple, the Living Word Fellowship, and revivals of American Indian religion. Some would also claim that many groups of evangelicals, charismatics, and mystics within Judaism and Christianity must be included as new religious movements within the "spiritual explosion."[87]

---

[83] Theodore Roszak, *The Making of a Counter Culture* (Garden City, 1969).

[84] *Ibid.*, p. 47.

[85] Jacob Needleman, *The New Religions* (Garden City, 1970).

[86] *Ibid.*, p. xi.

[87] Sidney Ashlstrom's essay, "From Sinai to the Golden Gate: The Liberation of Religion in the Occident" in *Understanding the New Religions* (New York, 1978), edited by Jacob Needleman and George Baber, pp. 3-22, especially p. 21 illuminates the issue.

The appeal of the new religious movements is related to the cultural situation in post World War II America. In general, increasing numbers of the American people have been unable to answer their fundamental human questions through the traditional religious and secular forms of American culture. The culture honors proximate questions by providing proximate answers. But even the culture is becoming less dependable and proximate answers less satisfying. In this situation, as Langdon Gilkey observes, "ultimate questions grow out of the loss of proximate answers."[88] Both Gilkey and Frederick Bird have emphasized the loss of the self in modern culture, either through a confused identity, a loss of "realness" and creativity at the center of the self, or through the compromise of the self by restricting the meaning of the self to its social roles which are themselves empty.[89]

As one would expect, Gilkey sees the significance of the appeal of the new religions to be related in part to two tendencies in American culture: the depersonalization of things and people outside one's self, and the separation of the body from the self. He contends that, among many factors, an important one is that many persons "who in modern society find themselves unsure they exist or are effective, receive a new sense of the reality, value, and possibilities of the self,"[90] especially in the cults of meditation and self-awareness. "The discovery of the self is the initial gift of Oriental religions of meditation in our midst."[91]

The incisive ideas of William Irwin Thompson support Gilkey's observation about the assault on the human self in modern culture while, at the same time, placing that issue within the broad context of a total cultural trend. In Thompson's vision, the civilization of modern culture has been built by the ego through competitiveness, consumption, externalization, mastery, separation, isolation, and specialization. That assertion of the ego posits the worth of a person not in terms of what one receives, feels, conserves, gives, and

---

[88] Langdon Gilkey, "Toward a Religious Criterion of Religion" in *Understanding the New Religions* (New York, 1978), pp. 131-137, especially p. 133.

[89] Langdon Gilkey, *op. cit* Frederick Bird, "Charisma and Ritual in New Religious Movements" in *Understanding the New Religions* (New York, 1978), pp. 173-189.

[90] *Ibid.*, p. 134.

[91] *Ibid.*, p. 134.

preserves, but on the thin basis of what one achieves and owns. "And so, if you are what you own, the more you own, the more you are."[92] The final tragedy of such a culture is that it consumes and destroys the human self, for the ego bent on consumption is insensitive to community, and an ego sustained by possessions is powerless (except for the pathetic gestures of remodeling the house, cosmetic surgery, and steel vaults) in the face of illness, old age, and death. ". . . Where the whole way of life is devoted to consumption, it is people who become consumed."[93]

Thompson sees even the universities and the churches as complicit in the processes of consumption and death, with scarcely a word from them of criticism, re-creation, or re-visioning of human life and culture. In this view, the churches have become the "morale booster" for the universities, the corporations, and the state, and for all people in them who need reassurance from time to time that this is really the "best of all possible cultures," what God really intended for the creation.

Thompson's hopes for the future center on a grand appeal for "resacralization," a re-visioning or a re-mythologizing of nature, self, and society. In this re-mythologizing," charisma shifts from technology to contemplative science, from industry to ecology, from factories to communities."[94] Here "one is not what one owns, but one's being is what one is."[95] His proposal leads toward "a spiritual awakening on the level of the great universal religions that have guided the cultural revolution of humanity" which will include a "change of heart and mind, a new wedding of nature and culture, and a new kind of human community which can express the resacralization of earth."[96]

People answer the question differently as to whether specific new religions embrace dimensions of constructive resacralization of nature, human life, and culture. One who has serious reservations about the total investment of the self and the processes of agency

---

[92] William Irwin Thompson, *Darkness and Scattered Light* (Garden City 1978), p. 67.

[93] *Ibid.*, p. 79.

[94] *Ibid.*, p. 43.

[95] *Ibid.*, p. 76.

[96] *Ibid.*, p. 101.

and consumption over communion and receiving or giving, [97] however, is likely to be a candidate for one of these movements. A religious movement which honors *any* aspect of a more deep, moral, comprehensive, and spiritual intimation about nature, the self, history, and culture would have great appeal.

In his essay for the National Conference on the Study of New Religious Movements in America, Theodore Roszak was sanguine about the ominous destructive potential in some of the new religious movements. Yet he chose to focus on what he labeled the "secular consensus" in American culture which has come so close to a closure against the viability of the "religious" that it has, in effect, pushed anyone with a positive religious sensitivity toward the new religious movements. While acknowledging that we live in a time of "religious awakening," he describes our situation in language strikingly similar to that of Thompson.

> "Science, technics, and social evolution—all radically divorced from religious tradition—sway the history of our time, and they do so globally, aggressively, militantly. They are fast taking over all the cultural ground, building a planetary synthesis that will soon bring our entire species within the urban-industrial dominance. We are very close to *End-game*." [98]

It is because of the near closure of the secular consensus against the religious that Roszak can speak of a spiritual void as being "the prime political fact of our time." [99] Precisely at that point Roszak sees a valuable lesson that can be learned from the renaissance of religion. "We can *use* what it tells us of human need and aspiration to question the assumptions of the secular consensus. We can use its conception of human potentiality to challenge the adequacy of our science, our technics, our politics." [100]

Roszak leaves us to conjecture about many aspects of the new religious movements, including whether or not they really promise

---

[97] cf. the incisive discussion by David Taken in *Pain, Disease and Sacrifice* (Chicago, 1968). cf. also *The Quality of Human Existence* (Boston, 1966).

[98] Theodore Roszak, "Ethnics, Ecstasy, and the Study of New Religions" in *Understanding the New Religions* (New York 1978), p. 49. The entire essay covers pp. 49-62.

[99] *Ibid*, p. 61.

[100] *Ibid.*, p. 54.

anything fundamentally different from the isolation, achievement, exclusiveness, and trivial morality of the secular or of the religious establishment. But he is quite emphatic in welcoming the religious explosion overall because of its challenge to the secular consensus, for that consensus does not go "deep enough to touch what is fundamental in human nature, and so it cannot understand our discontent or bring us fulfillment."[101] That, for Roszak, is because people are not fundamentally "power and profit-seeking creatures. . . Power and possession are without significance for the whole and healthy person. They become goals only by default and to the degree that higher purpose withdraws from our lives."[102] The gurus in all the new religious movements are significant, then, because they remind us of a project greater than that entailed in the secular consensus and because they "awaken the god who sleeps at the roots of our being."[103]

Robert Wuthnow offers other insights into the cultural situation that foster new religions. Especially helpful is his discussion of "anomie" and the relation of world order and disorder to religious movements.[104] In his essay, Wuthnow picks up two themes from Peter Berger,[105] those of "anomie" and "plausibility structures," and applies them to the varieties of religious experimentation which people have embraced in recent years. In his views, the multiplicity of religious movements in America is directly related to two facts: that the only "plausibility structure" comprehensive enough to perform a general norm-giving function is world order, and that since World War II there have been fundamental uncertainties and shifts in that world order. Wuthnow mentions a few examples of this wavering: the cold war, the rise of China to world power, uncertain relations with the Third World, the human rights movement, and the Vietnam War. The effect of the loss of any overarching plausibility structure has been to dissolve any general or universal moral authority and any general or universal source of personal stability.

---

[101] *Ibid.*, p. 60.

[102] *Ibid*, p. 61.

[103] *Ibid.*, p. 62.

[104] Robert Wuthnow, "Religious Movements and the Transition in World Order", in *Understanding the New Religions* (New York, 1978), pp. 63-79.

[105] Cf. Peter Berger, *Facing Up to Modernity* (New York, 1977).

In that situation, the fundamental drive for order, stability, and a "nomos," has taken a less general and universal form, but that drive is so strong that it will not be denied. As power will not tolerate a vacuum, persons will not tolerate anomie. "Americans have been forced to re-evaluate the moral basis of their institutions. . . . The effect upon religion has been that the plausibility of the whole Western tradition with its emphasis on modernity and rationality, can no longer be taken for granted quite as easily as it once was."[106] To be sure, this does not mean that the moral intimation and intention are lost, but only that the moral sense must place itself within a different plausibility structure. If the dominant orientation of American foreign policy has been an *amoral realpolitik* rather than the moral principles of religious vision and of the churches, persons must find a moral plausibility structure different from that of the nation.

That being the case, Wuthnow writes:

". . . In the *lacunae* of ultimate confidence, many have turned inward to reconstruct their own personal experiences of the sacred, often by borrowing heavily from the tribal, magical, and mystical religions previously reglegated to the fringes of Western tradition."[107]

On that analysis, Wuthnow proposes an explanation of why there is a kind of explosion of religious experimentation and of new and different movements. Without entering upon the difficult task of assessing them, he nevertheless urges patience toward them. Tightly constructed world orders have been achieved in the past "only at a tremendous cost in human freedom and social resources."[108] Over against that kind of order is "a loose confederation of local, national, and regional interests that can respond with flexibility to changing global conditions."[109] Steven Tipton studied three new religious movements and was led by that study to observe that a profound change resulted from the conflicts of the 1960's, "the de-legitimation of utilitarian culture,

---

[106] Robert Wuthnow, *op cit.*, p. 76.
[107] *Ibid.*, p. 76.
[108] *Ibid.*, p. 78.
[109] *Ibid.*, p. 78.

and with it the stripping away of moral authority from major American social institutions: government, law, business, religion, marriage and the family."[110] This change left its mark on both the utilitarian culture and on the counter culture. The utilitarian culture was left without affect and moral depth and, therefore, unable to deal with substantive discontents. The counter culture was left with so many unfilled expectations that many persons turned inward and to limited private associations for legitimation of their moral promptings.

The attractiveness of alternative religious movements is vivid against that background.

> "Disoriented by drugs, embittered by politics, disillusioned by the apparent worthlessness of work and the transiency of love, they found a way back through these movements, a way to get along with conventional American society and the demands of their own maturing lives. For some youths the social and ideological stability of these movements has meant psychological and even physical survival. For many more, membership in alternative religious movements has meant moral survival and a sense of meaning and purpose recovered through recombing expressive ideas with moralities of authority, rules, and utility. On one hand, these movements have thereby adopted and reconciled their youthful adherents to the traditional order. On the other, they have meant moral surival precisely by sustaining counter-cultural themes, albeit in altered forms."[111]

Although there are striking differences among the three groups, Tipton found that all three alternative religions enable their members to overcome the conventional opposition between instrumental conformity to modernized social conditions and expressive reaction to them. They "meditate and recombine existing meanings" to form alternative associations "better adopted to survival . . . than was the counterculture, supporting the attitudes of their members" in specific ways: 1. Ecstatic experience vs. Technical Reason; 2. Holism vs. Analytic Discrimination; 3.

---

[110] Now published as *Getting Saved from the Sixties: Moral Meaning in Conversion and Cultural Change* (Berkeley, 1982), p. 29.

[111] *Ibid.*, p. 30.

Acceptance vs. Problem-Solving; and 4. Intuitive Certainty vs. Pluralistic Relativism.[112]

The primary conclusion Tipton reaches from this study is that the alternative religious movements "enable sixties youth to make moral sense of their lives, . . . and they synthesize moral meanings important to the larger culture."[113]

This abbreviated consideration of the new religious movements points inescapably to three general conclusions: that American culture has increasingly moved toward insensitivity to the transcendent and to the most deeply human; that the traditional religions have accommodated far too extensively to the moral/social/political consensus; and that increasing numbers of persons have a strong intimation that there is something more profound than the secular consensus and competition for possessions, engaging them in a desperate search for physical, moral, religious, and intellectual integrity that many of them are finding in the new religious movements. Whether that felt, willed, and thought integrity is genuine integrity, whether it leads to peace, justice, and love is another question. At the least, we may conclude that the discontent is, for many, prompted by genuine religiousness. Beyond that, the question is still open as to whether these movements offer unflawed and long range options to the secular consensus.

Where Have All the Certainties Gone?

The purpose of this chapter has been to portray the unprecedented turbulence in American culture between 1945 and 1980. The intent has been primarily to understand, not to condone or to condemn. Two impressions emerge from our observations of those tempestuous and agonizing years. First, the period was characterized by a cumulative and pervasive assault on the human essence by the culture. Such an assault can be resisted only by an integrity, courage, and a strong sense of purpose that the culture itself cannot provide. Second, religious faith and vision through which

---

[112] *Ibid.*, pp. 21, 237-245.
[113] *Ibid.*, p. 223.

God is related to our deepest hungers and needs must provide an orientation of righteousness for the evaluation and criticism of all social, economic, political, and religious powers that attempt to "utilize" or demean the created dignity and value of persons.

We began this chapter with the claim of Robert Bellah that the post World War II period represents the third great crisis in the history of the United States. That is the case partly because of the increased power in this culture not only to do evil as well as good, but also to do *evil* under the impression that it *is* good, or, worse still, to do evil knowing that it is evil and to claim and pretend that it is good. We have tried to suggest just how confusing this is, especially to the young. Robert Bellah's autobiographical statement gives us a glimpse of one life passing through these turbulent years.

> "I grew up in the 1930's and early 1940's in a milieu in which there were few questions about Protestant Christianity or what were taken to be traditional American values. An essentially unbroken affirmation of American society was confirmed in my experience by America's leadership in the great antifascist war. It was not until after my graduation from high school in 1945 that I began to have basic doubts about my society. Thus my experience is fundamentally different from that of those born since the middle forties. I do not think now that the religious and ideological heritage that I was given as a child and as an adolescent was an entirely authentic version of the American tradition, but the subjective sense of continuity with the past is an indelible experience that undoubtedly colors even my present perceptions. My break with American values, when it came, was quite radical, and I went through a period of almost total rejection of my own society. That experience too must influence my present views. But for the last fifteen years or so my attitude toward American has embodied a tension-*odi et amo*—of affirmation and rejection. Of all earthly societies I know that this one is mine and I do not regret it. But I also know through objective observation and personal tragedy that this society is a cruel and bitter one, very far, in fact, from its own highest aspirations."[114]

In that confusion and darkness, the Christian Gospel should have been a dependable, steady, and empowering light. As difficult as were the times, we have now to see how effectively the chaplain ministry of The United Methodist Church sustained the Christian gospel during those years.

---

[114] Robert N. Bellah, *The Broken Covenant.* (New York, 1975), p. viii.

III. Ministry as Chaplains Understood It

The turbulence of recent decades has put in question every traditional form of religious ministry, including the ministry of chaplains. In this situation, the one thing that a clergyperson cannot afford to do, however, is to abandon the Christian vision as foundational to his or her existence and to accept the assessment of human nature and of human happiness that prevails in secular culture. Consequently, the ordained person is left with the difficult task of relating the search for human fulfillment in what Harvey Cox has called the "secular city" to the Christian vision, without identifying the religious answer with the answers most prominent in present culture.

Since World War II, that task has been easier for the local church pastor than for the chaplain/pastor. That is probably because of the constancy of support given by a tangible community in a stable parish situation. The other side of that easier way, however, is that the chaplain/pastor may be closer to the raw and uncharted edge of Christian ministry precisely because the chaplain is forced to sustain the deeper dimensions of faith and love by an individual effort and without protection from the critical issues of human morality and human survival. This study is focused on chaplain ministry and we must assess the success of the chaplain in accomplishing that task. We will be better able to do that after we attend to what chaplain/pastors actually say about their Christian ministry.

The research instrument asked chaplains: *Did the chaplaincy offer you opportunities for significant Christian ministry?* In all of the categories of chaplain ministry, the answers were overwhelmingly positive.

	No Response	Yes	No Opinion	No	Row Total
Army	10	410	4	5	429
Navy	4	216	4	5	229
Air Force	3	255	0	0	258
Reserve Forces	5	254	5	3	267
Veterans Admin- istration	4	90	0	1	95
Civilian Hospital	2	138	1	2	143
Confinement Fa- cility	0	23	1	0	24
Institutional	2	84	0	1	37
Industrial	0	5	1	0	6
Totals:					
Responses	30	1475	16	17	1538*
Chaplains	24(1.9%)	1186(96%)	13(1.1%)	13(1.1%)	1236*

Of the 1236 persons responding, ninety-six percent claimed that their form of chaplaincy provided significant opportunities for Christian ministry. Only thirteen persons, or slightly over one percent, saw their chaplaincy as not offering such opportunities, with exactly the same number having no opinion. Twenty-four persons did not respond to this question, less than two percent. Overall, then, 1185 out of 1236 persons, 96 percent, gave a moderate or a strong positive response to the question of authentic Christian ministry, with most of them (1034) answering with a strong yes. We do not know what the situation was with a particular clergyperson who gave no response to this question, or who responded but had no opinion, but the positive response here indicates a high sense of purpose, vitality, and usefulness, as well as a high state of conviction and commitment. This question is demanding because it entails reflection about what Christian ministry is, about the situations in which ministry is done, about people and their needs, and about the chaplain's own self, meaning, joy, and fulfillment.

In view of the recurring suggestions by some parish pastors that these chaplain/clergy have "left the Christian ministry," the responses tabulated above may appear striking and unexpected. Either the regular parish clergy or the chaplain clergy do not know

---

*Because some chaplains served in more than one kind of chaplaincy, the 1236 chaplains who responded to the questionnaire become a total of 1538 responses.

what the other group is doing or there are widely different understandings of Christian ministry in the two groups.

Reading the chaplains' comments, one is impressed immediately by the kinds of stresses and restraints which are present in special chaplain situations. Although there are many differences between a hospital, an orphanage, a jail or a prison, a school for mentally retarded, a military post, a ship, and a combat situation, there are also similarities. All of these settings come very close to being "closed communities." The person who is sick, without parents, confined against one's will, or under military authority, has limited freedom of movement. Thus, special stresses arise—stresses of pain, danger, loneliness, isolation, uncertainty, threat, and impotence which move all the questions about the meaning of one's existence to a more radical and threatening level than is ordinarily the case.

The limitation of freedom and the special stress in all of these settings might be understood under the designation, "total institution," a category developed by the sociologist, Erving Goffman, while working in a mental hospital.[1] Goffman suggests that sanitoriums, hospitals, homes for the blind and aged, jails, prisons and penitentiaries, boarding schools, monastic orders, and the military services also belong under this rubric. In the mental hospital and prison type of "total institution," Goffman finds a sharp division, even an enmity, between the "inmate" and the "staff." In most of these situations the staff performs a service function for the inmates—supervising, guarding, teaching, helping, or healing— and the freedom of the staff person is not limited as that of the inmate. The staff may appear as everything from the "primary hope" to the "primary enemy" of the inmate. Inmates lose privacy as well as self-control, and often are subjected to mortifying and insulting procedures. One way of coping in these settings is to identify with the "inmate world" and to struggle against the "staff world." Richard G. Hutcheson in his outstanding book, *The Churches and the Chaplaincy,* further discusses the Armed Forces as "total institutions."[2] Hutcheson sees the tension in the military as

---

[1] Erving Goffman, "On the Characteristics of Total Institutions," *Asylums,* (Garden City, NJ, 1961), pp. 3-124.

[2] R. G. Hutcheson, *The Churches and the Chaplaincy,* (Atlanta, 1975).

centering far more on the opposition between "insider" and "outsider" than on that between "inmate" and "staff."

The present study embraces the nature of Christian ministry in all of these kinds of "total institutions." Ministry in these situations of stress and constraint differs in important ways from ministry in a regular parish. The chaplain has the advantage/disadvantage of being a part of the "staff world" in many of these institutions and of being an "insider" in the military. The advantage of being a part of the "staff" is access to the patient/inmate in the total range of his or her activities, and of being a part of the "team" which in most of these institutions is provided to help the patient/inmate.[3] The disadvantage of being a part of the staff is that the chaplain's representation of the love of God may be seen by the patient/inmate as restricted to the limited purposes of a specific institution. The advantage of being an "insider" in the military is the full sharing of dangers, mortifications, and deprivation with others in the institution. Hutcheson considers that sharing of status with others in a total institution as so important to the possibility of ministry that it could hardly be over-emphasized.[4] The disadvantage of being an "insider" is that the institution may be absolutized, with the result that the breadth and depth of the love of God would be identified with the status and mission of a particular military organization.

In all of these institutions the role of the chaplain/minister and the "world" of those she or he serves could be different in significant ways from that of the regular parish clergy. What do the chaplains themselves say about this?

The chaplains report the same range of ministry activities that characterize the ministry of the regular parish clergy: preaching; teaching; administering the sacraments; visiting the sick and the imprisoned; comforting the dying, the bereaved, and the distressed; organizing activities and committees to enable education, healing, and ministry to happen; encouraging community organization and services; counseling; and praying and speaking at various kinds of religious, educational, and civic meetings. In spite of these similar understandings of the tasks of ministry, however, and in spite of differences *within chaplain*

---

[3] Note the exceptional nature of jail and prison ministry in this regard discussed in Chapter IV.
[4] Hutcheson, *op. cit.*, p. 47.

ministry between the military and civilian forms, rather sharp differences nevertheless prevail between chaplain and local parish ministry.

Chaplains understand their ministry to be more person centered than institution centered, as being far more ecumenical than parish ministry, and oriented primarily toward persons who are abused or abandoned by the system. Their ministry is a "presence with" rather than a "speaking to" people. It involves interdisciplinary teamwork in the process of encouragement, healing, rehabilitation, and spiritual ministry. It entails access to and explicit responsibility for all persons, including the "unchurched," in a home, school, prison, hospital, or military post or unit.

As a consequence, this ministry involves much more time in one-on-one relationships than in preaching to large congregations. It inevitably includes sharing the risks and cares of the people involved, and it usually entails some kind of staff responsibility for the overall quality and soundness of the structures that shape life in a particular setting. In the main, chaplain ministry represents a Christian ministry to and Christian presence with persons who are not likely to be included within the specific care and ministry of local church congregations. As one chaplain put it: "With rare exceptions, the parish clergy does not 'beat a path' to the invisible gates of any mental institution." Another chaplain, sixty years old, working in an institution, spoke in the same way: "Chaplaincy gave me the opportunity to work with people The Methodist Church neglected."

In an implicit but ironic way, chaplain ministry may carry forward the more traditional and inclusive meaning of a "parish" and a "parish clergyperson" within a general situation of disestablishment than the local, denominational "parishes" themselves do. We must return to that issue later. For the moment it is enough to take account of a shortcoming in the present "local parish" model implied by the claims of numbers of chaplains that they minister to persons who would receive no Christian ministry if they were not there.

A. Chaplain Ministry is Ecumenical

Almost without exception, chaplains claim that their ministry is ecumenical, a claim usually made in specific contrast to local, denominational, parish ministry. In some cases this claim is directly related to the words of John Wesley, "the world is my parish." In other instances, chaplains cite the parable of the sheep and goats as high authority for ministry to the sick, the imprisoned, the blind, and the hungry. Yet the word "ecumenical" has many meanings. The narrowest meaning is that of the universal evangelistic mission on behalf of the one true Christian faith, be that Baptist, Presbyterian, Roman Catholic, Methodist, or another. Such evangelistic, denominational ecumenism has little or no place in the chaplaincy. In contrast to this, however, stands the broadest meaning of ecumenism, founded on the universality of God's love in relation to all situations of human distress, and manifested through a *genuine care for all persons under all conditions.* Without this dimension of unconditional affect and concern, based upon God's love and a sympathetic understanding of the pains, conflicts, and ambiguities of existence, there would be little liklihood of effective chaplain ministry. Such a broad ecumenicalism is absolutely essential in the chaplaincy. This was made poignantly clear in the only comment one chaplain made on the entire questionnaire. Chaplaincy gave him the opportunity for significant Christian ministry, to show "care and concern for neglected persons."

Chaplain ministry is ecumenical in that it includes persons of all denominational and faith groups, in all kinds of situations. It is also ecumenical in that it enlists the resources of a healing or supporting team of persons with a variety of specialist skills in expressing this ministry to all people.

1. Ministry *to* All

Some chaplains mentioned the official obligation to minister to all persons. "The chaplain is expected to minister to all." I had a special obligation to every individual within the command regardless of faith or non-faith. My minstry was to people, not a chosen few." These comments by military chaplains describe a situation in ministry which prevails in all chaplaincy ministries. Every person in a hospital, prison, school, industry, sanitarium, or military unit has equal right and access to the ministry of the chaplain. Further, in many of these situations, the chaplain is obligated to go where the person works, lives, is sick, is confined, or in distress, rather than wait for a person to seek him or her out. A Navy chaplain puts it this way: "I have the opportunity of meeting and serving with people in the midst of crisis and pain rather than waiting till they come to me."

The implications of this "calling" in ministry are not easy for the ordinary parish minister to comprehend. In most civilian parish situations the minister has a special responsibility for members of his or her specific parish. In some cases this obligation might extend to persons of other parishes who are within the same denomination. It would not only be considered strange, but probably also a violation of ministerial courtesy if a civilian parish minister should visit persons of other parishes, denominations, or faiths in the prison, hospital, or institution. The special relation to persons in one's parish may give the pastor leave to call on his or her own in the role of an "insider" in any of these institutions. By the same token the pastor would be forbidden as an "outsider" to minister to any other unless that ministry were specifically requested.

In ordinary civilian life, every clergy person is an "outsider" to other denominations and faith groups. This is true in spite of the fact that, as one chaplain remarked, United Methodist clergy "should read and practice paragraph 453.2 of the Discipline: "Pastors are responsible for ministering to the needs of the whole community." It is surely the case that any person in need who called on a denominational parish minister would be received with compassion and helpfulness. At the same time, difficulties would arise if a pastor spent more time ministering to persons outside the parish than to those inside the parish.

Beyond that, however, the more serious limitation in the general civilian parish situation is that there are many "gaps in ministry" because neither the parish nor a combination of parishes constitutes the entire community. In the voluntary-parish-membership model, special groups are served well but that ministry is not comprehensive, and many are not served at all. The parish minister has special responsibility to a denomination and to a specific parish which is so preoccupying that one is not likely to think about the general health and welfare of the entire community. We often assume that because ministry is available to persons in one's own parish, it must somehow be available to all who want or need it.

That situation was dramatically illustrated in Atlanta, Georgia, in the tragedy of the missing and murdered children. The clergy were shocked not only by the tragedy but also by the fact that they had no structures available, apart from individual denominational ones, through which they could act for the security, health, and welfare of all the people in Atlanta. There was an awkwardness about their halting efforts to unite as clergy—Jewish, Christian, Moslem—to do something about a serious community problem which transcended all denominational boundaries.[5]

Ministries within the chaplain model are rather different. Ministry to all is a fundamental quality of responsibility, and functions of denominational ministry may or may not be added. Such additional functions might take the form of baptism, Holy Communion, confession, a Minyon, participation in Passover, etc. It would be rare for a chaplain to be effective as a minister while understanding his or her role as minister only or even primarily to Jews, Baptists, Episcopalians, Methodists, or Roman Catholics, rather than to persons in need, danger, distress, or crisis. This is not to suggest that the specific sacramental ministrations of a specific religious faith are unimportant. The point is rather that the basis for ministry by the insider in a "total institution" is defined by human need, not by the particular religious or non-religious identity of the person in need.

Chaplains come very soon to recognize the limitations of parish ministry in expressing the universality of the love of God. "Chaplain ministry fills a gap in Christiain ministry," wrote a sixty-three-year-old chaplain in an institution. "The chaplaincy gave me that unlimited

---

[5] After several efforts to define a base of unity and action, this group ceased to meet, unable to maintain a form of general religious concern for the entire community separate from their denominational/faith-group efforts and their work in the Atlanta Christian Council. In 1957 and 1958, the clergy of Atlanta came together and issued statements addressed to rising racial tensions and the possibility that the public schools would be closed rather than integrated. Eighty clergy signed the document (Manifesto) in 1957, and preserved the public school system. Perhaps it is enough if there is the possibility of a unified response to a community crisis. Increasing problems in complex communities suggest that it is as important to anticipate and prevent a community crisis as it is to solve a crisis, as important to avoid human casualties as it is to use skill and care to rescue and heal casualties. The recent effort in Atlanta took the name, Atlanta Interfaith Ministries.

opportunity to minister to persons the local church can't reach." "As a chaplain I have been given the opportunity to provide ministry for a large number of young men and women who probably would have never entered the doors of a church." "The chaplaincy gave me the opportunity for ministry among mentally retarded persons and their parents, and with professionals who work with them." So wrote other chaplains.

One spoke particularly of the "broad ecumenicalism" of chaplaincy in relation to grief. "My own understanding of grief has developed through a pilgrimage of more than a dozen years. It began in the mid-1960's when I attempted to minister to approximately thirty widows whose husbands were killed in Vietnam." Another spoke of hospital ministry. "The chaplaincy gave me the opportunity to contact and lead men who are normally missed and ignored by the Christian church. Much of my ministry has been directed toward people who are ill, and many of my assignments were to military hospitals." Another spoke of ministry to those in jails and prisons. "The chaplaincy gave me the opportunity to minister to men and women who are incarcerated and who have feelings of worthlessness, loneliness, and guilt; to help them understand that God cares, and that they can have a more meaningful and purposeful life." Another who works in an institution for the mentally retarded wrote about how compassion simplified theology. "The chaplaincy gave me the opportunity to be a minister and to do ministry among people with special limitations and skills (mentally retarded students). This also gave me the opportunity to rethink and simplify my theology."

Two chaplains spoke of ministry in terms of different forms of hope. An Army chaplain mentioned "the significance of offering people hope in the face of death in combat." An institutional chaplain wrote about the privilege of the "opportunity to serve people the church is not reaching, and to offer the down trodden, the rebellious, the disenchanted, a hand hold on their lives where they can get a grasp on hope and find some realistic ways of living a reasonably satisfying life."

Among the "all persons" the chaplain services, three groups are mentioned repeatedly: minority groups, "fringe" persons, and the "unchurched." In contrast to the situation in many "civilian church parishes," chaplain ministry has been interracial and inclusive of minority groups almost without exception since 1945. A retired Army chaplain described chaplain ministry as "direct personal ministry to the individual hurts of people." If one adds to that the recognition that chaplain ministry is direct personal ministry to the religious cares and hopes of individual persons, it is clear that any kind of interference with a person's access to the chaplain because of race, religion, membership, economic, or social status, would be unthinkable.

The scene that unfortunately occurred in many civilian parishes (including Methodist) of church officials barring entrance to blacks or others could never have happened in the chaplaincy. Some would say that this is the case only because of the authoritative nature of the institutions in which chaplains serve. That implies that chaplain ministry was "required by force" to be open to all, including minorities, whether chaplains really wanted it that way or not.

Chaplains themselves spoke of this question quite differently. In all 1236 responses, not one chaplain spoke of ministry that included minority groups as being an imposed obligation, which was contrary to one's desire or conscience. On the contrary, chaplains spoke with pride about the freedom and the integrity of ministry to all, especially to minority cultural groups. A Navy chaplain wrote: "Chaplain ministry enabled me to provide ministry for a broad spectrum of people from Flag Officers in the District of Columbia to a Marine Corpsman in combat—presenting the Lord where they are." An Air Force chaplain wrote even more positively: "Interracial and inter-cultural ministries in the Air Force are absolutely superior to anything I came near to experiencing in my home conference." Another wrote about the chaplain ministry as offering an "excellent opportunity to share one's concern for persons. It is like a course in anthropology, allowing a person to see those of other cultures, colors, and faiths." A retired chaplain, reflecting on his ministry, wrote even more sharply. "The chaplains could teach The United Methodist Church that Christian service is more than sending dollars to Africa to help the black, but being willing to sit beside a black in a civilian church. . . The Methodist Church has abandoned its heritage. It preoccupies itself with 'concerns' and not with people, 'the children of God.' Chaplains do."

One chaplain says simply: "We have led the way in ministries to minorities." A former chaplain who is now a pastor of a local church reflected appreciatively on the chaplain experience: "I feel the chaplaincy has enriched my ministry. As a local church pastor I feel I owe a great deal to the chaplaincy. My understanding of human nature, ethics, and cultural background has been enhanced." Another wrote of the broadening effect, personally and theologically, of the chaplaincy: "Being involved with world-wide cultures usually broadens one's views about religion, morality, and life. A narrow and dogmatic theology would seem inconsistent with the chaplaincy."

Commenting on the question, *Do chaplains know something about Christian ministry which The United Methodist Church overall should take into account?"* two chaplains wrote explicitly about provincialism/parochialism and the importance of critical examination of received attitudes towards minority groups.

> "Having to serve a wide spectrum of the population, chaplains learn to appreciate the uniqueness of personality and the broad principles of the Judeo-Christian faith. Too many of the churches I've attended are extremely parochial, limited in vision and with no dedication to serving the needs of their communities. Most think of mission in limited terms of church membership—the inside group. The chaplain has had to perform in an environment in which experiences are much more diverse and broad than the average pastor will ever have. He has had to bring a ministry and be a pastor to a broader sociological and psychological background in one year than the average pastor does in a lifetime."

Another chaplain spoke of fragmentation. "We see a much larger world of ministry in terms of races, denominations, and conditions, than the local church ministry—which is often narrowly focused. We see the need for denominational cooperation also. We are aware of the terrible absurdity of church fragmentation." The thrust of what many chaplains report is that in daily life and work they are able to represent a "wideness in God's mercy" that renders both cultural and religious fragmentation absurd. That may well be due to a combination of circumstances in the chaplaincy which shifts traditional priorities and focuses human questions at a more fundamental level than racial/cultural identities. "When people are facing death or enduring pain, the niceties of air-conditioned sanctuaries and polished brass are really not important." Another claims that the chaplaincy tends to emphasize not the issues that set cultural groups apart but those "broad human issues" which are really not numerous but that affect us all. Among these, he sees "quality of life, treatment of people, and non-sectarian ministry."

A military chaplain agrees: "The military chaplain is frequently dealing with very basic questions that the rest of society manages to avoid (life, death, violence)." But in all of the chaplain ministries there seems to be an urgency about broad and deep human questions which go beyond the trivial, the ordinary, and the conventional, and usually focus on a person-to-person relation. Two comments are terse and clear. "The chaplaincy makes critical the pastoral concern for people and their needs." The chaplain has the opportunity to minister to people at the point of their intense need in crisis, illness, and death."

One reason why chaplain ministry has taken the lead in interracial ministry and ministry to minorities is that persons are seen primarily in terms of survival, courage, health, and meaning, and not in terms of being members of a cultural group. This does not obscure the importance of cultural identity but it removes cultural identity as a factor in qualifying one for the time and interest of a chaplain. This is generally true, in spite of the fact that there are distinct racial subcultures in prisons, especially among long-term inmates.

Many chaplains also claim a significant Christian ministry to a fringe group of people, to those who are "down and out," the "outcasts." This designation includes those on the fringe of health, of acceptable conduct, and those who are emarginated in socio-economic terms. The testimony is that chaplain ministry places chaplains directly with persons for whom life is raw, threatening, painful, and in numerous cases, hopeless. The challenge is to make present the power and love of God without glibness, without superficiality, and without sentimentality.

Here is a critical opportunity to show "compassion and to practice evangelism," as one chaplain put it. Without compassion, no ministry would be Christian, and without the conviction that God's love gives an unconditional worth and meaning to one's life that is not destroyed by physical or mental illness, incarceration, abandonment by family and friends, or death, no one would be there day after day to share both the hurts and the hope. That is why a chaplain who works constantly in a hospital situation can write: "Our focus is probably more on direct ministry to human needs rather than . . . about perpetuating the institution for the sake of itself."

It is quite understandable that persons in this kind of ministry speak often of the chaplaincy as "offering more intensive opportunity to relate pastoral theology to life." One chaplain mentioned the importance of "really helping people who needed it," the freedom to "meet and minister to the spiritual and pyschological needs of individuals," the freedom to minister to "the underdog, the down-hearted, and the fellows in the guardhouse." Hospital chaplains spoke appreciatively of the privilege of ministry to the critically ill and of the educational help they received to prepare them for this ministry. "I have the opportunity to minister to the sick more deeply and at more crucial points in their lives than I could as a pastor because of my specialization." The chaplaincy gave me the opportunity to assist dying patients through their struggle with fears, frustration, and anger in facing their mortality. . . It also provided me the opportunity of assisting Protestant Christians to call up and recall their basic teachings of faith, to enable them to face the crisis of illness and hospitalization." Some mentioned the theodicy issue and the persistence of "why me?" questions to an understanding of God's justice and love. Another hospital chaplain emphasized the significance of the "proclamation of the gospel through caring, that is listening and hearing; responding in care and with sensitivity: confession/forgiveness/acceptance."

Many chaplains mention the limits, the frailty, and the imperfection of human life. "Chaplains go where the people are, share life with them as they are, and are aware that life isn't always pretty." Another speaks of the "awareness of the imperfections of the 'human condition' which seem never to be far removed. The awareness of faults and of limited achievements constantly reminds one of 'frailty.' " In a cultural system which is highly focused on achievement and success, and which tends to degrade the poor, the sick, and the imprisoned, this awareness of frailty, pain, and suffering seems to be critically important to the honesty and universality of Christian ministry. Hence, the emphasis is on sharing, hearing, acceptance, confession, fidelity, and forgiveness. A person working in a quite specialized ministry summed up many of these things.

> "When a young person is admitted to a Chemical Dependency Unit, that person is, in most cases, spiritually bankrupt. And here is where pastoral care has a significant role ministering to persons who are alienated from themselves, others, and from God."

Prison ministry seems to be the most difficult of all forms of chaplain ministry, because in addition to normal doubts about oneself and God, incarceration signifies a hard rejection by society. From the prisoner's perspective, incarceration is often seen as selective and unfair in a social situation where everybody is guilty in one way or another. In the cases of political prisoners, activitists for human rights, persons who refuse military service, or even some convicted in connection with Watergate, the "prisoners" thought of themselves as serving the best interest of the nation. Whatever the reason for confinement, the problem of chaplain ministry is both difficult and important because it must promote an honest and critical self-awareness that avoids arrogant self-justification and self-accusing worthlessness.

One prison chaplain felt that the church overall should be more aware of "the problems of the disenfranchised persons who feel unacceptable everywhere," for this is the plight of persons in most prisons. Others claimed that the church has a responsibility to those persons "who have been incarcerated and are making an attempt to start life anew." Another in a correctional institution spoke of real changes in peoples' lives.

> "I work with prisoners in a state maximum security prison, and the chaplaincy gives me significant opportunities for Christian ministry in the sense that lives are changed not only for individual prisoners, but for their families as well through the relationship that has been formed with the inmate."

Many prison chaplains stress the peculiar importance of patience and seed-sowing in relation to prisoners. Especially in this ministry, the pastor may give and give, month after month, and never see any tangible result of one's ministry. In such a situation, it is more important to be loyal to the substance of the gospel, confident that God will bring the "increase" in God's good time, than to be tempted by short range but superficial changes. One perceptive chaplain mentioned that explicitly. "The major role of prison ministry is seed-sowing. The seeds eventually grow, but the fast growth is not the firm growth. Gaining of stability is the greatest growth rather than the quick emotional high that soon passes."

Occasionally chaplains mention ministry to persons in the lower socio-economic scale. Some even speak of "outcasts." Three things are clear regarding this group of impoverished, sick, mentally retarded, and imprisoned persons: 1) society defines these persons as casualties and to some extent is responsible for producing the casualties, 2) these individuals must work through their calamities within their ambiguity and frailty, recognizing the flaws both in society and in themselves, and 3) by the grace of God, the cycle of resentment, cynicism, and self-condemnation can be broken and a new self-meaning discovered which transforms life whether or not illness is cured, death postponed, or incarceration ended.

That is a lesson which many chaplains are convinced is important and which they claim for their ministry. They are saying that "unsuccessful" persons are not as "evil" as they seem. More importantly, they are saying that the gospel of Christ is pertinent to all, stretching beyond the categories of cultural success and cultural definitions of good and evil. The restrained comment of one chaplain comes to mind: "Jesus called people to the love of God—God touched the outcasts." The disarming words of a chaplain who works in a hospital for the chemically dependent are applicable to many, inside and outside the chaplaincy:

"Perhaps more than I ever experienced in the parish, I have been an intimate part of people examining their lives, making major changes in their beliefs and lifestyles. I see God working miracles daily in the lives of people I work with. . . . I have found that people I work with are asking the kinds of questions about their lives that I need to be asking myself about my life."

Beyond the minority groups and the "fringe" persons, the most prominent category of persons who are ministered to by chaplains is the third group, usually referred to as the "unchurched." Some of these persons may have made a conscious decision against a religious affiliation. Most of them, however, seem to be persons who have been unaffected, uninfluenced, by the churches. This may mean that they know nothing about religion and that they do not consciously regard any of their actions, feelings, or thoughts as religious.

Chaplains sometimes refer to these persons as ones who would never attend a church and who would perhaps not be visible to the parish clergy. "The chaplaincy presented the opportunity to work and witness to a vast group of young people who are not available to the normal pastor." One chaplain speaks of ministering to persons "the local church can't reach." A chaplain in a school for delinquents speaks of the "opportunity to bring the gospel to youngsters who would never be reached by the denominations, and to bring a ministry to the staff who for the most part seem to be unchurched."

Another regards this kind of ministry as being his greatest challenge. "The biggest challenge has been to work with the unchurched, the 'no-preference' type, to witness to them in love, in daily living." Others spoke in similar ways. "I had the opportunity of continuous association with large numbers of men who had little or no concern about church/religion/God." "A significant aspect of my ministry was that to a large, non-church population that has left or has no background in the church." "I had the opportunity to reach many who would not otherwise talk to a clergyperson or seek his help." "I am involved in significant ways with people who are not involved in the church." "I had the privilege of being a friend and guide to people with little or no relation to the church."

Several chaplains thought that the church could learn something from chaplains because of the more diversified clientele and the fullness of the life-thrust in a group more comprehensive than merely church people. "The church should learn a greater sensitivity to the importance of being able to minister to all persons of any faith or of no religious affiliation." "The United Methodist Church is largely unaware that ministry goes beyond the bounds of the institutional church." "Chaplain clergy are exposed to life in a way church-protected parish clergy are not." Chaplains' clientele are much larger and more diversified in every way than that of the average pastor." "The church needs to learn to accept people who disagree and to recognize that Christianity is not a hothouse product." This point is poignantly expressed in the comment of a military chaplain.

> "The searching, probing spirit of persons to make meaning out of life gives opportunity to speak to basic life questions. The openness of persons in the military is more pronounced than in the local church. There is an opportunity to get closer to persons in a shorter time and have influence on their lives."

One senses in these remarks an excitement about the human quest that is fundamentally and inextricably related to "sharing an answer." It is almost as if the answer may be there but in an asbtract and dry, unfleshed form unless it is constantly related to the human question and the human quest. How bizarre it would be if the church said to the world: Christ is the answer. Now what is the question? What the chaplains seem to be saying is that the answer they affirm in Christ is present in such a way that it enables them to be open to the primary questions which ordinary people have about their lives. The answer in Christ thus becomes so rich and powerful a mystery that it can venture incognito among the strengths and weaknesses, the loves and fears, the rough and tumble of the diversified human family. It can share the full anxiety, even the agony, of that search for meaning without fear that somewhere there is something in a situation for which the love of God in Christ Jesus is not applicable, not an answer. The chaplains are saying that there is no sharing of the Christian answer unless there is a sharing in and of the human questions. They suggest that perhaps because the church has come to give inordinate attention to "seeking its own" the church may have forgotten something about elemental questions and answers which haunt ordinary people.

Some chaplains are more explicit about this and point out the "sheltered" life of the local church and the local church pastor. "I have the feeling that many pastors have lived a protected, even sheltered life and do not have the wide contacts with people of all walks of life which lead to an understanding of persons." "Chaplains know how to understand and help the unchurched." "I could visit troops almost anywhere. I was able to see and counsel men I would never have seen in my civilian church. I found a new world. In the civilian ministry one is sheltered to a greater extent." With strong imagery, another chaplain speaks to the same question.

> "The United Methodist Church might learn from chaplains that Christian experience and ministry are not restricted to a narrow parish wall, that they gain greater validity by sharing an open Christian life. Too many seek separateness/aloneness even in conference settings. I feel the chaplains are more like scattered manure doing a great good but the parish minister keeps himself piled up just rotting, afraid to live and be known."

It is impressive that many of these chaplain clergypersons are saying things about the "wideness in God's mercy," the depth of the passion, compassion, and love of God which includes all people—the same kinds of things that Bonhoeffer said while in prison. "To be a Christian does not mean to be religious in a particular way, to make something of oneself (a sinner, a penitent or a saint), on the basis of some method or other, but to be a (human being). . . . It is not the religious act that makes the Christian, but participation in the sufferings of God in the secular world.[6] On July 21, 1944, Bonhoeffer wrote: "I discovered later, and I'm still discovering up to this moment, that it is only by living completely in this world that one learns to have faith."[7] During his meditations in prison, he was led to reassess the meaning of Christian faith. That conviction takes the abbreviated form of an "outline for a book." In the outline of three chapters, he includes these statements.

---

[6] Dietrich Bonhoeffer, *Letters and Papers from Prison,* (New York, 1972), p. 361. Letter of July 18, 1944.

[7] Bonhoeffer, *op. cit.,* p.369.

"Our relation to God is not a 'religious' relationship to the highest, most poweful, and best Being imaginable—that is not authentic transcendence—but our relation to God is a new life in "existence for others," through participation in the Being of Jesus. . . . The Church is the Church only when it exists for others." [8]

One chaplain echoes Bonhoeffer and speaks for many when he says that chaplain ministry forces him to reconsider the central meaning of Christian ministry. Although he does not propose the outline of a book, he is drawn to radical changes in the style and substance of his preaching, and the implications of his statement are parallel to those in Bonhoeffer's *Letters and Papers From Prison.* This chaplain asks The United Methodist Church to recover the primary mission of the church which is "beyond building the institution and enhancing personal positions." He confesses: "I have had to rewrite practically all of my sermons used as a pastor, and discard many which I have realized were all too promotional with little universal substance left. Of course I know the churches need to be built and the budgets raised, but were I to start over, the worship hour would not be the time or place."

Two chaplains state the case for the ecumenical nature of chaplain ministry as including all persons in a simple and compelling way. They both commend this discovery to the church as a whole. "The Christian minister is responsible for the spiritual welfare of all. . . He learns to forget denominational lines." "We have learned to provide the broadest and most comprehensive ministry to the total community rather than just the church community." The strong conviction about the significance of a ministry to all persons, including the chronically sick, the incarcerated, the disenfranchised, the "down and out," and the "unchurched," is vivid and inescapable in what chaplains in many kinds of situations understand about their ministry as Christian clergy.

2. Ministry *With* All

Chaplain ministry involves a collegial relation with persons of other denominations and faiths that is relished by those involved.

---

[8] Bonhoeffer, *op. cit.,* pp. 381, 382.

Cooperation and collegial trust and support among clergy of different faiths were mentioned repeatedly by chaplains as a significant aspect of their ministry. This implies that in civilian parish life there is an operational, if not a formal, barrier between the faiths that requires some effort to overcome. And this suggests that there is a falseness about local parish and denominational competition that causes the emphasis of Christian ministry to be placed on membership and participation in the program of the denomination rather than on the nurture of the radical and unifying qualities of faith, hope, and love. The importance of the denomination does not disappear in chaplain ministry, but the focus is on the foundations of integrity, faith in God, care and love for persons, and the rooting of one's life within God's justice and grace. Compared to the joy and gratification of the chaplain who witnesses that kind of transformation, it matters little whether a person becomes a member of the Methodist, Presbyterian, Episcopal, or Roman Catholic Church, or whether that person becomes a believing Jew or an observer in one of the branches of Judaism. Rather, the primary tests of the effectivness of chaplain ministry are two: 1) Have you expressed to all for whom you are responsible the love of God in whatever forms are appropriate (friendship, care, compassion, counseling, teaching, admonishing, healing, preaching, administering the sacraments)? 2) Have you invited all for whom you are responsible to respond to the love of God in ways consistent with that love and appropriate to the highest prompting of conscience, will, and intellect?[9]

The usual priorities of the conference system and the reporting of organizational statistics for the *Conference Journal* have gradually come to dominate and to determine the understanding of Christian ministry among many United Methodist parish clergy. The sense of liberation and joy in collegial, ecumenical, team ministry is inescapable in accounts of chaplains, and often the contrast with

---

[9] H. Richard Niebuhr has given an impressive analysis of the "responsible self" as a social self. He emphasizes the "oneness" of the self in the "manyness" of God's actions. "The reponsible self . . . is a universally and responsive I, answering in universal society and in time without end, in all actions upon it, to the action of the One who heals all our diseases, forgives all our iniquities, saves our lives from destruction, and crowns us with everlasting mercy." (H. Richard Niebhur, *The Responsible Self* [New York, 1963], pp. 144, 145).

local church, parish ministry is explicitly stated. One of the first chaplains to return a questionnaire made the point in relation to human need. "A significant part of my chaplain ministry was the opportunity to minister to persons especially in crisis, at turning points in their lives: a more ecumenical ministry. I was a member of a team ministry in which each person was respected for his skills—not needing to fulfill everybody's expectations as in a local church."

Another simply speaks about "collegiality" and "ecumenicity." Another writes about the "value of a truly ecumenical ministry." One mentions the opportunity the chaplaincy gave "to relate to men and women of all faiths and the many denominations within Protestantism." Another relates the ecumenical ministry to the intensity of crisis needs and suggests a provincialism in the local church in this regard. "The chaplaincy gave me the opportunity for ministry to people in crisis situations, counseling; ministry to people of intellectual, moral, and spiritual levels well above those of civilian churches. This is supervision with the purpose of enhancing the spiritual life of people, not pushing institutional program goals."

Other chaplains wrote about enlargement and enrichment of the understanding of Christian ministry. One chaplain was appreciative of "time for a ministry of presence and for counseling, for opportunities for cross-fertilization with a wide range of faith groups with a consequent improvement in total ministry." Another speaks of broadening horizons. "The chaplaincy broadens one's horizons to see the vastness of the total Body of Christ beyond our tradition. Experientially one learns that The United Methodist Church does not have an exclusive franchise on the Good News." The issue of priority is emphasized by another. "People are in faith groups mostly as an accident of birth. Their basic human needs to feel loved, lovable, and worthwhile cross all boundaries. United Methodists need to forget that they are United Methodists and concentrate on being Christian human beings.

Another claims the spirit of Wesley in emphasizing the universality of the gospel. "We owe it to ourselves and to The United Methodist Church membership to demonstrate an overall ecumenical attitude. We have no corners on truth or correct polity." The phrase, "cooperation without compromise," was used often, and the claim was made by several that collegiality of all ministries and interdenominational cooperation was in no way a compromise or abdication of Methodist principles. Indeed, one person seemed to be proud of the fact that for chaplains the primary thing is "Christian ministry, rather than denominational ministry." It is not clear that the chaplains are claiming the same kind of theological support of this ecumenical ministry on the part of all denominations and faith groups. Yet, they seem to be claiming a support in Methodist undesrtanding of the love of God which undergirds the ecumenicity of their care and work, and which is obscured, if not eclipsed, by the functioning of the Conferences and the prominence of local parish church responsibilities and programs.

Chaplains see their ministry as a ministry *with others in other denominations and faith groups,* and they rejoice in the freedom from provinciality about the love of God that this discovery entails. Without exception, this aspect of ministry is seen as enlivening and enriching. The mutual support and cooperation arising from shared ministry reduces competitiveness and is a symbol of the oneness and universality of the love of God that all religious groups both express and often distort by an awkward and narcissistic exclusiveness.

3. Ministry *in* All Situations

Another aspect of ecumenism in chaplain ministry is the presence of that ministry both in the acute crisis situation and in the comprehensive circle of ordinary activities. The two claims about this ministry that stand out are that the chaplain is present within the community where the crisis/danger arises and that by sharing the general round of everyday life, the chaplain establishes a more honest, less pretentious, and more direct contact with people.

(a) *Crisis Situations*

As we have seen, in all forms of chaplain ministry there is something out of the ordinary among people ministered to. One is either confined, separated from a normal environment, seriously ill, or facing grave danger. The result of these forms of external stress is that more demands are put upon inward poise and stability. All of the chaplains tell about this in their different situations. One Army chaplain speaks of offering people hope in the face of death in combat. An institutional chaplain talks about "a chance to work with a population which I felt had a great need for help—that is long-term chronic mental patients." A Veterans' Administration chaplain speaks of "reaching people at the very time and point of their needs—life threatening situations." A Navy chaplain tells of "ministry to those in acute fear." A minister in a psychiatric clinic describes "counseling in crises, with couples, families, and the mentally ill."

A Navy chaplain claims that his "working with young men uprooted from their families and local churches" is significant. Another was gratified by a ministry which provided "spiritual, moral, and educational opportunities to men who lived under threat of death constantly." Another chaplain noted that "people are more ready to hear and learn about God when they are less sure they will be alive tomorrow." Although that way of putting it recalls Leslie Weatherhead's statement that "man's extremity is God's opportunity,"[10] neither statement suggests taking advantage of people who are particularly vulnerable. Yet both emphasize the importance of spiritual presence with persons in crisis situations.

"The strength of the ministry is in 'being there—where the parishioners are' sharing separation from families, combat, loneliness, joys of new places and people," writes a military chaplain. The integrity of the military chaplain is without a doubt related to the fact that he or she is an insider, sharing the full range of danger, separation, and inconveniences with all the others. As one chaplain put it, "they know that we do not have to be there, that we are there because we chose to be there." Even so, the more prominent consideration for chaplaincy overall is the presence to persons in extraordinary and critical situations. They express this in many ways. One speaks of the chaplaincy as being "up-front." "Chaplain ministry is more 'up-front' than is parish ministry,

---

[10] Leslie Weatherhead used the statement often during the 1940's and 1950's, but he did not create the statement. It apparently comes from John Flavel, *A Faithful and Ancient Account of Some Late and Wonderful Sea Deliverances*, written about 1680, and quoted by Lord Belhaven in a speech to the Scottish Parliament on November 2, 1706.

especially in the areas of death and dying, alcohol, drugs, and in hospital ministry."

> Chaplains deal with people who are really face to face with the meaning of life and death, with pretenses shorn away. . . . I've found that in the chaplaincy masks are ripped away and people had to face and deal with naked issues. I guess I'm saying that chaplains very often have to exercise greater honesty in dealing with people.

Another chaplain was convinced that many people had never seen or heard a Christian pastor before they met him. "I ministered in hospitals, in war, in basic training—all situations where the gospel is desperately needed and welcomed by many." Another chaplain wrote of ministry at the "living edge of life." That double use of the word, life, suggests that death for humans is peculiar among living beings because the human being is an animal who knows that he or she will die. For the human, then, the primary issue of life is not longevity, but meaning. As the hunger to make "sense out of nonsense," to find meaning for one's own life," is universal, minstry at the "living edge of life" begins to suggest an important presence at those critical and decisive moments when one despairs or hopes, trusts or becomes cynical, gives up or accepts peace, is joyful or resentful about one's own life. There is a power and integrity about a light that shines in darkness, a love that continues to be love in the tragedies and crises of life. Within the generally unprotected, vulnerable, and exposed situations of many people the chaplains are claiming the special privilege of being present in the name and spirit of Christ. This view is well expressed by a chaplain who wrote: "Chaplain ministry is at the center of the action, not the periphery. I am where people are the most open and the most vulnerable."

(b) *The Daily Round of Life*

We discussed "total communities" above and observed how all chaplain ministries take place within a form of "total community." We noted that the military is a "total community" in which the conflict of identities is more that of "insider vs. outsider," than that of "inmate vs. staff." We also recognized that "insider" status conferred an authenticity and an authority on chaplain ministry that could never be achieved by an "outsider." We noted that chaplains share all the dangers and deprivations with others in the community. One chaplain put it this way: "There is a special relationship in the military chaplaincy between the soldier and the chaplain—the same clothing, the same pay, the same hardship, the same rewards, the same danger, the same sacrifice, the same separations from loved ones." There are other aspects of chaplain ministry in the military as a "total institution," however, which deserve comment even if they do not apply in exactly the same way to the non-military types of chaplaincy.

Many military chaplains claim that they share fully in the daily round of life with their people where they work, play, socialize and live, and that their full participation in the daily events of life establishes a plateau of realism, forthrightness, directness, and honesty which is of immense significance to Christian ministry. One spoke of the "great opportunity to interact and be a part of the mainstream of the lives of his constituency." Another spoke of "visiting the people where they are—where they work, live, recreate, and so forth. . . . It shows that we genuinely care for our people. We want to know them by being with them."

This suggests that the separation of the religious from the secular is largely avoided in the ministry of the chaplain. Chaplains derive authority and calling from an explicitly religious base, but they are given a position in the military which enables them to express the concerns of God within the total spectrum of human life and work. Thus the totality of the human struggle is placed within the reach of the care of God. The chaplain ministry declares functionally and verbally that nothing can separate anyone absolutely and finally from the love of God. This is surely an important part of the meaning of the chaplain's claim to be a "Christian presence in a secular community."

In some instances chaplains emphasize the comprehensiveness of this shared life in physical terms, for example, having access to and meeting people in the work areas of a base, ship, or post, "where people do their jobs." In other instances, the more subtle dimensions of that presence are highlighted. One chaplain speaks of being "with people where they are, both geographically and emotionally/spiritually," while another writes of the importance of a "personal" ministry, "really being where our people are, where they work, live and 'have their being.' " Chaplains are claiming a kind of ministry that is close to the depths of peoples' lives, their fundamental doubts and confidences, fears and loves. At this level many of the socializing and conventional concerns of people become trivial and superficial. This claim was expressed in different ways, but in all of them is an emphasis on the honesty, openness, and forthrightness of chaplain ministry.

A chaplain with only fourteen months service in the Navy was impressed with both the necessity and the actuality of honesty among the people as well as the clergy. "The most *real ministry* I have found is that with real people with real problems, who must be honest because we live, eat, and work together." That direct contact with people that makes weak persons positively vulnerable also creates a situation with which a strong person can minister through a wide range of human qualities including personal character and example as well as through insight, advice, counsel, the sacraments, and preaching. A chaplain wrote about the privilege of an ecumenical ministry, a counseling ministry, and a diversified ministry, but above these he cherished the opportunity "to be oneself not only in ministry but accepted as an individual person, to affect change in people's lives by example as well as by other pastoral ministrations."

The other side of chaplain ministry is the frankness with which the people disclose the real problems of their lives. As one put it, "the chaplaincy provided me a unique insight into people 'being themselves,' that is with their 'Sunday masks' off." An institutional chaplain reports the same kind of frank and real contact with people in his work. "I appreciate the opportunity to assist people toward freedom in working through their spiritual dilemmas, personal problems of an emotional nature, and to resolve financial and other difficulties. These are usually kept from a pastor by a parishioner needing help. Parishioners didn't want people to know." A chaplain reports an incident which contrasts chaplain ministry and parish ministry even more sharply. "I recall a woman who was a member of a local church coming to see me about a personal problem, and she stated that she could never reveal this to her minister because of what he might think of her."

We must be careful not to generalize about ministry in such a way as to reach false conclusions. The fact that some chaplains have had experiences with particulary inept local pastors or particularly narrow parishes does not establish the general quality of congregations or pastors. On the other hand, chaplains are claiming a kind of Christian ministry that is in closer touch with the real life issues than that of ordinary local church ministry. This does not imply that local parish ministry is dishonest or that local parishioners are superficial. It does suggest quite clearly that because of many aspects of these special situations, chaplain ministry is less cushioned by the civilties of social acceptability and is closer to the radical roots of good and evil in all of us as well as to the meaning of life and death.

One chaplain stated the claim quite concisely. "The chaplaincy gave me the opportunity to live, work, and play with my congregation so that we know one another—the bad and the good—and I could minister to the real person." Actually, the "realness" is on both sides as we have seen. The chaplain can be present without pretending to be better or worse than he or she is. And the people can be present with their strengths and weaknesses frankly acknowledged. This is true partly because minister and people live so close to each other that one could not get by with evasion or pretending. More importantly, it is true because the gospel is a claim for the love of God in the face of the most radical forms of human duplicity and evil. If the gospel is a story of the encounter of real guilt and evil with real goodness and holiness, then the ultimate betrayal of that gospel would be to allow it to be taken as a charade, a "pretended evil" conquered by a "pretended grace," leaving the vitalities of real human life untouched, unchanged, and unredeemed.

The claim by the chaplains of an ecumenical Christian ministry is so overriding in its implications that it affects every other aspect of ministry. But there are still other pointed things the chaplains say, falling into the general categories of counseling, significant presence, and team ministry.

B. Counseling Ministry

"During my first six months at a reception center, I did more counseling than in the previous six years in the pastorate." So wrote a retired military chaplain. Another spoke of "doing more counseling in the first three months in the Air Force then in five years in the parish." One claimed he counseled 863 persons in his first year as a chaplain. Another reported that for the last year he counseled an average of twenty-four persons a week and counseled in about one divorce situation a week. The numbers vary, but the claims about one-to-one ministry are overwhelming. Chaplains are not denying the role of counseling in parish ministry, but they understand themselves to be involved in a higher ratio of counseling to preaching and administration than is the case in civilian parish ministry. They value this ministry highly, and are grateful that they are freed from various kinds of distracting activities and are available for counseling. One reason for this is the greater need for counseling in chaplaincy situations than in the ordinary civilian parish. We have already seen that almost every chaplain situation is one in which the "extraordinary" prevails, with the attendant strains on self-meaning caused by crisis, illness, separation/loneliness, confinement, or danger. But the chaplains' are claiming more than that they are doing a greater quantity of counseling than the parish minister. There are so many references to person-to-person ministry that something more subtle and complex seems to be involved. The other dimension is related to a number of things in addition to the "extraordinariness" of the situation: more acute need, more fundamental search for human meaning and purpose, more honesty, and more urgency.

Repeatedly, the chaplains speak of the importance of a "person-centered ministry." It is as if the world turns not on the stock market, on the outcome of the battle, on recovery from this illness, on the image of the church, or even on the family. But the world and everything in it turns on whether or not that one person before the chaplain is able to "hold together"; to trust others, the world, and himself/herself; to sustain a center of confidence and hope against all the threats, intimidations, and enticements that would draw that person "out of the self" and destroy him or her as a person in the process.

Chaplains seem to be "called" to persons in these situations. Often they speak of "feeling" or "listening" to the hurts of persons. As one chaplain put it: "Chaplain ministry made critical the pastoral concern for people and their needs." Without doubt, the universality of "personness" is a factor here. *Any person in need has a claim on the chaplain's time and ministry.* That fact cannot be overestimated. But something else is still involved. That was suggested by a chaplain who wrote: "People in difficulty come to the chaplain first. My experience in the civilian parish in the last five years led me to believe that when things went wrong people did not want their pastor to know. . . . Confidentiality and trust were important in counseling—confidence that there will be understanding and help, not just condemnation." Implicit in the emphasis on counseling ministry is a claim to a quality of confidentiality and understanding by the chaplains, a quality which is integral to Christian ministry whether or not there is a crisis or an extraordinary situation.

Chaplains apparently regard confidentiality in counseling more highly than the parish minister. This is due in part to the situation of stress, danger, or conflict of conscience. Persons in those extraordinary situations cannot repress the radical and fundamental human questions. As a result, both they and the chaplains "lay bare" their souls. That kind of self-exposure, self-revelation, and vulnerability requires the most profound dimensions of confidentiality traditionally associated with the confessional.

Since Protestantism has largely abandoned the role of the clergy in confession, the meaning of confidentiality has eroded in the ordinary parish situation. As the parish clergyperson has assumed a more social/political function reflecting the dominant prejudices, values, and attitudes of the self-selecting parish membership, fundamental questions about morality, hope and meaning are obscured. Persons fear the loss of status in the eyes of the clergy and of the community if their passions and actions become known.

There seems to be a relation between self-honesty, confidentiality, and condemnation. Several chaplains spoke of "accepting persons" as they are and understanding them in a non-judgmental way. A retired chaplain suggested that The United Methodist Church at large should learn from the chaplains a "non-judgmental dealing with people's problems." Another retired chaplain said the church should learn "how to accept persons where they are." A middle-aged hospital chaplain contrasted "imposing a model" of

character upon another with "enabling" another. "In my experience in Methodism, ministry generally meant making others into
what they were supposed to be. In chaplaincy the process has
been more of enabling others to develop toward their own
potential."

A Veteran's Administration chaplain thought that Methodist
clergy tend to be too judgmental and questioning. "Chaplains are
willing to work with alcoholics, and so forth, without questioning
them. We as United Methodists should do the same." One chaplain
suggested that chaplains "are perhaps better able to minister to
alcoholics, homosexuals, and so forth, ('sinners')." Another spoke
more tersely to the same point, "Chaplains are willing to eat, drink,
and live with sinners."

The thrust of many of these comments is a positive theological
claim concerning the unconditional dimension of God's grace.
"The church must learn 'to recognize individuals as they are and not
reject those who transgress, and to love the unlovely,'" wrote one
chaplain. It is important for the church to recover the nature of
ministry and the acceptance of persons as persons of value,"
claimed another. What are we to make of these claims about
ministry?

One might conclude that chaplains have been brainwashed or
intoxicated by the ethical relativism of Clinical-Pastoral-Education,
or of "situation ethics," atheistic humanism, or of some combination
of these. That would be a tragic mistake! The chaplains are
confessing that their experience in The United Methodist Church led
them to embrace a standard of sexual morality, total abstinence,
heterosexuality, religious observance, non-violence, and personal
purity that caused them to identify Christian morality with their own
morality and to look down upon persons with different standards
and lifestyles. When they went into the chaplaincy, however, they
discovered a genuineness and an integrity among persons with
widely different cultural and ethnic traditions. Beyond that they
discovered that the love of God was applicable to all persons in
their ambiguous and confused conditions: child and spouse
abusers, liars, deceivers, killers, alcoholics, homosexuals, manipu-
lators;—persons who were sick, arrogant, self-centered, broken,
unable to love. They learned that the love of God was present with

them *as they were,* which means that one may refuse that love and attempt to separate oneself from the love of God, but that nothing—our sinfulness, evil, refusal, and denial—can separate us from the love God has for us.

This does not mean that chaplains condone child abuse, killing, violence, homosexuality, alcoholism, hate, drug intoxication, or any form of destructiveness. It rather means that none of these, or all of them together, destroy the value of the person or cancel the love of God for that person. To put it differently, faith and behavior are related, but faith is more important to human integrity and dignity than behavior. For behavior can change. It can become more compassionate and more fair and just within faith.

This discovery has important implications for behavior and the way in which lasting changes in behavior are made. People in Alcoholics Anonymous, Parents Anonymous, and in the Christian church, have known this for a long time. It may be surprising to hear that word coming from chaplains, or even from secular social scientists who are able to describe accurately how changes in behavior occur among people, quite apart from whether or not they have the personal power to bring these changes about in themselves or in others.

David R. Walters is a hard-data clinician who has been consulted in more than two thousand child abuse cases. He is convinced that the abuse of children is not usually due to either mentally-ill (pathological) parents or to morally evil parents. He sees child abuse as mainly "the logical outgrowth of our cultural heritage and predilection toward violence,"[11] a part of which heritage is Judeo-Christian with the sanction of the parents' responsibility not to "spoil the child" by "sparing the rod." As a social scientist, Walters writes about "how people (child abusers) change," with no explicit reference to religion.

"They do not change as a result of threats by professionals to remove their children. They do not change as a result of police or detectives conveying their feelings of disgust or abhorrence. They do not change as a result of paternalistic or maternalistic lectures by physicians,

---

[11]David R. Walters, *Physical and Sexual Abuse of Children* (Bloomington, 1975), p. x.

caseworkers, or other professionals. Finally, they do not change as a result of prosecution that results in fines, probation, or imprisonment. In fact, most of these approaches aggravate the problem rather than reduce it, for the parents become only more angry, bitter, and frustrated and project the blame on the abused child.

"People change because other people care about them as persons without necessarily approving of their behavior. In lay terms, people change because of positive feelings toward another whether those feelings are based on a need for acceptance, friendship, or love."[12]

In whatever different ways the chaplains express, it, they are emphasizing that the person is more important than the behavior. Christian love is an unconditional care about the value of the person in spite of unacceptable behavior, rather than a response to acceptable behavior. Non-judgmental, therefore, does not mean that there are no moral standards nor that "unacceptable behavior is acceptable." It means that, before God, the presence of gracious love cannot be nullified by unacceptable behavior nor gained by acceptable behavior. At this primordial level of honesty, soul-revelation, conscious vulnerability, and perhaps culpability, persons come to the chaplain with trust in his dealing gently, confidentially, fairly, and compassionately with their "beings."

They see the chaplain as representing not the state, the system, the institution, cultural respectability, nor acceptable behavior, but the ultimacy of God's power, justice, and love. That is why there are repeated references to persons, credibility, trust, honesty, and confidentiality. This kind of confessional function in counseling is different from acknowledging a transgression, repenting and "making amends" so that one might receive communion. It is more like assisting another directly and indirectly to relate one's doing to one's being in decisions freely made about who one is, about loving and being loved, about healing and being healed, and about finding peace with all that is outside and all that is inside oneself.

C. Ministry of Significant Presence

A retired chaplain who spent most of his active ministry in hospital

---

[12]David R. Walters, *op. cit.*, p. 95.

work with the mentally ill and in a school for the developmentally delayed, spoke quite directly about the importance of presence: "You have to be there to be effective." Another chaplain wanted The United Methodist Church to realize more fully the importance of "being with" those to whom we minister. For him, there is no alternative to being fully and personally present with another person, no substitute for a "caring presence."

> "The United Methodist Church could learn from the Chaplains that ecumenicity works, encouraging understanding, personal growth, and caring relationships. There is no substitute for frequent, caring presence. Clergy are critical in power structures, but will gain authority and access by affirmation and day-by-day struggling with problems rather than by the issuing of proclamations and 'prophetic pronouncements.'"

Assuming what has been said above about the "insider" vs. the "outsider" and about the importance of being present with persons for whom we have the responsibility/privilege to minister, whether in a crisis or simply in the daily round of life, what is it that is special and important about the chaplain's presence? In the discussion of counseling, we noted many comments by chaplains which emphasized a non-condemning affirmation and acceptance of persons, an acceptance that is rooted finally in the love of God. Paul Tillich's words come to mind. "Faith is our acceptance of God's acceptance of us in spite of the fact that we are unacceptable."[13] Yet in the discussion of ecumenical ministry we noted that chaplains work with and are "present to" all kinds and conditions of persons, many of whom may have no knowledge or interest in religion, and some of whom may even be contemptuous of religion. These observations inevitably raise the question as to what significance a "religious presence" can have to a person with no interest in religion.

The chaplains say many things which throw light on that question. They suggest that although their own presence is grounded on, authenticated, and legitimized by religious faith, that presence takes different forms at different levels of relation. These levels are those of friend, staff officer, and pastor. From the perspective of the

---

[13]Paul Tillich, *The Courage to Be* (New Haven, 1952), p. 164.

chaplain, the highest, most definitive, and most inclusive level is that of pastor, but being a pastor also includes being a staff-officer and a friend. From the perspective of the person for whom the chaplain is responsible, the chaplain may be only a friend, only a staff-officer, only a pastor, or some combination of these, depending upon what the person wants, allows, or expects the chaplain to be. How does this work out in fact?

1. Presence as a Friend

Persons become human through relations with others and few are able to "go it alone" in spite of the importance of individual growth and responsibility. This suggests that there is something universally important about friendship. Yet in many of the situations in which chaplains work, a person is either isolated or in such excruciating stress or danger that he or she has no one at hand who may simply be trusted as a friend.

Chaplains understand that situation and apparently find it important in their ministry simply to be warmly, directly, and personally present as a "friend" to another. Whatever expertness the chaplain may have acquired in being on the staff of a hospital, prison, institution, or military unit, and whatever knowledge and authority he or she may have received in theological education and ordination are pertinent only as they enable the chaplain to be present as a friend. The person may not be seeking staff help in working out a problem, nor seeking spiritual counsel. He or she may simply be seeking a personal presence to break the destructive tyranny of being made a non-person in an impersonal environment.

Many chaplains described their work as including the identification of human need and responding to that need. The role of "friend" was often made specific. "My ministry included preaching, counseling, and relating to people who were away from home, lonely, afraid—and needed a 'friend.'" "We must never forget the importance of person-to-person relationships through counseling sessions and 'just being friends.'" The desperation felt by some persons who are without a single available human friend who can be trusted is fortunately remote from most of us, but chaplains apparently confront many persons for whom this is the case.

In many instances of chaplain ministry the presence of a person as a friend was a link to human meaning which enabled a person in distress not only to hold together the "threads of sanity," but also to resist the slide into cynicism and despair. That kind of presence is what chaplains are indicating when they use those simple and disarming words, "just being a friend," to describe an important part of their ministry.

2. Presence as a Staff Official

The position of the chaplain differs structurally in civilian and military settings. Yet in all of them the distinct advantage of the chaplain is that the chaplain is a part of a team of experts within an institution and can call on other staff persons for help and influence the treatment of persons within the institution. That identification with the staff may at times create difficulties for the chaplain. In a prison, for instance, the inmate may regard all those responsible for his incarceration as enemies, including the chaplain. In most chaplain settings there is a double loyalty. But the two loyalties are not equal, and the primary reason for a chaplain's position in addition to that of physician, nurse, social worker, guard, custodian, and so forth, is to share whatever light is available from the perspective of an ultimate loyalty to God.

Even so, chaplain ministry is difficult because of the explicit tensions which develop at times as to how an ultimate loyalty is related to several limited loyalties. The answer for the chaplain is not to reduce or remove the tension but to live with it in such a way that the conditional loyalties are kept open to the sanctions and resources of the ultimate. It would be too much to claim that the chaplain is the "conscience" of the institution, but he or she is given a peculiar status in an institution because he or she is there to represent the interest of the deeper human, moral, and spiritual integrity of all persons in the institution. The Christian can use persuasive skills with those who set the policies of the institution so that those policies serve the needs of moral, spiritual, and human growth.

Chaplains as a group feel that teamwork among different skilled professionals and the opportunity to influence the policies of the institution are special opportunities in the chaplaincy which do not exist for the parish minister. A hospital chaplain tells of "working with terminally ill patients and their families with a multi-disciplinary team, consisting of a chaplain, psychologist, and others." Another speaks of the "opportunity to meet crisis needs as part of a professional team." Another emphasizes how "gratifying" it is to be recognized and respected by persons in other disciplines as on a par with them in the joint effort of healing and encouragement.

In these instances, religion and the work of the chaplain are integrated with other functions of life without being compromised. Religion is regarded neither as taking the place of other concerns, nor as being supplanted by them. What chaplains find particularly satisfying is that religion is regarded as being important without having to function in isolation or having to carry the whole burden of human distress and happiness on its own.

Further, many chaplains claim success at influencing conditions within the institution they serve. Most of the institutions with chaplains do not have an explicitly religious purpose. No one is claiming that a hospital, prison, school for the developmentally delayed, or military unit is itself a church. Yet, within a secular context there is an opportunity to the chaplain as a member of the staff to make the institution more attentive to human need and dignity. One chaplain writes: "Many civilian clergy can only offer spiritual help. A chaplain is prepared to do much more. He knows how to move officials and help systems to meet human needs." Another makes a more modest claim in the military for an "occasional opportunity to influence command decisions by religious insights and religious considerations." The central theme was perhaps best expressed by a military chaplain who spoke appreciatively of the opportunity for an "organizational ministry," making the organization "more concerned for the welfare of persons."

Just how this function takes form in the different environments varies considerably. With regard to the military chaplaincy, the thirty-three recommendations of the report to the 1976 General Convention of the Episcopal Church included an insistence shared by many United Methodist Chaplains about humanly degrading treatment in the Armed Services.

"The Episcopal Church, through its Chaplains, should continue its vital 'ministry of presence' on military installations, and, therefore, be especially alert and resistant to cases of maltreatment and to the undermining of human diginity, particularly during basic training.

"The Episcopal Church should ask other communions to join it in expressing concern to the Department of Defense that the human diginity of all persons in the armed forces be scrupulously respected at all times, whether they be recruits, troops, or prisoners; and that the Department of Defense be requested to reinforce its directives to all commands concerning the implementation and maintenance of this policy.[14]

On the other end of the spectrum, in many hospital settings the ministry of the chaplain includes an explicit responsibility to use his or her power to assure that everything possible is being done to assist the life and human fulfillment of every patient in that hospital. It would be a rare case for the chaplain to have power over the institution, but it would largely nullify the function of the chaplain if he or she did not have the power to influence the institution and his or her staff colleagues toward providing the kind of environment and presence which would preserve human dignity and promote human happiness and fulfillment.

In this regard, two chaplains emphasized ministry to the staff as well as to the patient or inmate. Within a hospital setting, one mentioned the "stress management needs of helpers, including medical staff and clergy, and the importance of correlating behavioral insights with theology in order to make ministry more relevant." That suggests that stress-management along with healing is better done together as a team than individually as heroes.

Another chaplain who has worked for years in a prison situation spoke of the importance of ministry to the prison staff to keep them from becoming hardened and cynical about all prisoners. Prison work is as long and demanding a vigil as it is an important one. The staff fails if it is duped by the prisoner's claim for trust and privilege or if the staff becomes cynical and gives up on the possibility of any change in a prisoner's life. Even in the difficult work in a prison some

---

[14] *Participation of the Episcopal Church in the Ministry to the Armed Forces of the United States: an Evaluation.*Report to the 1976 General Convention of the Episcopal Church from the Study Commission on Ministry to the Military, p. 38.

hope and openness to change, however fraught with risk and danger, are essential.

We have stated the ideal situation. The actual accomplishments of chaplains depend upon their own strengths of spirit and character as well as skill, and upon a large number of other factors. It would be easy to say that there is no influence of the chaplain on the policies of an institution and to point to My Lai, to murder or suicide in prison, or to death because of an error in a hospital. Very few ideal claims would stand if they were nullified by imperfect performance. We constantly operate in a fallible system with persons who are fallible, and chaplains are themselves fallible. The failure to achieve perfection voids neither the ideal nor the effort.

In a fine study, *The Military Chaplain*, Clarence L. Abercrombie, III acknowledges human fallibility and comments on the influence of military chaplains in specific situations in Vietnam. In his survey, chaplains were asked what they would do if they were present when a commander ordered his troops to kill enemy prisoners. Six chaplains claimed to have personal knowledge of that kind of situation.

> "One was personally familiar with the My Lai massacure. Another had brought formal charges against the perpetrators of a similar though much smaller incident. In each of the remaining four instances, *the chaplain concerned had successfully prevented the killing of the prisoners*. However one might interpret the duties and responsibilities of the chaplain, the actions of these four priests and ministers alone more than justify the existence of the Chaplain Corps."[15]

Although Abercrombie is indulgent to justify the entire Chaplain Corps because of the life-saving action of four priests and ministers in Vietnam, he has suggested through those episodes that the Army is less destructive and more observant of human diginity because of the presence of chaplains. And that illustrates the significant presence of a chaplain as a staff-officer.

As was the case with "presence" as a friend, the ministry of significant presence as a staff-officer is not always explicitly religious. There is not anything necessarily or explicitly religious

---

[15]Clarence L. Abercrombie III, *The Military Chaplain* (Beverly Hills, London 1977), p. 98.

about the help that the chaplain offers as a staff-officer. But these activities are included in the primary vocation of the chaplain as a minister of the gospel of Jesus Christ and they bring us to the edge of the explicit form of religious presence, that of a pastor, a shepherd, of God's people.

3. Presence as a Pastor

The primary quality which gives "significance" to the presence of the chaplain is ordination and induction into the Good News of God's love for all persons in Jesus Christ. That is the center of the power, morality, and authority for the chaplain, a center that is never simply equivalent to the state, hospital, prison, military unit, or church. The opportunity to be present as a "friend" or as a "helper" in the role of staff-officer is made possible only by the chaplain's identity as a Christian or Jewish clergyperson. The endorsement of a clergyperson by the church is usually required for anyone taking a chaplain position. That is a formal recognition that the chaplain has a "special" status in the institution in which he or she serves. That status is directly related to what gives the unique "significance" to the chaplain's presence—the privileged relation to every person that honors the dignity of conscience.

The chaplain's presence is that of restrained, persuasive, peaceful, and compassionate encouragement of all persons to understand themselves, others, and their situation in the light of the ultimacy of the love and righteousness of God's holiness. The chaplain is present not to manipulate, force, condemn, "use," or command persons, but to act always *as a servant of God's love,* which is beyond human comprehension, *and as a servant to persons* who are striving to find meaning and to achieve integrity, worthiness, happiness, and peace in their lives.

In this process, the chaplain does not "accept" all kinds of aspirations and behavior. The chaplain is committed to the love of God which is inevitably set against the denial of that love. Part of the "significant presence" of the chaplain as a pastor is that he or she can confidently call persons to seek those things which make for *their true happiness and fulfillment.* Such is possible because the very being of the chaplain is formed by two qualities and convictions: the fulfillment of the creation in redemption, in the Kingdom of God, and the presence of the love of God from which nothing can separate us. The chaplain is a steward of the mysteries of faith, hope, and love. The human hunger for these treasures is so pervasive that the chaplain is usually welcomed and appreciated, even blessed, precisely because he or she carries a presence that "comes in the name of the Lord."

In a way, this treasure of the vocation of the clergy is qualitatively the same in all situations—civilian or military, local parish or chaplain assignment. In another way, the chaplain must carry that treasure in situations in which he or she too is vulnerable, alone, and isolated from the visible, gathered church. It is not surprising that chaplains speak of the freedom to live this faith and to share it not so much in set ways, but in the strength, freedom, insight, and responsibility of one's self. The positive side of this status is that the chaplain stands as a humane person among persons, with no special privileges, no "clergy discounts." He is able in the rough and tumble of daily life to make present a transcendent context within which life is both judged and blessed. The chaplain cannot really hide behind rank, a clerical collar, an institution, a bishop, a study, a library, or anything else. Through his or her own strength, faith, and love, the chaplain either carries this presence or does not. This is the terrible nature of the opportunity and the risk of the chaplaincy.

The negative side of this status is the temptation to put the values of the institution in which one serves in the place of the values which are dominant in the righteousness and love of God. That danger is expressed more about chaplains in the military than about chaplains in civilian institutions. However, the temptation may well be present not only for all chaplains but for all clergy as well. In general, chaplains claim that they find new personal resources and strength in the chaplaincy. Through the help of God, the church, and many persons, they say they are able to keep their function as pastor as the dominant and legitimizing quality of all that they do simply as "friend" or a "staff-officer." However much the persons who receive this ministry of the chaplain may or may not recognize it as "religious" or "Christian" ministry, for the chaplain that ministry in its totality is rooted in the pastoral function, in the ordination to serve people of God's creation by sharing all of the dimensions of the love and power of God to bless, fulfill, and redeem human life.

Much of what the chaplains say may raise questions about the full authenticity of the ordinary parish ministry. Statements of that sort may reflect their own individual experience in parishes and in the chaplaincy. They may, on the other hand, be an accurate reflection of a problem within The United Methodist Church. That will be for others to decide, but the question is so important that we must return to it in the final two chapters of this study.

In general, chaplains are claiming important dimensions of Christian ministry in their work, and to some degree charge that much of the work and interest of United Methodism does not really understand, appreciate, or support these activities. The chaplains are given their own voices to recapitulate their claim and to put their questions to the church at large.

> "I believe that we are about the task of setting people free. But so often the pastor, because of traditional roles of parish ministry, is in great bondage—not to God so much as to the mystique of being a "minister." This has the tendency to make him dependent on his job and title for his personal identity. That, in turn, has the tendency to foster feelings of hostility and anger about that dependency, thus negating much of his or her self-worth.

> "I don't think The United Methodist Church *really recognizes* the many forms of ministry. I think the church is stuck with ministry as the traditional Sunday service, scripture, prayer, and the sacraments. I don't think the church is really aware of the ministry of suffering, or the ministry of joy, or the ministry of just being an open person with another person. I think the church is afraid of ministry that is not within control of the pastor, or board, and so on."

Is it possible that what the chaplains describe and claim is outside the "scope of ministry" in the local parish? Is it possible that what the chaplains describe and claim is not Christian ministry? Does The United Methodist Church sustain a Christian ministry which embraces the activity of both the local church pastor and the chaplain/pastors? Those questions are crucial for the church. Before turning to such questions we must allow the chaplains to speak about the problems and conflicts of conscience that trouble them and the people they serve.

IV. Troubled
People ... Troubled Pastors

Clergypersons constantly confront the temptation to emphasize the positive factors in every situation to the neglect of the negative and tragic aspects of human life. Focusing on things that can be done to better a situation or to solve a problem, clergy are sustained by a basic confidence that "all things work together for good for those who love the Lord" (Romans 8:15).

This confidence is easily "trivialized," however, into the achievement of "success" according to cultural standards of power, status, health, popularity, and wealth. When this happens, the acceptance of limits and of tragedy is slighted, if not denied altogether. The pastor in preaching and counseling easily becomes "one-sided" in activistic efforts to solve all problems. The old Marine motto, "The difficult we do immediately, the impossible takes a little longer," suggests a kind of Pollyanna optimism about the human ability to solve any problem. But in the complex human struggles reflected in the civil rights movement, the war in Vietnam, child and spouse abuse, bio-medical-ethical issues, persons are not just confronted by solvable problems. They must embrace mysteries containing contradictory elements: the responsibility for action, the ambiguous effects of action, and limits that human action cannot remove.

Even in the midst of these complex mysteries, the love of God entails an active conscious compassion for the travail in nature and in human life. The prayers of the church for the coming of the Kingdom of God carry the compassion and hope that all people and all of the creation will participate in a "peaceable kingdom." Such hope is carried in a broken world among broken persons. It thus may be impossible to communicate hope and love without living and sharing in the brokenness of present life. The chaplain who said that he never experienced conflicts of conscience in his ministry seems to be an anomaly. Chaplains who were totally neutralized by the suffering they encountered were also few in number. The latter are understandable, the former utterly puzzling! Most of the chaplains tell a story of conflict and trouble among their people and within themselves which is both illuminating and inspiring in regard to what, using Paul Lehmann's phrase, "God is doing to make and to keep human life human in the world."[1]

1. Conflicts Between Ordination and Employer Demands

Since World War II, the suspicion has grown among many that it is impossible to fulfill a calling as minister of the gospel of Jesus Christ and at the same time be in the employ of the Army, Navy, or Air Force as a chaplain. That issue has been raised most sharply by a report of a United Church of Christ task force to the Ninth General Synod, St. Louis, June 22-26, 1973,[2] and by the various writers in the Harvey G. Cox, Jr. (ed.) book, *Military Chaplains: From a Religious Military to a Military Religion*[3] and by Gordon C. Zahn in *The Military Chaplaincy.*[4]

Harvey Cox puts the issue tersely, not only for the military chaplain, but also for all clergy. Speaking positively about the "rediscovery of the critical-prophetic dimensions of biblical faith," and welcoming the theological voices in Christianity and Judaism that have "exhorted the religious community to extricate itself from its bondage to the idols of race and state, and to call people back to a covenant of justice and peace," Cox then asks the crucial question:

"How does a chaplain proclaim the prophetic gospel when he is wearing the uniform of the military, is paid by the state, and furthermore,

---

[1] Lehmann, *Ethics in a Christian Context* (New York, 1963), p. 99.

[2] *Ministries to Military Personnel* (published by United Church Press, Philadelphia, 1973).

[3] Harvey G. Cox, Jr. (ed.), *Military Chaplains: From a Religious Military to a Military Religion* (New York, 1971).

[4] Gordon C. Zahn, *The Military Chaplaincy. Study of Role Tension in the Royal Air Force* (Toronto, 1968).

is dependent on his superior officers for advancement? Notice I do not ask if 'it is possible . . .' There is too much evidence that many chaplains believe they can proclaim such a message, though they concede it is difficult. No, we ask *how* because in many ways, *all* professional ministers share in some way the chaplains' dilemma. All clergymen are paid by the state. How? All are paid (or certainly a vast majority) by funds collected under charitable tax-exempt provisions. . . .

"The question of how one speaks the truth to power is not a question that chaplains alone must grapple with. In a sense their difficult situation has the merit of being at least a *clearly* difficult one. Its limitations and constrictions are out in the open. But these difficulties really amount to a more severe case of what in some way infects us all."[5]

The United Church of Christ[6], the Presbyterian Church in the U.S.A.[7], and the Episcopal Church[8] have all acknowledged the dangers of role tension in the military chaplaincy and have studied and debated the possibility of "civilianizing" the chaplaincy to the military. All of them reject the "civilian" option but recognize that the chaplain's primary role as pastor is compromised if the chaplain establishes his or her primary identity as military officer and not as clergyperson.

To justify the privilege of status within the military, the chaplain must serve the interests of the military. Yet he or she must serve the interests of the military within the primacy of the clergy function. Role tension and possible role conflict are inescapable for the chaplain. As an "insider," he or she is trusted with the special "quality of presence" that primary loyalty to God provides.

---

[5]Harvey G. Cox, Jr., *op. cit.,* p. xi. In this same volume, George H. Williams points out that President James Madison opposed paying the clergy from public funds in order to keep religion from falling under the control of the government. Cf. Williams' excellent essay, "The Chaplaincy in the Armed Forces of the United States of America in Historical and Ecclesiastical Perspectives," pp. 11-57.

[6] *Ministries to Military Personnel* (Philadelphia, 1973). Also *The Report of the Office for Church Life and Leadership on Ministries to Military Personnel.* Executive Council, United Church of Christ, 1975.

[7] *Ministry to Persons in the Armed Forces.* A Report to the 187th General Assembly. United Presbyterian Church in the U.S.A., 1975.

[8] *Participation of the Episcopal Church in the Ministry to the Armed Forces of the United States, An Evaluation.*Report to the 1976 General Convention of the Episcopal Church from the Study Commission on Ministry to the Military. N.D.

Paradoxically, the "privileged position of access of an insider is really effective for clergy (only) if the quality of presence in that privileged situation is quite clearly that of the clergy."[9] The studies by these churches acknowledge the role tension but recommend retaining the present form of chaplaincy. At the same time, these studies stress the importance of clarifying the primary role of the chaplain as clergyperson and advocating changes in the designation of "insider" status (particularly the wearing of rank) which, while functioning as signs of access, may in fact, tend to compromise the "quality of presence."

Lawrence V. Tagg has written a brief but excellent account of the struggle within The United Methodist Church about the military chaplaincy, "Methodism and the Military Chaplaincy: A Continuous Tension, 1920-1980."[10] He acknowledges the peculiarity of Methodism in providing a very large number of Protestant chaplains to the military forces and, at the same time, sponsoring a sustained and vigorous movement against war. Ernest Fremont Tittle and Henry Hitt Crane, for example, were eloquent leaders of the pacifist cause. They influenced many persons in society, in the church and on college campuses.

The conflict between the pacifists and those who supported the chaplaincy through the Methodist Commission on Chaplains (known as the Methodist Emergency Committee and the Methodist Commission on Camp Activities before 1942) came to a climax in the General Conference of The Methodist Church in 1944 when World War II was far from decided. Ernest Fremont Tittle led the move to disassociate The Methodist Church completely from the war effort, urging that the church "should not *bless* war,"[11] should not officially endorse war, should not promote the war through any of its agencies, and should not pray for military victory. Professor Umphrey Lee of Southern Methodist University and Professor Lynn Harold Hough of Drew University opposed Tittle and urged the

---

[9]Jack S. Boozer, "The Relation of State and Military Authority to Religious Authority," *Chaplaincy*, Vol. III, No 1, 1st Quarter, 1980, p. 42.

[10]Lawrence V. Tagg, "Methodism and the Military Chaplaincy: A Continuous Tension, 1920-1980." *Chaplaincy*, Vol. III, No. 1, 1st Quarter, 1980, pp. 29-31.

[11]Letter from Tittle to Shy Banks, June 2, 1944. Quoted in Robert M. Miller, *How Shall They Hear Without a Preacher? The Life of Ernest Fremont Tittle* (Chapel Hill, 1971), p. 463.

church toward a stronger support of the war. The Conference approved *by one vote* a report which invoked God's blessing on the "million young men from Methodist homes" who were engaged in the war and offered prayer for all persons in the armed forces and for ultimate victory.[12]

The General Conference of 1948 established the Commission on Chaplains as a permanent agency of the church, giving the Commission responsibility to recruit, endorse, and give general oversight to Methodist clergymen serving as chaplains in the armed forces. At that same conference, a Methodist laymen, Chester A. Smith, proposed an amendment: "We look with disfavor upon the chaplains being members of the armed forces and being subject to the military authorities and being recipients of commissions, thereby making the church a part of the war system"[13] Mr. Smith's proposal was heard, but failed to be approved in 1948, 1952, 1956, and in subsequent General Conferences.

In 1968, Professor John Swomley of St. Paul's School of Theology, Dean Kelley of the National Council of Churches, and Dean Philip J. Wogaman of Wesley Theological Seminary, petitioned the General Conference to "Demilitarize the chaplaincy." This petition did not arise from a pacifist position but from a conviction about the integrity of Christian ministry. Its explicit purpose was to "extricate the chaplaincy from non-ecclesiastical sources of authority."[14] The petition was not reported out of committee but it indicates a reticence among both pacifists and non-pacifists concerning clergypersons' being commissioned officers in the armed forces. The Vietnam era brought forth a general suspicion of the military which tended to sharpen even further the questions about military chaplaincy which had been raised for decades.

The growing concern in the church as to whether a military officer can at the same time carry the full meaning of "ordained servant of God" and "minister of the gospel of Jesus Christ" was expressed

---

[12] *Daily Christian Advocate,* Second General Conference of the Methodist Church, May 3, 1944, p. 123. *Proceedings of the Forty-First General Conference of the Methodist Church.* Kansas City, Missouri, p. 176. Report of vote, 170 to 169, p. 200.

[13] *Daily Christian Advocate,* Proceedings of the General Conference of the Methodist Church, May 10, 1948, p. 378.

[14]cf. Lawrence V. Tagg, *op. cit.,* p. 28.

even more strongly in a petition to the General Conference of 1976. The petition asked:

> "That the General Conference of The United Methodist Church take immediate steps to disengage the church from the military chaplaincy system and replace it with a civilian chaplaincy, whereby ministers will be appointed to serve military personnel without themselves becoming members of military establishment although subject to assignment by the military but with salary, maintenance and pension provided by the church, and

> "That the General Conference seek the cooperation of other religious bodies but in case such joint action cannot be achieved, or if the military authorities will not permit such a civilian chaplaincy, that The United Methodist Church shall end its participation in the present system after giving one or two years notice of such withdrawal, and the reasons therefor, to all concerned, including the military authorities, the Congress, the chaplains, the Annual Conferences, the church at large and the general public."[15]

Both the strongly worded petition and the action of the General Conference upon it indicated the urgency and the importance to The United Methodist Church of the question of role tension and conflict of loyalties within the chaplain ministry. The Conference referred the proposal to the Board of Higher Education and Ministry for study. The Board then delegated the task to the Division of Chaplains and Related Ministries, with instructions to study carefully all aspects of the question and to prepare a report with recommendations for the Board to present to the General Conference in 1980. The Division appointed an Advisory Committee to conduct the study.[16]

The Advisory Committee examined the extensive studies that three denominations had made of ministry to the military,[17]

---

[15]Quoted in *Military Chaplaincy: A Study of the Participation of the United Methodist Church in the Present System of Military Chaplaincy* (published by the Division of Chaplains and Related Ministries, The United Methodist Church, 1979), p. 1.

[16]Composed of Wes Aitken, Chairperson, John Barr, Earl Andrews, James Thurman, Marlin Siders, and James Rickards (representing the Staff of the Division of Chaplains and Related Ministries).

[17]Studies by the United Church of Christ, the Presbyterian Church in the U.S.A., the Episcopal Church. Cf. notes 7, 8, 9 above.

reviewed books about military chaplaincy, and studied the military regulations governing chaplain activities, as well as the procedures followed by the Division of Chaplains and Related Ministries in endorsing and overseeing the work of Methodist clergy as military chaplains. Further, the Advisory Committee asked selected persons of The United Methodist Church to write position papers on the theological and sociological "assumptions underlying ministry to the military."[18] These papers, with introductory remarks, were printed under the title, *Methodist Chaplaincy: A Study of the Participation of The United Methodist Church in the Present System of Military Chaplaincy,* and were distributed to the delegates to the General Conference in Indianapolis, Indiana, in 1980.[19]

The Advisory Committee recommended "that a civilian chaplaincy not be established" but recognized critical problems in the present system and spoke "against the assumption that the issue is settled forever." The Committee further recommended "that no major changes in the structure of ministry to the military community be undertaken unilaterally by The United Methodist Church," and that "consideration of any major change should be made in consultation and cooperation with the other religious bodies endorsing chaplains to the military community."[20]

In the survey instrument used for this study, three questions were designed to elicit the chaplains' views of role conflict they confront, the kinds of problems which disturb their people, and conflicts of personal "conscience" and "being" which chaplain ministry entails for them. The first of those questions was a rather general one: *Was there conflict between your role as minister and your role as representative of your employer (command or management)?* Although the responses indicate no conflict for most of the chaplains, the amount of conflict reported cannot be taken lightly.

---

[18] These persons were: Prof. Clarence L. Abercrombie, III, Wofford College; Prof. Jack S. Boozer, Emory University; Dean Harold DeWolf, Emeritus, Wesley Theological Seminary; Dean Thomas Langford, Duke)University; Bishop Mack B. Stokes, Jackson Area; and Bishop James S. Thomas, Ohio East Area.

[19] Printed by the Division of Chaplains and Related Ministries, Board of Higher Education and Ministry, The United Methodist Church, 1979. Copies are available from the Division of Chaplains and Related Ministries.

[20] *Military Chaplaincy,* p. 2, Cf. also *Daily Christian Advocate,* The General Conference of The United Methodist Church, Nashville, Tennessee, 1980, advance Edition G-65, 66.

	No Response	Strong Yes	Moderate Yes	No Opinion	Moderate No	Strong No
Army	17	18	59	13	159	164
Navy	5	9	33	7	78	96
Air Force	8	6	37	7	78	122
Reserve	6	10	46	19	104	82
VA	2	4	8	5	34	42
Civilian Hospital	6	3	13	5	58	58
Confinement Facility	1	4	4	0	6	9
Institution	6	9	12	3	32	25
Industrial	0	0	1	1	2	2
Total	51 3.3%	63 276	213 (18.1%)	60 4.0%	550 1150	600 (74.5%)

Of the 1236 valid responses,[21] 1150 (74.5 percent) report no conflict between the two roles, 276 (18.1 percent) report conflict—of whom 51 (4.1 percent) indicate strong conflict—while 111 (7.3 percent) have no opinion or give no response to this question. These figures indicate that while three-fourths of the chaplains do not experience role tension or conflict at all, four out of one hundred experience *strong* role tension. The latter figure, although only 4 percent, is high enough to be examined carefully, and should not be dismissed as being due simply to the peculiarities of individual chaplains and commanding officers or boss/supervisors. Even so, while the extent of role conflict is sufficient to give some pause about the structure and system of chaplaincy, it is still true that the overwhelming majority of chaplains report no serious conflict of roles in their actual work.

If we separate the responses of the military chaplains to the question from those of civilian chaplains, the following picture emerges. (See table on p. 148.)

Slightly less role conflict is felt in civilian chaplaincies than in military chaplaincies (16.3 percent to 18.5 percent). The ratio, however, is surprisingly similar, hovering around one out of five and one out of six chaplains reporting conflict. Among those who

---

[21]The discrepancy between 1538 and 1236 questionnaires coded is due to the fact that many chaplains have served in more than one type of chaplaincy during their careers. The percentages should be accurate, whichever total is used.

Military Chaplains

	No Response	Strong Yes	Moderate Yes	No Opinion	Moderate No	Strong No
Army	17	18	59	13	158	164
Navy	5	9	33	7	78	96
Air Force	8	6	37	7	78	122
Reserve	6	10	46	19	104	82
Total	36 3%	43 218	175 (18.5%)	46 3.9%	418 882	464 (74.6%)

Civilian Chaplains

	No Response	Strong Yes	Moderate Yes	No Opinion	Moderate No	Strong No
VA	2	4	8	5	34	42
Civilian Hospital	6	3	13	5	58	58
Confinement Facility	1	4	4	0	6	9
Institutional	6	9	12	3	32	25
Industrial	0	0	1	1	2	2
Total	15 4%	20 58	38 (16.3%)	14 4%	132 268	136 (75.5%)

experience conflict of roles, *one* out of *five* military chaplains reports strong conflict whereas *one* out of *three* civilian chaplains reports strong conflict. That variance is due to the higher incidence of conflict reported by chaplains in institutions and confinement facilities.

Of twenty-four chaplains in confinement facilities responding, eight note moderate or strong conflict of roles and fifteen indicate no conflict. Of eighty-seven chaplains working in institutions, twenty-one report moderate or strong conflict of roles while fifty-seven indicate no conflict. In these cases the ratio of chaplains with role conflict to the total number of chaplains reporting is from one out of three to one out of three and seven-tenths. The most striking statistic is that among those who report conflict, almost one out of two chaplains in institutions and confinement facilities indicate that there is *strong* role conflict.

The small total number of responses from chaplains in institutions and confinement facilities prohibits sweeping statements about that kind of chaplain ministry. Even with the limited number of responses, however, there is a clear indication that, generally speaking, the most serious situations of role conflict and role tension for chaplains are those in institutions and confinement facilities, rather than in the military chaplaincies as one might have expected. The lowest amount of role conflict is in the Veteran's Administration and civilian hospital chaplaincies. Overall, the survey seems to indicate the following: (1) there is about the same amount of role conflict in the civilian and military chaplaincies; (2) role conflict is a problem which has structural dimensions that need steady surveillance and scrutiny by the church; and (3) role conflict is so extensive for chaplains in institutions and confinement facilities that chaplain ministry in these settings warrants not only a constantly critical appraisal of the openness of these settings for Christian ministry but also special forms of support for chaplains in these assignments by the church and, perhaps, consideration of a rotation system for persons in this kind of chaplain ministry in order to avoid unnecessary burn out.

B. Troubled People: Complex Anguish

Two forms of one question were placed on the questionnaire to shift emphasis from the chaplains to the persons seeking their ministry. How do these persons understand themselves and what are they asking of the chaplain? The data do not warrant constructing a profile of the typical person who seeks the ministry of the chaplain. Yet, what the chaplains in their various ministries report makes quite vivid the kinds of burdens, dilemmas, and pains that are felt by a wide spectrum of people. The first form of the question invited an easy response. (See table p. 150.)

One sees immediately that the chaplains' perceptions of the people for whom they are responsible indicate an overwhelming percentage of people with personal conflicts or conflicts of conscience. Perhaps one should have expected such in an age that W. H. Auden has called an "Age of Anxiety."[22] An interesting question arises, however: Is there any difference in the anxiety level (or conflict level) between persons in military settings and those in

---

[22] W. H. Auden, *The Age of Anxiety* (New York, 1946).

During your active chaplaincy, did the persons under your pastoral care have personal conflicts or conflicts of conscience?

	No Response	Strong Yes	Moderate Yes	No Opinion	Moderate No	Strong No
Army	88	174	149	2	14	2
Navy	46	105	70	2	4	2
Air Force	39	97	114	3	4	2
Reserve	75	88	91	9	2	2
VA	20	45	23	2	4	1
Civilian Hospital	25	68	48	1	1	0
Confinement Facility	4	15	4	0	0	1
Institution	19	46	20	0	2	0
Industrial	0	3	3	0	0	0
Total	316	641	522	19	31	10
		Total yes - 1163			Total No. - 41	

civilian settings? If we place the figures for all the military settings and for all the civilian settings side by side, what will this comparison show? (See table below.)

Of 920 military chaplains giving a response other than "no opinion," 888 (96.5 percent) indicate moderate or strong conflict.

Military	Yes	No	Total
Army	323	16	429
Navy	175	6	229
Air Force	211	6	259
Reserve	179	4	267
Total Military	888	32	1184

(No opinion: 16; No response: 248)

Civilian	Yes	No	Total
VA	68	5	95
Civilian Hospital	116	1	143
Confinement Facility	19	1	24
Institution	66	2	87
Industrial	6	0	6
Total Civilian	275	9	355

(No opinion: 3; No Response: 68)

Of 284 civilian chaplains giving a response other than "no opinion," 275 (96.8 percent) indicate moderate or strong conflict. This points to an extremely high percentage of persons with personal conflicts or conflicts of conscience. If the chaplains are correct, a large majority of the people they serve are seriously troubled. The significance of these facts is directly related to the kinds of things that trouble the people. In order to specify what the chaplains sense about the causes of conflict among their people, the second part of the questions listed a number of items, and chaplains were urged to check these items in the appropriate space or to write in stresses or factors that were not listed. The specific formulation was:

IF YES, what are these conflicts about?
a) Love, sex, and marriage
b) Alcohol and/or drugs
c) Failure to do one's duty, lettings others down
d) Moral questions about what one is expected to do
e) Misrepresenting records, hours, scores, and so on.
f) Loneliness, abandonment, loss of self-worth
g) Problems regarding friendship and respect for others
h) Loss of meaning in life and work
i) Other _____

If one combines the answers into Yes and No and into Military and Civilian categories, the chaplains report the following:

	Military		Civilian		Total	
	Yes	No	Yes	No	Yes	No
a) Love, sex, and marriage	1026	15	313	1	1339	16
b) Alcohol and/or drugs	942	60	392	15	1334	75
c) Failure to do one's duty	587	285	212	38	799	323
d) Moral questions	781	159	261	22	1042	181
e) Misrepresenting records	410	381	104	101	514	482
f) Loneliness, abandonment	946	55	298	8	1224	63
g) Problems regarding friendship	722	171	254	25	976	196
h) Loss of meaning in life and work	740	157	271	14	1011	171

Almost all persons are troubled about love, sex, and marriage. The reports about alcohol and drug problems are very similar to those about love, sex, and marriage, with an overall total of 1334 responding Yes and 75 responding No, an overall percentage of 94.3 percent. Again the problem with alcohol and drugs is slightly higher among those in civilian settings with 96 percent over against 94 percent for those in military settings.

Close to that statistic are 1224 instances of problems with loneliness and/or abandonment over against 63 who report no problems of this sort. That means that 95 percent of those reporting indicate that persons are troubled by loneliness and abandonment. Contrary to what one might have expected, this statistic is higher for civilians than for military persons, with 97.4 percent (298 out of 306) of the civilians and 94.5 percent (946 out of 1001) of the military persons showing anxiety about loneliness and abandonment.

The problems with the next highest number of instances are "moral questions about what one is expected to do," "loss of meaning in life and work," and "problems regarding friendship and respect for others." In these instances, the affirmative responses are, respectively, 85 percent, and 83 percent. Again in these three instances, the problems are slightly more pressing among persons seen by civilian chaplains than among those seen by military chaplains. This does not mean that a higher percentage of civilians have these problems than do military personnel. Civilian chaplains are ministering to people who are in special situations of illness, deprivation, limitation, affliction, or distress. The majority of people in civilian life generally are not in these categories. It must be remembered that the statistics reported here apply only to persons seen by military and civilian chaplains. They certainly indicate generalized problems in contemporary culture that affect all persons, but the special situations in which chaplains minister dictate caution in generalizing from their constituency to the citizenry as a whole.

Still, it would be illuminating to assess what the chaplains report alongside what interpreters of the climate among American youth generally report and what surveyors of churches and religious attitudes are saying. Most of these critics make distinctions between the 1950's, 60's, 70's, and, in projection, the 80's, cognizant of many of the orientation-shattering events discussed in Chapter II. In the 1950's, there was a complex and fluid mixture of contradictory trends, all within the nature of postwar recovery, rebuilding, and consolidation. On the one side, there was an effort to reestablish and strengthen the American way of life, along with a fusion of religious faith with peace of mind and prosperity. Senator Joseph McCarthy, President Eisenhower, Billy Graham, Norman Vincent Peale, Monsignor Fulton J. Sheen, and Rabbi Joshua Liebman in their different ways represented this perspective. On the other side, serious questions were being raised about the health and justice of American life and about the easy identification of religious faith with "peace and prosperity."

The 1954 Supreme Court decision striking down segregated public schools forced a reexamination of accepted social institutions. Critics within the churches began to question the authenticity of "just any kind of faith" and of the claim that "the power of positive thinking" was a genuine expression of Judaism and Christianity. Pope John XXIII legitimized serious questioning when in 1959, he called into being the Second Vatican Council in order to "open the windows" and let a little fresh air in.[23]

The 1960's was a decade of unprecedented turbulence. Jackson W. Carroll and David A. Roozen summarize the decade for us.

"Consider the following: the election of the first Roman Catholic as President of the United States and his tragic death in 1963; the continuation and escalation of the cold war, including both the Berlin Wall and the Bay of Pigs; rapid technological advances, initiated earlier, but beginning to be implemented on an ever widening scale, inspiring hopes and fears of a technopolitan utopia; the full flowering of the civil rights movement—sit-ins, freedom rides, white citizens' councils, bombings, racial murders, the March on Washington, and the passage of the 1964 Civil Rights Act; the urban riots of the 1960's and the assassinations of Martin Luther King, Jr., Malcolm X, and Robert Kennedy; anti-war protests over Vietnam; the rise of student protests against both the military-industrial complex and the universities; the beginnings of the women's liberation movement; and, finally, the rise of the counter-cul-

---

[23] *Aggiornamento* was the word most often used for Pope John XXIII's bold vision of "updating the church" in his call for Vatican II in 1959.

ture, including the search for alternative life styles, drug use, communes, and a variety of new religious movements."[24]

These forms of social turbulence that shattered the stability of received traditions were accompanied by equally intensive struggles within the churches. People within the churches found themselves split, some supporting traditional theology and morality, segregation, and conservative church and social order; others involving themselves in protests against the Vietnam War, demonstrations for civil and human rights, and efforts toward a new morality, a more inclusive understanding of the church, and new forms of human community.

The overall effect of the 1960's was the questioning of the authority and ability of every institution in American culture to provide orientation and meaning. As a result, conscientious persons were forced to find the sinews of authenticity, integrity, and meaning wherever they could. It may well be that no decade in American history ever confronted citizens with such a heavy burden. The youth of the country turned *en masse* to social idealism and social activism, pushing for the American ideal of "liberty and justice for all."

The 1970's saw a change again, this time toward disillusionment if not cynicism as all unifying confidences began to dissolve. The Yankelovich study for General Mills, for example, includes a statement by Dr. Dayton Hultgren about the family which points up the ambiguity of things. "The major difficulty facing the family today is the absence of any communal shared values which give directions for parents."[25] Social efforts through new laws and less restrictive opportunities failed to bring the "new age." The scars of Vietnam and Watergate frustrated and confused the search for personal happiness and fulfillment.

But if the critics are in agreement about the different forms the search for meaning takes during these postwar decades, they are also in agreement about the persistence and pertinence of the

---

[24] Jackson W. Carroll, Douglas W. Johnson, and Martin E. Marty, *Religion in America: 1950 to the Present* (San Francisco, 1979), p. 6.

[25] The General Mills American Family Report, 1976-77, *Raising Children in a Changing Society* (General Mills, Inc., 1977). Conducted by Yankelovich.

search itself for meaning and human happiness. The picture which George Gallup, Jr. and David Poling give of America's faith indicates a widespread hunger for meaning and values in life. In addition, they hear a strong indictment of the main line churches for concerning themselves primarily with institutional concerns to the neglect of key personal needs.

"There is a greater hunger among the churched as well as the unchurched for a sharper focus on the primary questions of life. A large bloc of the unchurched seem to be saying that they would like to be part of a living fellowship that dealt directly and personally with the larger, more sensitive issues in our world. But 49 percent of the unchurched and 39 percent of the churched agreed with the statement that 'most churches and synagogues today are not effective in helping people find meaning in life.' Closely related is the assessment of 56 percent of the unchurched that 'most churches and synagogues today are too concerned with organizational as opposed to theological or spiritual issues.' Church members agreed by 47 percent."[26]

Douglas Johnson speaks for the other authors of *Religion in America: 1950 to the Present* when he claims that the need for meaning and purpose is fundamentally characteristic of human life, and that, as a spiritual drive it will have its way either in constructive human relations, in the destructiveness of demonic seduction such as Jamestown, or in a chemical attempt at escape or sedation. Persons cannot remain human and be indifferent to meaning and purpose. "The innate desire of people, regardless of station in life, to find meaning and purpose must be satisfied, and if one institution fails, another will arrive to accommodate the need."[27]

There is considerable agreement between the troubles (interests) the chaplains report and the general picture of human society Johnson sketches, although Johnson makes an explicit claim for the religious nature of this hunger.

---

[26] George Gallup, Jr. and David Poling, *The Search for America's Faith* (Nashville, 1980), p. 85.

[27] Douglas Johnson in Jackson W. Carroll, Douglas W. Johnson, and Martin E. Marty, *Religion in America: 1950 to the Present* (New York, 1979), p. 99. Cf. also the earlier work of Viktor Frankl, *Man's Search for Meaning;* Michael Novak, *Ascent of the Mountain, Flight of the Dove;* David Tracy, *The Blessed Rage for Order;* Langdon Gilkey, *Naming the Whirlwind.*

"The search is to find that creative force in life that results in a sensitivity to others' needs while providing a firm hold on one's own understanding of the nature of existence. . . . This religious impulse is the basic ingredient in the search for meaning. . . . For individuals, this search ranges from the activities of institutional churches to engagement in quasi-religious secular activities. . . . It means people do things to increase self-knowledge, develop communities of caring souls, practice techniques for personal development, and engage in exercises of disciplined thinking.

"The objective of this search, the joining of groups and the use of disciplined practice, is to take oneself seriously enough to want to discover how each person figures into the ultimate scheme of life. The search is a serious business now and will continue to be. It requires commitment and discipline. The search is religious even though a given group may deny any connection with religious ideas and ideals."[28]

As we saw above, the complex problems that cause persons to seek out chaplains includes sex and love, loneliness, alcohol and drugs, moral questions, loss of meaning in life and work, and problems in human friendships. These problems, related to persistent needs of human existence, are so central to human joy and fulfillment that persons impulsively cloak their failure to satisfy them through the self-destructive use of drugs and alcohol or through acts of violence which harm or destroy others. During these decades, especially the 1960's and 1970's, it happened not only that parents became strangers to their children, but that children became strangers to themselves.

Peter Berger has written a poignant essay, "Languages of Murder,"[29] in which he compares the trial of Lieutenant William Calley for his murders at the My Lai massacre with that of Charles Manson for the Tate/La Biancha murders. Berger sees these trials as cultural paradigms. In the Calley case, American society was on trial; in the Manson case, the counter culture was on trial. In both cases there was a deindividualization and dehumanization of those murdered. Human beings became the "enemy" for Calley and "pigs" for Manson. But the deindividualization also embraced the murderers as they were caught up in the doctrinaire

---

[28] Douglas W. Johnson, *op. cit.*, pp. 93, 94.
[29] In Peter L. Berger, *Facing Up to Modernity* (New York, 1979), pp. 83-94.

"innocence" of a communally-sanctioned righteous case. "The victims must be dehumanized and the killers deprived of their humanity."[30]

The tragedy in both cases entails the placing of all persons in the group designation of either "friend" or "enemy." Against the "enemy" any form of violence was seen as legitimate and "justified" when the moral relationship of "fellow human being" between persons, even enemies, was removed. Berger sees Calley and Manson as representing "possibilities" of the American spirit today because they reveal the potential for various kinds of "legitimation of inhumanity" in our culture. "The underlying option for America is between the sacredness of human life . . . and the various ideologies of death, no matter under what cultural or political guise they may present themselves."[31]

It seems that the hunger for meaning which has always been present among persons has become acute in a radical way since World War II. There are strange cultural currents in contemporary society which would "use" all human qualities and persons for the sake of the economy or for the sake of the state, making sport of those who still search for genuine love and friendship; who expect morality of their government, of others, and of themselves; and who persist in the belief that God has created us to live in a peaceful and supportive interdependence in which all persons have a place. In such a situation sensitive persons are thrown in opposition to an aggressive and fabricated society in which many must lose in order that a few might win.

Why should persons seek out a chaplain because of problems of status, popularity, fear, sex, morality, loneliness, and abandonment? In spite of some technical peculiarities about the chaplain and others in the total military community, there is a profound significance in the fact that persons seek our clergy for help with a wide variety of problems, many of which, in themselves, could more properly be addressed to experts skilled in the special areas of need. The answer to the question is suggested by two statements quoted above. Douglas Johnson speaks of the "innate desire of

[30] Peter L. Berger, *op. cit.,* p. 89.
[31] Peter L. Berger, *op. cit.,* p. 94.

people" for meaning and purpose, and Gallup and Poling speak of the hunger of people generally for "a sharper focus on the primary questions of life." People are troubled by many things, but the persistent and underlying factors which prompt them to seek out the clergyperson have to do with "loss of meaning in life and work" and the relation of morality and loneliness to that loss.

This suggests that every surface issue has become related in recent decades to the fundamental issue of human integrity and meaning, and, significantly, that the traditional confidence in human integrity and meaning has been shaken to the point of radical self-doubt and "lostness." People bring various problems about promotion, security, disappointment, illness, sex, status, and so forth, to the chaplain because their central problem in any or all of these matters is that they are not really "doing better." A recent issue of *Daedalus* on the theme, "Doing Better and Feeling Worse"[32] states the issue clearly. The critical problem for most people has to do with what Roszak calls the "very sense men *(sic)* have of reality,"[33] a fundamental uneasiness, dis-ease, anxiety about the possibility of a human and humane life for oneself and for others. Howard Zinn describes in a striking way the self-examination and internal reassessment that Americans in the early 1970's were forced to make.

> "The most personal, most intimate of human relationships began to be examined. It was an attempt to pierce the many layers of artifice piled up by "civilization" and rediscover the root need of man and woman, to hear again that primeval cry for companionship and freedom. That cry had been stifled by modern technology, by unnecessary things, by false relationships, money, success, status, superiority; all these things had replaced genuine affection. At the pinnacle of American success—unprecedented wealth, power, resources—people suddenly felt a failure at the core. Some were unhappy and distraught, others vaguely, confusedly dissatisfied, but almost everywhere in the country, Americans were uneasy about what they were and where they were going."[34]

If the sense of "lostness," "failure," and "radical rootlessness" is "at the core," that situation must be carefully understood and

---

[32] *Daedalus*, "Doing Better and Feeling Worse: Health in the United States," Winter 1977.
[33] Theodore Roszak, *Making of a Counter Culture* (Garden City, 1969), p. 267.
[34] Howard Zinn, *Postwar America: 1945-1971* (Indianapolis and New York, 1973), p. 232.

frankly addressed. Robert Coles locates the problem precisely at that point and ridicules the "collective egoism" of the new self-centered individualism and its withdrawal of energy from what Coles calls "civility" or "civilization," and from what Martin Buber has termed the "interhuman." For Coles, civilization is a small price to pay for "sparing ourselves thousands, indeed millions, of breastfeeding, fist-clenching, constantly jabbering and self-scrutinizing I's, with their haunting, unsettling refrain of recent years: I am all right; I know what I want—and that's all that counts."[35] Coles attributes the idolization of individual impulses directly to the loss of what he calls "certain shared imperatives" which place the good of the nation or the good of the human family above one's personal preference or gain (good).

> "Civility means all of us subordinating our feelings to certain shared imperatives. . . . When the self becomes our transcendence, politics becomes, along with everything else, a matter of impulse, whim, fancy, exuberant indulence, bored indifference, outright angry rejection. A political analogue to 'doing one's own thing' is a one-issue politics. Civility is meant to guard diversity—because the unifying object of transcendence is something, by definition, above and beyond personal taste or inclination. . . ."[36]

Quite ironically, precisely at the time when there is mounting evidence in social-scientific data of the interrelation between persons, cultures, and ecosystems, many persons in America are at the point of losing confidence in their desires for love, trust, honesty, and moral integrity and in the possibility of a social, political, and economic fabric that offers opportunity and justice for all persons. One of the reasons for this is that the functional myth of chosenness, of manifest destiny, which has continually informed Americans, has never, in spite of Abraham Lincoln and others, really allowed the recognition of the possibility of America's flaws, America's evil, America's limited power, America's fallibility and finiteness.

If such is the case, how could the primal myth underlying

---

[35] Robert Coles, "Civility and Psychology" in *Daedalus*, "The New Consensus," Summer 1980, p. 141.

[36] Coles, *op. cit.*, pp. 140-141.

American self-consciousness assist Americans during the last three decades to comprehend the inescapable evidence of the evils in American life: discrimination against native Americans, women, blacks and other minorities; waste, abuse of the air and the earth; violation of the rights of citizens through police brutality, government-sponsored medical experimentation, invasion of privacy, denial of the ballot; and the increasing primacy of economics and military/police power over the moral strength of justice and opportunity for human fulfillment?

The strong moral justification of World War II against Hitler and his arrogant ideology of a new humanity (eliminating sub-humans such as Jews, Slavs, and Gypsies) obscured for most people the extent of America's complicity in evil not only in the ways mentioned above but in actual instances of unjustified and unnecessary killing. But what was relatively obscure to Americans in the euphoria of the triumph in 1945 gradually became inescapably clear over the next few decades, as we saw in Chapter II, culminating in the two national tragedies of Vietnam and Watergate.

Robert Benne and Philip Hefner have written with exceptional insight about the crisis. "We Americans have no way of comprehending for ourselves why we should be defeated or why we might wage a mistaken war. We simply have no public language for even discussing these possibilities."[37] Actually, the situation is more pressing than a limitation of language. The issue permeates our beings and threatens us by requiring of us *a viable integrity* in spite of our self-doubt, *a viable confidence* in the nature of the human and the inter-human in spite of constant trivializations of the human, and *a viable myth* of the meaning of America in spite of America's loss of innocence and complicity in evil. It is as if the nation overall is undergoing an advanced state (stage) of adolescent crisis, begun but not resolved in the Civil War. For Richard Rubenstein, the Holocaust is a manifestation of a fundamental flaw not only in America but in all of modern western society, the creation and destruction of surplus population. The machine, technology, and bureaucracy have become so

---

[37] Robert Benne and Philip Hefner, Defining America: *A Christian Critique of the American Dream* (Philadelphia, 1974), p. 84.

powerful and pervasive that they "use" and "destroy" people. Through a shortage of cheap labor, overpopulation, and limited food supply, events move inevitably toward solving all the problems at once. Ordinary and emergency powers are assumed in order to acquire "total domination." Trading on old fears and suspicions, the government pronounces Jews, Gypsies, and others as "stateless." Their possessions are seized, they are placed in mass housing with food only for survival, and they are to provide the labor for I. G. Farben and other industries for a few weeks until, according to efficiency studies, it is cheaper to incinerate them in gas chambers than to keep them alive and working. Why not? Was there any crime committed at Auschwitz?[38]

This is Rubenstein's way of expressing the flaw at the center of modern culture. It is not altogether clear that he is committed to his answer, but he is certainly committed to the task of forcing us to face the question. His answer is that the Nazis "probably committed no crime at Auschwitz." That is the case because, as he sees it, there is no universal dignity of the human and there is not a "natural or God-ordained law binding on all men and nations in terms of which the Holocaust can be judged."[39]

For Rubenstein the death and labor/death camps of Europe show conclusively that "rights do not belong to (human beings) by nature. To the extent that (humans) have rights, they have them only as members of a polis, the political community, and there is no polis or Christian commonwealth of nations."[40] For Rubenstein, rights derive from political, economic, social, and military power. To be powerless is to be without rights. Rubenstein's caustic analysis of western culture and of its Judeo-Christian roots is mentioned not necessarily because it is correct, but because it prompts a radical questioning of the rhetoric of those political and social altruisms which may well conceal from us not only an honest appraisal of our culture, but a genuine assessment of ourselves as well.

Without at the moment providing an appropriate religious or Christian response to Rubenstein, I suggest that the possibilty that he is right has now invaded the consciousness of many and has

---

[38] Auschwitz was a combination labor and death camp, in distinction from Treblinka, Balzec, Maindenick, and Sohibor which were "death factories" only.

[39] Richard L. Rubenstein, *The Cunning of History* (New York, 1975), p. 90.

[40] Richard L. Rubenstein, *op. cit.*, p.89.

created a radically new sense of ontological, primal, and critical uncertainty about the human enterprise. That is the reason that most present human problems are related to "loss of meaning in life and work" and, one might add, "loss of meaning in citizenship and community." And that is the reason persons who are troubled about many things come to the chaplain/pastor for help. Their primal anxiety is not about one particular problem, but about the entire enterprise of human culture.

Images of the mushroom cloud, of the death chambers at Auschwitz, of buried chemicals oozing to the surface of the soil, and of leaks in nuclear power plants penetrate the consciousness and displace Browning's image of "God's in his heaven; all's right with the world," leaving an inescapably foreboding and threatening question at the center of persons. In *An Inquiry into the Human Prospect,* Robert L. Heilbroner writes at the outset, "There is a question in the air, more sensed than seen, like the invisible approach of a distant storm, a question that I would hesitate to ask aloud did I not believe it existed unvoiced in the minds of many: 'Is there hope for man?' "[41]

The poignancy of that question, "Is there hope for the human?" is vivid in the findings of Dr. William Beardslee and Dr. John Mack in their studies of the dominant images, fears, and hopes in the lives of children.[42] As part of a Task Force Association on the Psycho-social Impact of Nuclear Developments of the American Psychiatric Association, they find a pervasive fear to have become primal in the minds of many children, robbing them of both confidence and hope for the future. Many scenes of bloodshed and violence influence that perception, but the threat of nuclear war with its seeming destruction of everything is the overriding cause of the fear. Dr. Mack describes the research on 1000 grammar and high school students around Boston, Baltimore, and Los Angeles. "The implications are disturbing indeed. We may be raising a generation without hope, without promise of a future, cynical about the adult world and helpless to change it."[43]

---

[41] Robert L. Heilbroner. *An Inquiring into the Human Prospect* (New York, 1974), p. 13.

[42] "The Fear that Haunts our Children." *McCalls,* May 1982, p. 77.

[43] "The Impact of Nuclear Developments on Children and Adolescents" is part of Task Force Report #20 of the American Psychiatric Association and may be procured from the A.P.A., Publication Sales Division, 1700 18th Street, N.W., Washington, D.C. 20008.

Without the "coping strategies" that older persons develop, the children are peculiarly vulnerable to the numbing effect of these images. Even so, many of them, unable and unwilling to submit to the inevitability of destruction, have launched a kind of "children's crusade" of writing letters to children in Russia. This is an innocent and gentle effort to affirm a human future for others and for themselves that the adult population has either forgotten or forsaken. Hugh Downs gave attention to this movement when, in a nationally shown issue-centered television program, he showed a six-year-old, Lute Breuer, reading a poem by Dick Smith, which was the prayer of both of them.

"Peace Bird"
Listen to the peace bird, pretty and bright,
Stop and think before you start to fight.
Fighting is not nice, fighting is not right.
So listen to the peace bird, pretty and bright.

With the dissolution of internal as well as external certainties, people are vulnerable to all kinds of proclaimed certainties, from the hucksters of snake oil on the right, to all forms of destructive cynicism from the critical doubters on the left. If people are troubled, what about their pastors? What have Christian faith and the Christian community to do with the foundational anxiety that many people feel today? If the pastor is not troubled by the troubles of the people, how can he or she help? Yet, if the pastor is made a casualty through being troubled in the same way other people are troubled, how can he or she help?

The vocation of the chaplain/pastor is the call to be wounded by the reality of the threat and to make present the unconditional love of God in spite of the threat. That is a part of the meaning of Paul's words: "But we have this treasure in earthen vessels, to show that the transcendent power belongs to God and not to us. We are afflicted in every way, but not crushed; perplexed, but not driven to despair; persecuted but not forsaken; struck down, but not destroyed. . ."[44] We turn to that issue as we examine what happens to the chaplains themselves in this life at the edge of Christian ministry.

---

[44] Second Corinthians 4:7-9, Revised Standard Version.

3. Troubled Pastors: The Treasure Only a Broken Vessel Can Carry

Chaplains were vivid in describing the personal conflicts and conflicts of conscience which prompted persons in their care to seek help. They were equally frank and forthright in talking about their own fears, doubts, and conflicts as they carried on their ministry. The question put to the chaplains and their answers, by type of chaplaincy, were as follows:

During your career as chaplain, did you have conflicts of conscience?

	No Response	Strong Yes	Moderate Yes	No Opinion	Moderate No	Strong No	Raw Total
Army	28	35	99	19	118	130	429
Navy	8	17	50	12	71	71	229
Air Force	6	9	52	6	76	109	258
Reserve	17	19	45	16	100	70	267
VA	3	7	22	6	22	35	95
Civilian							
Hospital	12	5	47	6	42	31	143
Confinement	1	4	1	1	10	7	24
Institutional	5	8	22	7	28	17	87
Industrial	0	2	1	1	1	1	6
Total	80	106	339	74	468	471	1538
	5.2%	6.8%	22.0%	4.8%	30.4%	30.6%	100%
		445(28.9%)			939(61.0%)		

The combination of strong and moderate negative responses indicates that 61 percent (939) of the chaplains had no conflicts of conscience in their work as chaplain/pastors. The answers were equally divided between "moderate no" and "strong no." On the other side, the combination of strong and moderate positive responses shows that 28.9 percent (445) of the chaplains had conflicts of conscience, with moderate conflicts outnumbering strong conflicts about three to one. The statistics on both sides are impressive. Three of ten chaplains have known conflicts of conscience, while six of ten chaplains do not have such conflicts. These data are important indicators of the quality of personal presence chaplains maintain in their ministry. Therefore, we ought to look at the outset for any difference between military and civilian chaplains as to conflicts of conscience.

During your career as chaplain, did you have conflicts of conscience?

Military Chaplains

	No Response	Strong Yes	Moderate Yes	No Opinion	Moderate No	Strong No	Raw Total
Army	28	35	99	19	118	130	429
Navy	8	17	50	12	71	71	229
Air Force	6	9	52	6	76	109	258
Reserve	17	19	45	16	100	70	267
Total	59	80	246	53	365	380	1183
		326	(27.5%)		745	(63%)	

Civilian Chaplains

	No Response	Strong Yes	Moderate Yes	No Opinion	Moderate No	Strong No	Raw Total
VA	3	7	22	6	22	35	95
Civilian Hospital	12	5	47	6	42	31	143
Confinement	1	4	1	1	10	7	24
Institutional	5	8	22	7	28	17	87
Industrial	0	2	1	1	1	1	6
Total	21	21	93	21	103	91	355
			114	(32.1%)		194	(54.6%)

Perhaps contrary to expectations, again, more civilian chaplains (32.1%) report actual conflict of conscience in their work than military chaplains (27.5%). Military chaplains in larger percentage than civilian chaplains report no conflict of conscience with 63 percent and 54.6 percent respectively.

In the followup request to this question, chaplains were asked to "indicate briefly the nature of these conflicts." Four hundred and forty chaplains who took the trouble to write a comment, mentioned many kinds of specific conflicts. The factor most often mentioned, although only by military chaplains, concerns serving people who work in an institution, the mission of which is to kill, thereby placing the chaplain in the situation of serving a "killing machine." Sixty-three chaplains mentioned this conflict. The next most prominent conflict was about Vietnam—about why the United States was involved there, as well as about the way the war was being carried on.

A young National Guard chaplain wrote: "I don't see how anyone who serves around a 'war-machine' could avoid struggles of conscience concerning the possibilities he faces." Several spoke of war as a necessary evil. "I am not a pacifist. I found very few war lovers in the military. Many people saw war as a necessary evil." Others wrote of the conflict between the "military and ministry" or the "military and pacifism." An older, retired chaplain spoke of the conflict between ideals and practical demands. "It is difficult to condone murder and yet I was a member of an organization which had killing as its reason for being."

Another older, retired pastor who had spent much time as a hospital chaplain wrote poignantly: "The question of taking life even in battle bothered many, even the chaplain. This is one question I constantly had to counsel about with men in the hospital at Normandy. There were many other questions, too, such as self-inflicted wounds, the why of war at all, men who would never be whole again, physically or mentally." Still another retired chaplain raised an over-arching question about conscience and the military. "My service in the military relegated conscience to second place."

A former chaplain in his forties shared thoughts about the complexity of the issues of self-preservation, self-sacrifice, death, and Biblical injunctions to righteousness.

"Conflicts of conscience always occur when you encounter death of your close friends at the hands of "the enemy." One of the conflicts in the face of war is self-preservation. How is one to protect himself, yet be willing to die if he can save a comrade? And if one does take the necessary measures of protection, how can it be justified by God's word, especially if it involves taking another life?"

Chaplains see the tension and conflict at different points, and they show quite different levels of success in handling these conflicts. One chaplain saw the war and use-of-force issue within the church-state conflict in a way reminiscent of the comment by Harvey Cox, quoted at the beginning of this chapter. "There is conflict between church and state which each chaplain must realize and deal with. He should not forget his proper role which I regard as a representation of the church to the military. But such problems must exist in the civilian church also, on a different level."

One of the most puzzling yet most indicative comments about personal conflict entailed in chaplain ministry was written by a middle-aged National Guard chaplain who had apparently never been on regular active duty with the military. "I'm a pacifist and have had difficulty justifying my being in the military—basically I do it because I think the military needs my kind of thinking and because I can provide pastoral care to individuals. I like the pay better than anything else about it." The complex anguish of troubled people is matched by the complex priorities of troubled pastors.

For many of the chaplains in the military, the Vietnam War created the most serious conflicts of conscience, bringing to the surface latent general questions about church and state and the specific issue of how a Christian pastor could minister within the military. One chaplain indicated that only gradually did the Vietnam situation constitute a strong moral challenge to him. "Toward the end in Vietnam, I wondered if it was moral and also wondered why young people had to die in such folly." Another confessed that the issue became clear to him only toward the end, but then in such a way as to constitute a complex moral dilemma: to be loyal to his own conscience about the war, or to be loyal to persons in the armed forces who had no choice but to obey orders and fight, whatever moral questions they may have about the war.[45]

"I questioned my role as a military member and the Vietnam conflict. The matter of conscience came near the end of the Vietnam conflict as the issue became clearer and many of the earlier beliefs seemed less

---

[45] It was, of course, possible for a person in the military to become a conscientious objector and to apply for non-combatant service or for release. Such an action would likely have no chance of success unless the person had undergone a moral/religious conversion and was absolutely conscientious and convinced about the new values on which his or her life rested.

certain. I felt strongly that I could not act to undermine those persons charged with fighting in Vietnam; my only legitimate option would be to separate and then voice my opinions."

One chaplain spoke about how Vietnam both confounded moral clarity and compromised courage. "The Vietnam War created numerous problems in the counseling situations with those combat crews as they probed their own consciences regarding validity of targets, and so on. I can think of two incidents where 'fear of authority' caused me not to object to unfair treatment of a fellow chaplain." Another acknowledged being a part of the protest movement and the power of the moral dilemma for him. "I was in the protest movement while serving as a chaplain. This kept me in trouble both ways. The problem was not the trouble, but the complexity of the decision about what to do. I stayed in basically because I felt we needed chaplains who opposed the war. Many disagreed on both sides and I'm still not certain that mine was the right course of action."

In quite a different perception of the morality issue, at least one chaplain who wrote agreed with those who point to political decisions which compromised military action. "My conflict was caused by the fact that the Vietnam War was wrong—not because of the war, but because of the Civilian Power Structure. Ambassador Ellsworth Bunker sacrificed many lives to satisfy both Vietnamese politicians and the Congress of the United States. We were not allowed to win the war militarily."

Short comments by two chaplains showed crisply the major thrust of comments about compromise. "During Vietnam, I questioned the war effort as a whole, but never questioned the appropriateness of the church's being represented among the people fighting the war." "Vietnam was such a morass for all of us. The gray was so pervasive that even the ends of the continuum were blurred." For the civilian population of the United States, the Vietnam action was at first generally clear (although there were strong counter-voices); then the situation became blurred, eventually becoming clear again, but finally for withdrawal rather than for involvement. But for most of the chaplains who were thrown into conflict by Vietnam the situation was blurred, as stated, at both ends of the spectrum. The chaplain could not see his or her way to support and justify the war. Neither could he or she abandon those persons sent by the highest authority in the United States to do their patriotic duty for the security of the United States.

The fact that most chaplains report no conflict of conscience about the military or about Vietnam becomes in itself a troubling datum for some chaplains, raising serious questions about collegiality in ministry among chaplains which reach far beyond the level of differences of opinion. An Army chaplain in his forties wrote with disarming honesty for some chaplains.

> "There are always conflicts of conscience—usually small ones. My major one was over whether I could stay in the Army during the sixties while knowing that the Vietnam War was a disaster for the nation. I decided to stay in and, as a result, almost got kicked out. This was a real problem when my turn came to *go* to Vietnam. I went (70-71) and found that *almost everyone that I came in contact with* in Vietnam felt pretty much as I did!

> "We kept our mouths shut and did what we had to do—I suppose Vietnam is the last place to ask questions about whether one should be there or not! But I came to believe that chaplains in general . . . were more hardline on Vietnam than anyone else! There is much to ponder over that—perhaps under the heading that converts are often more ardent in their faith than those born into it."

Both facts, that many chaplains *were* in agonizing personal conflict, and that the majority of chaplains were apparently *not in conflict* about anything, does indeed give much to ponder. We will return to that issue after we look at some reasons for conflict of conscience among chaplains.

Many chaplains are disturbed about the question as to *when* an issue becomes serious enough to justify action by the chaplain and, when one decides that one must act, *what* specific actions should be taken. The particular problems cover a wide spectrum, from official lying and human rights (prisoners, patients, and military personnel) to issues in personal morality, particularly regarding sexuality and the use of drugs and alcohol. Yet the conflict in this instance is not about the specific moral problem but about what the chaplain should do in the official capacity as "staff-person" in a hospital, prison, corporation, or a military establishment.

This conflict is created by the role-tension discussed earlier in this chapter. The chaplain's position as a staff person which entails the influence and power to change a destructive condition, itself becomes weakened if the issues he or she chooses to challenge or the way he or she chooses to challenge them turn out to be threatening or embarrassing to the chaplain's administrative superiors. The chaplain knows that administrative superiors will evaluate his or her performance as chaplain and that tenure depends upon the cumulative average of these appraisals. Thus, the chaplain will not be able to continue a ministry he or she regards as important unless that ministry is approved and supported by administrative superiors. At the same time, the primary qualities of Christian ministry are derived from faith, ordination, and the commission of the Christian church, not by military regulations or the judgments of administrative superiors.

This kind of issue came to the surface in several ways among the chaplains. Some spoke of the situation as the struggle to decide which causes one should "fight for with the command," of "being diplomatic but truthful to senior commanders." This is all the more difficult when one knows that the commander might interpret the chaplain's forthrightness as disloyalty and penalize the chaplain in an appraisal of the chaplain's work. One chaplain spoke of the tension and of the self-doubt it creates.

> "Most conflicts center around questions of integrity and how to maintain integrity prophetically. The tension between being a martyr on an issue and maintaining a position of relative strength over the long haul is a difficult one. How do you know that you have not copped out?"

Another mentioned the tension entailed in serving two masters and of the constant temptation to ease or resolve the tension in favor of one or the other. "There are times when the simplest way through such a moral dilemma is to abdicate moral responsibility, to get along by going along, and to forget one's ordination vows and obligations. The tensions which arise from this are real and sometimes result in inappropriate compromise for the sake of greater acceptance by one's military commanders and promotion enhancement."[46]

In the military it is assumed that power and authority are essential to discipline and effectiveness, but there is the constant possibility of "abusing" that power. Chaplains are special kinds of staff officers in the military, however, in that they are commissioned to speak for the rights and dignity of all persons and against the abuse of power. They are morally free and morally obligated to do more than to implement the decisions of a commander. The tensions and obligation to challenge a commander in certain situations are inescapable in the role of chaplain in the military forces.

Although the situation is somewhat different in prisons, hospitals, industry, and other settings, the same kind of tension is present in all chaplain roles. Several hospital chaplains described their conflicts. One of the earlier and clearest challenges entails whether or not it is right to "pull the plug" of a life-support device. That issue cannot be resolved with a neat formula and there is always possible conflict with others on the hospital staff. One chaplain wrote: "I have finally resolved this—it depends on each case and all the factors in each case."

Another was concerned over the ethics of medical experimentation and transplants. Another mentioned conflict about "whether to encourage nurses and/or families and doctors to use drugs that I am fairly sure would hasten the patients' death." Another speaks of inevitable inadequacies in a large Veterans' Administration hospital. "When I see a patient whose spiritual and emotional needs are disregarded and treated like a number or a slab of beef I get disturbed in conscience. This doesn't happen often and when it does happen it is not done intentionally. But it does happen."

Chaplains who work in jails and prisons reported the same kinds of conflict but with a more critical urgency because of the limits on the prisoners' freedom and his or her access to measures of recourse.

"The climate of the treatment of inmates when I first entered prison

---

[46] Another chaplain spoke of conflicts over "social and ethnic issues with senior officers who wanted to hide real problems and also to cover up traffic in alcohol and drugs as well as other destructive moral issues."

ministry was one of almost total disregard for life, limb, and mental well-being. I saw the inmates as persons of worth and as human beings entitled to humane treatment. Yet, I was subjected to having to minister to them in environments that were subhuman and which I could do little to change. I had to choose constantly between leaving in disgust or staying because these men needed someone who at least cared about them."

Another prison chaplain spoke about the build up of resentment against prisoners by the staff. "The primary conflict for me was trying to decide how to handle brutality in prisons, and involvement in court cases related to brutality. Part of my work is with prison officers—to help them to be patient and caring with prisoners."

In prison and jail ministry the role tension for many chaplains is the sharpest possible: Is the chaplain primarily a part of the "correctional team," or is he or she a bearer of the judgment and grace of God to the prisoner? If the latter, then he or she represents the judgment of God against the unfairness and selective enforcement of the laws of a society as well as God's judgment agaist the person in prison. The chaplain as the bearer of divine judgment and grace is not allowed to take lightly the laws of a city or state, but neither is he or she allowed to identify them with the Kingdom of God.

If the difference between being a "sinner" before God and a "criminal" before the state is obscured, then the chaplain/pastor becomes a part of the "correctional team" and has no *foundation* for questioning the law and tactics of the state while totally questioning the conduct and attitudes of the incarcerated. Breaking a law makes a person a "criminal," whether the law is about segregation, possessing drugs, violating a curfew, refusing to register for the draft, marching without a permit, passing bad checks, stealing, mugging, or murder.

Karl Menninger deplores the consequences of identifying "crimes" with "sins" and appeals for the recovery of the awareness of sin and, with it, the recovery of new possibilities of human integrity for society and for individuals. The sin on both sides is evident in the case where a Texas judge sentenced an adolescent to thirty years imprisonment for possessing two marijuana cigarettes, presumably for sale.[47] Menninger wrote the speech of the "sinner" in response to an overly accusing and self-righteous society's attack: "Why do you strike at our society?"

" 'Please!' begs the sinner. 'I confess my guilt and I concede my defenselessness. I cannot adequately answer your 'why.' My hand was forced. Your 'society' has attacked me. I confess my resentment, my aggressiveness but also my misery, my terror. Call it my sin; sentence me, punish me. Avenge yourselves on me but ultimately shrive me. Forgive me and take me back. Might it not have been you?' "[48]

One chaplain described a new approach to ministry to the imprisoned, the New Horizons Treatment Center. Eight churches joined together to support a clergyperson who represents them in making the Gospel present to persons who are captive. He described the work and the importance of a presence other than that of the correctional team.

"Solidarity with the poor and oppressed—with the imprisoned—will undoubtedly involve us in a painful confession of corporate sinfulness and human frailty. But such a realization of our common humanity may also be the bridge which gives us access to one another. . . We feel this is an exciting and promising model for prison ministry. . . For not only does it bring a diverse group of church people into some kind of relationship with the prison population; it also gives the chaplain the freedom to be a pastor to the residents. Representing the church, she has the chance to maintain a uniquely independent stance: neither resident nor guard.

"In most correctional institutions, chaplains eagerly define themselves as part of the institution's over-all 'correctional program' and thereby forfeit the opportunity to function as a genuine bridge to the outside world and a clear voice of gospel freedom."[49]

Tony Sayer, co-director of a community ministry to prisoners in Asheville, North Carolina, sponsored by several churches, feels that the integrity of the gospel to prisoners requires taking their situation seriously by offering "confidentiality" and "freedom to

[47] Karl Menninger, Whatever Became of Sin? (New York, 1973), p. 62.
[48] Menninger, op. cit., p. 187.
[49] Whit Hutchison, "Local Churches Support New Horizons Center," Ministry and Mission, Atlanta: Candler School of Theology, Emory University, Volume 4, Number 3, October 1979, p. 3.

criticize the system." His experience in Asheville is that such integrity is next to impossible if the "preacher carries keys to the jail," that is, is a part of the "correctional team." A truly alert church

> "would relinquish its keys and other emblems of the Chaplain's identification with the correctional structure, and it would vigorously preserve the two pastoral initiatives most conductive to solidarity with prisoners: confidentiality and the freedom to criticize the system. It is distressing to see many instances where the church is basically unwilling to minister to the imprisoned unless state funds are forthcoming."[50]

Although there are some limitations to confidentiality which are openly acknowledged in prison situations, tensions about confidentiality are experienced by chaplains in many settings. Problems arise particularly about information given "in confidence" which might indicate impending harm or death to other persons. Is confidentiality absolute, covering all information given, as well as the identity of the person being counseled? Or is there some principle which, in emergency, overrides the requirements of confidentiality? A chaplain working in an industrial setting makes the point. "My conflict is about when to break confidentiality. That situation recurs in the event of imminent danger to oneself or to others or to the institution. Whatever I have done has begun with the individual being counseled."

Returning to specific conflicts of conscience, many United Methodist chaplains are disturbed about the use of alcohol and the pressure to drink alcoholic beverages, especially in the military. These usually involve the Officers' Club in some way, and, as a rule, includes pressure to pay dues and to be present at functions where alcohol is served. For some chaplains, merely being present is a moral compromise because that seems to condone and to encourage the use of alcohol. Others feel compromised because drinking is accepted to the extent that an abstainer is under pressure to explain his or her "oddness." One young Navy chaplain was both surprised and affronted by what he found upon entering the chaplaincy. "Alcohol is the number one conflict faced each

---

[50] Tony Sayer, "When the Preacher Carries Keys," *Southern Exposure*, Volume 6, Number 4, pp. 57-58.

day in the military. We are *expected* to drink, toast, and so on, even by my present Southern Baptist Senior Chaplain. I am constantly amazed at the alcohol mentality." Another was disturbed at the "total acceptance of the use of alcohol by fellow chaplains."

Several chaplains, all presumably military, spoke of the pressures that long periods of separation from spouse and children put on those relationships. In some cases these were expressed as ordinary conflicts between job and family. In other cases, however, the military situation puts particular stress on the family relation primarily because of the separation involved, although the chaplain's exposure to danger may well accentuate the significance of long periods of separation.

A young chaplain speaks of conflicts and adjustments which the military entails. "Especially difficult are family separations and guilt/worry about our relationship." An older chaplain looked back on this kind of "price" paid to serve as a military clergyperson with some regret. "I constantly had feelings of conflict when away from the family on overseas tours. 'Should I be at home with my wife and children or here serving military personnel?' I feel now that I would not sacrifice my wife and children."

Quite a number of chaplains mentioned conflicts concerning religious services, particularly zealous commanders who wanted to or did require those under their command to attend chapel. One chaplain risked his entire career in the Navy to challenge the position of the Chief of Navy Chaplains as well as that of the Senior Commander to prove unconstitutional the requiring of chapel attendance of military personnel.[51]

Conflicts covering the administration of Holy Communion centered on three issues. The first involves being asked to serve open Communion to cover for other chaplains who are not allowed by their churches to offer the Sacrament to a general Protestant constituency. The second was described as consecrating the elements according to Methodist tradition and liturgy and yet wanting the communion table to be open to all who desired the Sacrament. The third concerned the elements used in the Eucharist:

---

[51] Cf. oral history document, Roland W. Faulk. On file: Division of Chaplains and Related Ministries, The United Methodist Church, P. O. Box 871, Nashville, TN 37202.

whether to use wine, grape juice, or both in Holy Communion. These conflicts indicate a search for a theological foundation for adminstering Holy Communion that neither the new chaplain environments nor administrative regulations provide.

A number of chaplains also mentioned issues which touch on the impropriety of regulations, disregard for human life, and flaws in the justness and fairness of an organization or system. One spoke forthrightly about lying by commissioned officers. "I was in serious conflict about the government saying we were not bombing Hanoi nor did we have troops in Cambodia. I was there and we were doing both." Another spoke of the Task Force Commanders' covering up the information about a serious and brutal event at My Lai on March 16, 1968, reported by a helicopter pilot (W. O. Thompson) and other soldiers involved in that action. There were frequent comments about the injustice of the system, the dehumanizing and degrading aspects of the system, and the abuse of power and authority.

One chaplain spoke of the difficulty of ministering in a "subhuman environment." Another wrote: "I am uncomfortable wherever the little person is misused or overlooked." In one way or another, many of these comments are related to the Vietnam War. "I was in serious conflict about our nation's role in Vietnam and after, and our care or lack of it for veterans as well as for the people of southeast Asia." One chaplain longed for more justification of the Vietnam effort by the United States government and for more theological support by the church for his ministry. "The things that bothered me most were 1) my uncertainty about the validity of our involvement in Vietnam, and 2) my grief at the inability of the church to give me more support in my ministry in Vietnam. My presence there resulted from the fact that my 'people' were there, not because I supported our being there—which I really did not."

Although many chaplains called attention to inadequacies or problems in the church, in fellow chaplains, or in the organization within which they work, there was also an admirable frankness about personal faults and errors which marred the effectiveness of their ministry. At times those personal flaws were covered by a general remark such as "I did not do as much as I should have" or "I could and should have done better" or "I found it difficult to love those who were morally repulsive" or "I should have taken *firmer* stands on many issues." In other instances the issues were more specific. One chaplain was disturbed that he found no meaningful way to relate to the church at large. "I felt that the church had emotionally abandoned me in my area of ministry. The tension has been between how much of this is my own personal problem and how much is the church's problem." Another frankly confessed that he had "sold out." "After the Korean emergency was over I felt I should return to my Conference and a regular appointment, but I had enough World War II time that, added to my time of chaplain service in Korea, seemed too much to throw away. I felt I was guilty of 'selling out' for the promise of a government pension."

The vulnerable and fragile side of the story was indicated in the frank words of another chaplain.

"My most serious conflict was about personal morality. I was assigned to independent shipyard duty at twenty-five, while single. I began social drinking and had several illicit sexual affairs with women during four years of active duty. I capitulated to my weaknesses and contemplated leaving the ministry. Rightly or wrongly, I did not leave the ministry but, with God's help, my life changed directions. My misconduct was inexcusable and I did experience much remorse. I do not blame the military for my actions. But lack of peer pressure, congregational pressure, or supervision by a senior chaplain allowed my baser self to emerge. I know personally three chaplains who had similar experiences."

In contrast to the testimony of these chaplains, there was the claim by one chaplain that he experienced no conflict of conscience because he "knew he was called by God." And there is that striking evidence among 1236 chaplains that over 60 percent experience no conflict of conscience in their ministry, cryptically and tersely expressed by one chaplain in words mentioned before: "I never experienced any conflict of conscience in the military.' What is one to make of these different if not contradictory claims? Are these differences simply the differences among persons? Have persons understood the questions so differently as to account for these almost contradictory comments? Or are there more serious theological differences entailed here?

It must be admitted that the question put to the chaplains may have been ambiguous, and that different interpretations of the question may have brought forth different answers and comments. That possibility implies that a more carefully worded question would have elicited answers revealing much more anguish of conscience in chaplain ministry. Without denying that as a possibility, it would still be naive to dismiss the issue on that assumption.

We find here two rather different interpretations of Christian ministry, interpretations that may be as applicable in the traditional parish ministry as in the chaplain ministry. Paul Tillich has expressed that tension in relation to theology and preaching in the oft-quoted meditation, "You Are Accepted,"[52] and in relation to morality in the distinction between the "sensitive" conscience and the "good" conscience.[53] Tillich claims that it is impossible to unite a "sensitive conscience" with a "good conscience."

Delaying a full discussion of the theology of chaplain ministry for the moment, it seems that the chaplains who report conflicts of conscience are claiming a kind of Christian ministry which can only be conducted by persons who can understand and identify with persons who are troubled, outcast, flawed, lonesome, sinful, or lost. They know the manifold forms of unrighteousness, ambiguity, and pain in themselves and in others, and they know the conditions of society which have not been fair to all. Hence they are not surprised by the manifold forms of abuse and wrong that people and institutions cause for themselves and for others. Because they understand these things they are not unaffected by or indifferent to those persons and situations. They know that in the situations and in the persons, there are violations of the will, purpose, and presence of God.

Yet to understand these violations is not to condone them. On the contrary, understanding them is essential to Christian ministry. For it is precisely in the awareness of our imperfection and incompleteness, of our lonesomeness and lostness, and in our knowledge of our evil, that we are able to receive the gift of God's confirmation,

---

[52] Paul Tillich, *The Shaking of the Foundations* (New York, 1948), pp. 153-163.

[53] Paul Tillich, "The Transmoral Conscience," *The Protestant Era* (Chicago, 1948), pp. 136-149.

acceptance, and forgiveness. That gift is the unmerited and unconditional love of God which does not abandon us, in spite of what we have been and are. Human evil does not separate us from the love and care of God. However, God's love also does not sanction selfishness, jealousy, destructiveness, and evil.

The gift of unconditional love is a treasre incommensurable with other "goods" and "values," but it is always carried in "broken" vessels. Perfect vessels cannot carry it because they have no need of the gift of God's grace. Persons most aware of the richness of God's compassion know most fully how God's love is expressed for all persons, especially those who have no voice, skill, or strength to defend themselves against a mocking, strident, and judgmental society.

The chaplains who report conflicts of conscience are clergy who "know" and "live with" human brokenness. They know unrealized obligations and the unfilled hungers and hopes for the peace and righteousness of the Kingdom of God. For them the treasure of the gospel can only be carried by a person who is wounded, a vessel that is broken. Human wholeness is not our achievement, but is the gracious gift of God. The gospel is "good news" precisely because it is pertinent to us just as we are, a light in our darkness, which places both our goodness and our evil under the righteousness and love of God. "Blessed are those who hunger and thirst for righteousness, for they shall be satisfied" (Matthew 5:6, Revised Standard Version).

V. Chaplains and the Church: Is Reconciliation Possible?

"The Church and the chaplains must find their way back to each other."

(Air Force Chaplain)

A. Anatomy of the Estrangement

There is widespread agreement that a sharp separation has arisen between pastors in local churches and pastors in different kinds of chaplain ministries. This may be the case in all churches, but it is now an acute problem in The United Methodist Church. The gulf is wide and deep administratively and theologically, and almost as wide and deep ethically and financially. Since the General Conference of 1976, all pastors not assigned to local churches are placed in a special category, "Appointment Beyond the Local Church," either to strengthen or dissolve their status as clergy in full connection with the church. Many different understandings of Christian ministry influence the present impasse on both sides. At the same time there are wide differences of attitude and effort among the different conferences of the church.

From the standpoint of the conferences, the mixture of chaplain and other non-local church appointments leads to an ambiguous situation with no clear administrative or theological accountability. There are specific issues which arise such as: "Methodist clergy sanctioning the war effort," "their freedom from the constraints of the parish," "the non-Christian nature of their work," "their better compensation and retirement system," "their greater freedom to negotiate their own position," and "their increasing numbers add to the number of lay members who vote at the annual conference."

The overriding suspicion, if not resentment, however, is administrative. The local church pastors resent the fact that these clergy are within the appointive power and responsibility of the conferences, but not sufficiently accountable to the conferences. Conference officials fear the day when many of the "others" might ask for conference appointments. These suspicions may rest on the strong impression that genuine accountability is mutual. They may also rest on the somewhat more pedestrian hunch that pastors not in local churches really contribute little to the Methodist system in membership, support, counsel, and participation, yet they receive the benefits of the connection. In either case, the central issue seems to be accountability, usually understood as carrying an administrative rather than a theological meaning.

The legislation of the 1976 General Conference, re-affirmed with minor changes in 1980, claims an even handed and reciprocal responsibility for "Appointments Beyond the Local Church." "Clergy persons in these ministries shall be accountable to the annual conference and given the same moral and spiritual support by it as are persons in appointments to pastoral charges."[1] In the detailed description of the category, accountability to the annual conference is specified. For example:

"Conference members under appointment beyond the local church are amenable to the annual conference of which they are members and insofar as possible should maintain close working relationships with and effective participation in the work of their annual conference, assuming whatever responsibilities they are qualified and requested to assume.

"They shall submit annually to the bishop, the district superintendent, and the Board of Ordained Ministry a written report of their performance of the ministerial office. . .

"A conference member serving an appointment beyond the local church shall be available and on call to administer the Sacraments of Baptism and the Lord's Supper as requested by the district superintendent of the district in which the special appointment is held (Discipline, 1976, par. 454, pp. 209, 210).

"Every ministerial member of an annual conference appointed to any other field than the pastorate or district superintendency shall furnish

---

[1] The Book of Discipline of the United Methodist Church, 1976, par. 454, p. 208.

annually to the conference secretary, at the time of the conference session, a statement of his remuneration, and the salaries or remunerations of all ministers in special service shall be published in the Journal of the Annual Conference". (Discipline, 1976, par. 937, p. 363.)

The impression is inescapable that the General Conferences of 1976 and 1980 sensed that the relation between annual conferences, pastors of local churches, and clergy under appointment beyond the local church was too poorly defined, and that the vagueness in this relation was not healthy for the church or the clergy. The specific action that the General Conference took suggests two things: 1) moral and spiritual support of clergy in these situations by the annual conference on "their performance of the ministerial office" and the reporting of their salary are specifically required; 2) the primary "tie that binds" the clergy together in The United Methodist Church is an administrative structure, not a theological or religious substance.

A question concerning the moral and spiritual support that chaplains and other clergy "appointed beyond the local church" have received from The United Methodist Church was put to persons in civilian and military chaplain ministries in the following way:

Has The United Methodist Church supported you in your ministry as a chaplain?

	No Response	Strong Yes	Moderate Yes	No Opinion	Moderate No	Strong No
Army	28	206	160	5	19	11
Navy	13	97	97	2	10	10
Air Force	13	129	101	0	11	4
Reserve	23	98	121	7	11	7
VA	7	48	36	1	1	2
Civilian Hospital	7	42	80	3	9	2
Confinement Facility	2	4	11	0	4	3
Institutional	3	31	42	1	7	3
Industrial	1	3	0	1	1	0
Total	97	658	648	20	73	42
		1306 (90.6%)		20 (1.4%)	115 (8%)	

Total Responding: 1441

Chaplain pastors gave overwhelming testimony to the support they are given by the church. The 1306 positive responses and 115 negative ones, out of 1538 questionnaires, indicate that 85 percent of those questioned acknowledged good support while all other categories comprised only 15 percent, including 97 who gave no response to the question. If one tallies only the positive and negative responses, the 1306 positive responses represent a 92 percent positive vote.

If one gathers these responses under two categories, military and civilian chaplaincies, the following picture emerges:

	No Response	Strong Yes	Moderate Yes	No Opinion	Moderate No	Strong No
Military Chaplains	77	530 1009 (91.2%)	479	14 14 (1.2%)	51 83 (7.5%)	32
Civilian Chaplains	20	128 297 (90.2%)	169	6	22 32 (9.7%)	10

Counting only those who gave some kind of response, the percentage of positive responses for military chaplains is 91 percent and for civilian chaplains, 90 percent. The similarity of responses from all chaplains accentuates the very high percentage of chaplains who understand themselves as well supported in their ministry by The United Methodist Church. That statistic is without doubt gratifying to persons in The United Methodist Church, yet it puts in question the accuracy of assertions about a cleavage between chaplain/pastors and local church pastors.

The questionnaire also asked chaplains how The United Methodist Church's support was expressed to them, whether through their annual conferences or through the Division of Chaplains and Related Ministries (formerly the Methodist Commission on Chaplains). Answers to that further question were quite revealing:

Was this support through the Division on Chaplains?

	No Response	Strong Yes	Moderate Yes	No Opinion	Moderate No	Strong No
Army	31	244	131	3	14	6
Navy	11	122	74	3	10	9
Air Force	14	143	93	1	4	3
Reserve	25	121	97	10	10	4
VA	4	56	31	0	2	2
Civilian Hospital	16	46	62	3	12	4
Confinement Facility	4	5	12	0	2	1
Institution	6	41	29	0	7	4
Industrial	1	3	1	1	0	0
Totals	112	781	527	21	61	33
		1308	(92%)		94 (6.6%)	

Total Responding: 1423

Combining these different forms of chaplaincy into two categories, military and civilian, the picture is more clear.

	No Response	Strong Yes	Moderate Yes	No Opinion	Moderate No	Strong No
Military Chaplains	81	630	395	17	38	22
		1025	(93%)	17 (1.5%)	60 (5.4%)	

Total Responding: 1102

	No Response	Strong Yes	Moderate Yes	No Opinion	Moderate No	Strong No
Civilian Chaplains	31	151	135	4	23	11
		286	(88.2%)	4 (1.2%)	34 (10.5%)	

Total Responding: 324

Was this support through your Annual Conference?

	No Response	Strong Yes	Moderate Yes	No Opinion	Moderate No	Strong No
Army	34	65	108	22	121	79
Navy	10	28	64	12	56	59
Air Force	18	27	75	11	70	57
Reserve	26	31	87	26	54	43
VA	14	15	30	1	20	15
Civilian Hospital	9	25	55	4	26	24
Confinement Facility	3	3	5	2	3	8
Institution	8	10	30	6	21	12
Industrial	0	2	2	1	1	0
Totals	122	206	456	85	372	297
		662 (46.8%)		85 (6%)	669 (47.2%)	

Total Responding: 1416

Again, placing all the forms of chaplain ministry in the category of civilian or military, the percentages become more vivid.

	No Response	Strong Yes	Moderate Yes	No Opinion	Moderate No	Strong No
Military Chaplaincy Total Responding: 1095	88	$\left(\begin{array}{cc} 151 & 334 \\ 485 & (44.3\%) \end{array}\right.$		71 71 (6.5%)	$\left.\begin{array}{cc} 301 & 238 \\ 539 & (49.2\%) \end{array}\right)$	
Civilian Chaplaincy Total Responding: 321	20	$\left(\begin{array}{cc} 55 & 122 \\ 177 & (55\%) \end{array}\right)$		14 (4.4%)	$\left(\begin{array}{cc} 71 & 59 \\ 130 & (40.5\%) \end{array}\right)$	

The contrast between chaplains' perception of support from the Division of Chaplains and Related Ministries and support from the Annual Conference is striking.

	Military	Civilian	All
Affirming support by church	91.2%	96.2%	90.6%
Affirming support by Division of Chaplains	93%	88.2%	92%
Affirming support by Annual Conference	44.3%	55%	46.8%

Responses by the chaplains indicate that:

1) A large majority (90.6 percent) of the chaplains understand themselves as supported in their work by The United Methodist Church. Slightly over 50 percent of that number acknowledge strong support. While 52 percent of the military chaplains report strong support, only 27.5 percent of civilian chaplains saw church support as strong. Thus, while the percentage of civilian and military chaplains reporting support from the church is about the same, civilian chaplains perceive that support as more moderate than strong (72.5 percent to 27.5 percent) whereas over 50 percent of the military chaplains see support by the church as strong.

2) There is an almost direct correlation between support from the church and support that chaplains have from the Division of Chaplains and Related Ministries. The strange wrinkle is that the 92 percent of the chaplains who perceive support from the division is slightly higher than the 90.6 percent of the chaplains who perceive themselves as supported by The United Methodist Church. (Is this simply a statistical variance or could it indicate that a few

chaplains do not regard the division as an agency of the church?) Within the overall figure of 92 percent, however, more military chaplains (61.5 percent) report strong support from the Division of Chaplains and Related Ministries, slightly exceeding that from The United Methodist Church overall. Yet within that high percentage there is evidence that civilian chaplains are less satisfied with that support than are military chaplains.

3) When one considers the support reported for the annual conferences, the picture is strikingly different. Less than half of the chaplains (46.8 percent) affirm support from an annual conference, with a significantly higher percentage (55 percent) of civilian chaplains reporting annual conference support than military chaplains (44.3 percent). If one adds the unusually high number of "no opinion" responses to these negative responses, it seems that 53.2 percent of the chaplains report no support for them and their work by the annual conferences. Further, if one also takes into account that 44 percent of the military chaplains and 45 percent of the civilian chaplains who gave a negative response indicated a *strongly* negative response, it is clear that The United Methodist Church confronts a critical situation if the church intends to overcome the cleavage between chaplains/pastors and local church pastors through the offices and the powers of the annual conference.

In view of the high investment that the church is making to affirm specialized ministers while simultaneously tightening up the administrative side of a chaplain's relation to the annual conference, more specific observations of chaplains as to whether support from the annual conference is pastoral, logistical, educational, or collegial are important. Divided again into the two categories, military and civilian, they reported the following:

	Responses and No Responses	No Response	Yes	No Opinion	No Response	Total Response	% Yes of Response	% Yes Overall
Pastoral Support								
Military Chaplains	(1183)	326	353	87	417	857	41%	30%
Civilian Chaplains	(355)	98	136	15	106	257	52.9%	38.3%

Logistical Support								
Military Chaplains	(1183)	390	156	135	502	792	19.6%	13%
Civilian Chaplains	(355)	115	80	43	117	240	35.3%	22%
Educational Support								
Military Chaplains	(1183)	404	125	126	528	779	16%	10.5%
Civilian Chaplains	(355)	113	84	33	125	242	34.7%	23.6%
Collegial Support								
Military Chaplains	(1183)	344	321	102	416	839	38%	27%
Civilian Chaplains	(355)	101	125	25	104	254	49%	35%

If one counts "no response" as indicative of nothing, the only instance in which over half of the chaplains give a positive response (52.9 percent) is the reporting by civilian chaplains of pastoral support. If one counts "no response" as a negative response, that percentage slips to 38.3 percent.

About half of the civilian chaplains report pastoral and collegial support, 11 percent higher than military chaplains report in that category.

In the other categories of logistics and education, however, only 33 percent of civilian chaplains perceived support while less than 20 percent of military chaplains did. All of these percentages fall still further if "no response" is taken as a negative response.

Logistical support is probably not an important item in most instances of chaplain ministry because Bibles, vessels and elements for serving Holy Communion, and transportation, when needed, are now usually provided by the organization the chaplain serves. Educational support is more important in pastoral ministry generally. That support usually centers on education for special skills and a variety of formal programs of "refresher study" for clergy at intervals during their careers as augmentations of the Pastors Schools. In this regard, the chaplain/pastors are probably in less need of educational support than the local church pastors because education is considered to be more important in chaplain ministry and is therefore provided by many of the organizations that the chaplain/pastor serves. Educational opportunities for chaplains in the military are outstanding. Therefore, military chaplains do not generally expect educational support from their annual conferences.

The issues of pastoral and collegial support, however, are fundamental. How might a structure function to promote collegiality in the travails and joys of ministry when that structure is seen by chaplains as being only 38 percent to 52.9 percent effective in its support of the chaplains? The easy answer is that chaplains do not see the situation correctly. It would be simplistic to accept that answer as adequate, however, in light of chaplain descriptions of their Christian ministry discussed in Chapters III and IV. If one takes chaplain claims for ministry seriously, then it is obvious that the chaplains are raising a theological claim for Christian ministry which is not honored generally by local church ministry or by the annual conference.

At the outset of this chapter, we cited the provision of the *Discipline* which makes clergy in all appointments beyond the local church "accountable to the annual conference and given the same moral and spiritual support by it as are persons in appointments to pastoral charges." It must be noted that this new category, "Appointments Beyond the Local Church" (ABLC) entered into use with the 1976 General Conference, and that it applies not only to chaplains but also campus ministers, district superintendents, teachers and others who work in educational institutions, staff members of boards and agencies, missionaries, students, and all other persons who for whatever reason were previously regarded as being in "special appointments." In this and subsequent legislation in 1980 there is a new stress on accountability to the annual conference which is intended explicitly to entail reciprocity. For the first time, the Discipline requires that the District Superintendent evaluate the ministry of every person in the ABLC category, such evaluations to be based on information one gives in the annual report to the conference.

These changes in the structure of relationships are obviously directed toward recovering and strengthening the theological and administrative dimensions of collegiality in ministry. The distance to be traveled is extensive, however, and the administrative remedy by itself probably will not be effective. Consider the following case:

Member of annual conference in full standing: 38 years

Appointments:
Student
Chaplain, World War II (U. S. Army)
Teacher in United Methodist University
Requested by the conference:
Figure of annual salary
Brief annual report to the conference
Provide and clarify information for Board of Pensions
Support given by conference:
Assistance and Certification to Methodist Commission on Chaplains in World War II
General:
Within the last thirty years when there was peculiar strain between youth and the church, I was asked to serve on no committee or for any interpretation of what was going on in the culture, on college campuses, in religion, or in Christian theology. I was asked in 1980 to contribute toward the Crusade for Pensions in the conference, but beyond that was never asked what I might need nor asked to respond to needs within the conference.

Correspondence with the bishop resulting from the legislation of the General Conference of 1976, designed to increase accountability and collegiality, further illustrates the problem.

February 13, 1979

Bishop John Christian Lord

Dear Bishop Lord:
A few days ago I received a request from the Secretary to the Cabinet of the New World Conference, asking for the second year for a statement about my activities as an ordained minister and for an

indication of my salary for 1978. In addition he asked that someone in the University who supervises my work send you a statement certifying that none of my duties at Trinity involve a compromise of my ordination vows. I have asked Dean Schmidt to send you a letter on behalf of the University. The other form is being returned to Dr. Stipe forthwith.

I am a little puzzled about what interpretation you put on the action of the General Conference of 1976 regarding ministers who are appointed beyond the local church. I have been under special appointment to the faculty of Trinity University since 1950. My impression is that, using the language of the *Discipline*, there has never been in my case a close working relationship with and effective participation in the work of the New World Conference, and, in the twenty-seven years, I have never been asked by the conference to do anything except report my salary, until the request came last year. I do not wish to compromise you, the conference, or myself in the matter, but I cannot tell whether you want persons in my category to get into closer relationship with their home conferences, or to transfer into the conference within whose bounds such persons now live and work.

It is particularly embarrassing to me that I have such a nebulous contact with you, and I would like to remedy that situation in whatever manner you prefer. I would gladly come to your office for a conference at your convenience. On the other hand, if your regular responsibilities bring you to the University periodically, I would be extremely pleased if you would have dinner with me, giving the occasion to discuss matters of mutual interest, of faith and hope and love.

Cordially,
Benjamin Worldly

February 22, 1978

Dr. Benjamin Worldly

Dear Dr. Worldly:

Please let me thank you for your most gracious letter and assure you that all of us who work with appointments are just as puzzled as you are concerning the action of the General Conference of 1976. An attempt was made evidently to tie ministers under special appointment closer to the church than they had been in the past. There have been ministers who have been appointed to work that has no acceptable structure whatsoever. We have had some ministers who have wanted appointments to jobs that have bordered on the ridiculous. All of us are trying to work our way through the General Conference legislation so I hope you wil be patient with us.

I hope to have the opportunity to have some fellowship with you one of these days when I am visiting the University or possibly when you are near my office. With every good wish I am

Sincerely,
John Christian Lord

Dictated by Bishop Lord
Written and signed in his absence

There was no further conversation between Bishop Lord and Professor Worldly on the matter. Both had good intentions, and both wanted to understand and implement the new General Conference legislation, But, sadly, both were already overburdened with the daily round of required activities. Both wanted dutifully to obey the legislative mandate, yet neither could draw on the spontaneous resources of collegial care to "keep the situation in mind" or to find a time and a place to meet as fellow clergy.

This is said neither against the bishop nor against the professor, but simply to indicate the *presence* of a structure of administrative accountability and the *absence* of a structure for mutual accountability in ministry. All of the developments point to the ambiguity if not the contradiction between administrative and theological considerations and between the annual conferences and the Division of Chaplains and Related Ministries (DCRM) as the primary agency of the church in assuring mutual support and mutual accountability. The theological factor can hardly be overemphasized and will be discussed later. First we need to assess the annual conferences and the Division of Chaplains and Related Ministries as administrative agents of collegial ministry.

B. Annual Conferences and Chaplain Ministry

The increasing number of persons in ministry beyond the local church creates an administrative problem and arouses fears in the annual conferences. This occurs at a time when the General Conference mandates tighter accountability and when the chaplains are predominantly negative about collegial support from the conferences. What are the problems and the opportunities in relying on the annual conferences as the primary vehicle of accountability and support for chaplains and others in non-local-church ministry?

1. Problems in the Annual Conference Structure

a) *Differences Among Conferences.*

As there are wide differences among conferences in attitude toward chaplain ministry, so there are wide differences in attitude toward and support of all clergy in the "Appointment Beyond the Local Church" category. We saw this difference among chaplains as extending from complete cynicism about attending annual conference to high praise from the continuing contact with a district superintendent and a bishop. That same difference was also apparent in the attitudes conferences had toward incorporating former chaplains into the regular programs and assignments of the conference.

On the surface, the differences in number of clergy, priorities in ministry, general strength, and attitude toward General Conference Legislation influence what a specific conference does about its chaplain clergy, and whether any distinction is recognized between chaplains and other persons in the ABLC category. For example, each Conference Board of Ordained Ministry should designate a liaison person to facilitate understanding and cooperation in ministry between the Board of Ordained Ministry and clergy appointed beyond the local church in that conference.[2] Yet all conferences have not appointed such a liaison person, and many of those who have been appointed have not begun to function.

A few conferences have taken leadership in nurturing an *esprit* among persons in the ABLC category and in relating their ministry to

---

[2] The 1980 General Conference passed legislation requiring meetings to strengthen liaison and understanding of ministry in each episcopal area and to integrate clergy not appointed to local churches.

that of local church pastors. In January, 1982, the Division of Ordained Ministry of the Board of Higher Education and Ministry joined with the Division of Chaplains and Related Ministries in a national meeting at Nashville of liaison persons from all annual conferences within the United States. Especially informative for newly appointed liaison persons, the meeting revealed much confusion about which clergy among those not appointed to a local church should be "endorsed" by the Division of Chaplains and Related Ministries. Does "related ministries" cover all ministries beyond the local church other than that of civilian and military chaplains?

The two day discussion focused on a fundamental contradiction between United Methodist theory and United Methodist practice—between the claim that there is but one ministry of Christ whatever the setting and the almost universal practice of a second-class attitude toward all kinds of ministries beyond the local church. The meeting illustrated the wide differences among conferences in the way special ministry clergy are regarded, supported, and integrated into the work of the conference.

b) *Geographical Barriers.*

The church recognizes that distance from one's conference makes participation in the regular work of the conference difficult in spite of good intentions. Chaplains and others who are outside the bounds of their annual conference are encouraged, therefore, to establish an affiliate connection with the conference in which they actually live and work, and to establish an affiliate relation to a charge conference. Although that is an administrative step in the right direction, such a contact is likely to be on the level of a guest or service club member who is "making his meeting" in another city he is visiting. Even that category is of little help to the ordinary military chaplain because of limited assignments in one place and frequent assignments where there is no charge or annual conference.

In spite of fortuitous situations for affiliates in some conferences, this arrangement has not seemed to offer much promise for the majority of chaplains. If mutual collegial support cannot be established for a chaplain in his or her own annual conference, an affiliate relation with another conference is likely only to adulterate the conference relation further. The geographical barrier is real, but the administrative arrangement of affiliate membership designed to overcome the geographical barrier will not touch the primary problem of the estrangement between local church clergy and all other clergy, an estrangement that prevails whether or not there is geographical separation.

c) *Administrative Barriers.*
Functionally, the administrative structure and priorities for local churches in conferences dominate the time, thought, resources, and activity of the pastor. Effective ministry is measured in terms of obvious measures: conversions, membership, baptisms, growth, meeting the budget and apportionments, attendance, and doing well with conference specials and priorities. Every one of these activities may be legitimate and constructive. The total effect of this orientation, nevertheless, is to consume energies for the program under the assumption that the qualities of the Kingdom of God are inevitably promoted with the program.

Identifying success in the conference program with the qualities of the Kingdom obscures radical and prophetic discernment of the word of God in the midst of our individual and social life. That also intensifies the comradeship of those who give themselves fully to the program, creating an "insider" consciousness which is suspicious of other forms of ministry, parochial toward other denominations, and distrustful of the ubiquity of the grace of God. Gradually, the impression grows that if it isn't reportable in conference records, it isn't ministry.

As we saw in Chapter II, chaplains claim a Christian ministry to many persons in critical and isolated situations that most local pastors never enter. Because of the chaplain's presence, new possibilities of hope, self-worth, acceptance of God, and participation in the joys of the Kingdom of God are offered to persons. In theory, all Christian clergy rejoice that these moves of faith and love are made. In practice, however, the preoccupying concerns of conference programs are so consuming that joy at those dramatic changes in peoples' lives and gratitude for the fellow-clergy "who are there" to minister are pushed involuntarily to the outer edge of one's consciousness. In effect, then, the Methodist administrative structure "controls" the substance of the gospel.

Given these factors and the extensive responsibilities of bishops and district superintendents, it is unlikely that the new emphases on collegiality in one ministry and on mutual accountability will be effective in overcoming the estrangement between clergy in local church appointments and those in appointment beyond the local church. The problem is deeper than the administrative structure. There is no administrative measure that can or will, by itself, remedy the situation. This is because the most serious and fundamental difference is over the interpretation of Christian ministry.

d) *Religious Barriers: Conflicts Over the Meaning of Ministry*

The primary cause for the lack of collegiality in ministry among United Methodist clergy is the reductionist vision of what God is doing in the world, coupled with a defensiveness on the part of all pastors which makes breadth of perspective and understanding exceedingly difficult. In such a general situation of "mis-meeting" and misunderstanding, polarizing stereotypes flourish. To local church pastors, the chaplains have left the Christian ministry because they have sold their souls to their institutional sponsors. To chaplains, local church clergy have lost touch with those persons in society who are radically threatened if not destroyed by the "principalities and powers" of the culture.

To local church clergy, chaplains are "out of relation" to the gospel because they are not an integral part of the local church and conference program. To chaplains, the local church clergy have neglected, if not abandoned, the heart-beat of the gospel, the love of God which includes all persons in all situations. To local church clergy, chaplains are "strangers" who use—perhaps waste—the resources of the church without helping in the difficult task of generating resources. One chaplain put it this way: "The local church clergy understand human problems in relation to the church. Chaplains understand the church in relation to human problems.

There may be more validity to one or the other side of this argument in different situations, but the tragedy of the present cleavage is that what "God hath put together," the clergy of The United Methodist Church have, in fact, put asunder. It seems clear that no one ever intended that these aspects of ministry be in opposition to one another. And it may well be that local church clergy also understand themselves to be involved in ministry to persons whose existence is marginal, a ministry either through the activities of the local congregation or through regular and special support of various kinds of "missions" of the church. There are growing numbers of instances of local church ministry to marginal groups. Two instances illustrate this:

In the December, 1981 issue of *Forward*, an evangelism journal of The United Methodist Church (Vol. 2, Issue 6), there is an impressive story of the ministry of Detroit's Metropolitan United Methodist Church to mentally retarded adults. The pastor of the church, Dr. William K. Quick, describes that special ministry of the church.

> "In an age when most folk walk on the other side of the street to avoid the mentally retarded adult, these 'special' children of God have found what it really means to be accepted within the Christian fellowship. . . . Our entire church has become conscious of a world of persons who have, for the most part, been 'hidden away' from the rest of us. Their presence has sensitized the church to the reality that persons of limited possibilities are indeed inheritors of God's grace."[3]

The author of the article concludes the story with an appeal to other local churches to be more alert to "individuals within their community to whom no one is offering Christian ministry." He presents the program of Metropolitan Church as a model to inspire other congregations "to become aware of retarded persons and to do something to make them a part of a loving Christian fellowship. This, too, is evangelism."[4]

In terms of a vision of Christian ministry as participation in what God is doing in the world, both local church clergy and chaplain clergy would seem to agree and rejoice in this ministry at Metropolitan Church. In day by day functions, however, the local church sees its primary mission in terms of those in reach of the congregation, persons the congregation sees and hears. Chaplains usually work among persons about whom the local church

---

[3]"Ministry to Mentally Retarded Adults." *Forward*, Vol. 2, Issue 6, December 1981, pp. 1, 5.
[4] *Ibid.*, p. 5.

has no knowledge, persons who may themselves have no way of knowing that a local church cares about them.

For another illustration, consider a statement of a Veterans' Administration chaplain. In my letter to chaplains which accompanied the questionnaire, I explained the project and asked for cooperation. Among other things, I said: "Please give me the benefit of knowing the most positive, the most troubling, the most discouraging, the most challenging, and the most meaningful aspects of your ministry as a chaplain." In reply, this hospital chaplain wrote as follows:

Dear Jack:

I have just struggled through your questionnaire, which I found quite stimulating and painful. I then read your letter, which I should have done to start with. I want to answer the questions you asked in the third paragraph of your letter.

a. The most positive aspect of my ministry is seeing people on the cutting edge of life, in the midst of trials and suffering using their faith; not using it as a crutch to beat back reality but using it to bring meaning out of despair.

b. The most troubling for me is trying to work with patients whose religious pathology is so negative that their faith acts as a millstone around their necks instead of a source of help.

c. The most discouraging for me is seeing so many die who leave us with cherished memories of trusted moments—the smiles, the silences, the holding of hands, and the treasured words of faith. These I find myself missing from time to time. As time passes, the value of those experiences grows and I become less discouraged.

d. The most rewarding for me has been a spiritual pilgrimage I have undertaken in which my concept of God has changed from an authoritarian figure to a caring, loving God.

Good luck in your work. I hope that it is as stimulating for you as it has been for me.

Sincerely,

Although the chaplain in this instance is employed by the Veterans' Administration rather than by a church, his work is made possible by ordination and the religious, as well as modest financial, support of The United Methodist Church. Many participants in a local church would rejoice that this level of ministry is taking place under the sponsorship of The United Methodist Church. These persons cannot in most instances be where the chaplain is to express the love of God to persons the chaplain sees each day. But they would want their prayers and their contributions to their local church to support and sustain that chaplain and many others in the kind of ministry which this letter describes.

The irony of the situation is that crucial transformations in the lives of persons from indifference toward caring, from fear toward trust, would not be prominent in the reports of local churches and to the annual conferences unless those persons moved toward baptism or membership in The United Methodist Church. A fundamentally pervasive sense of God's love in Christ for all persons, especially those in acute need or jeopardy, is still present. Yet the functional forms of The United Methodist Church tend to dominate if not control the understanding of Christ's presence. The meaning of Christian ministry includes the gathered community in worship, sharing, love, and work. It includes as well all kinds of outreach to protect, defend, heal, comfort, and encourage those who are alone and abused. It would be tragic if the meaning of ministry is ever taken to separate these functions or to put them in conflict.

As ministries beyond the local church have increased, suspicion and tension, even conflict, have developed in such a way as to define Christian ministry predominantly in terms of one or the other of these functions. Comments to chaplains about their "leaving the ministry" are too serious and pervasive to be dismissed as joking. The pilgrimage of individual chaplains suggests a pilgrimage of The United Methodist Church as well. The most rewarding aspect of our life together may well be in the constant submission of the limitations of our structures, powers, and ideas to the ultimacy of God's compassion and love.

2. Values of the Annual Conference Structure

Given all that has been said about the past record of support of chaplains by the conferences as well as the different kinds of barriers between local church pastors and chaplain pastors, it is nevertheless essential to the future health of the church that the conferences find ways to include chaplain ministries in their comprehensive vision of God's work and calling. The conference body enables lay and ordained people to become a comprehensive Christian community in faith and order, life and work, responsibility and forgiveness, justice and mercy. The conference is the skeleton that enables the hands and heart and mind and feet to move together.

As part of the comprehensive community of faith, the local churches are kept aware of those who are in distress and are challenged to confront and neutralize the "principalities and powers" of public life that demean and abuse nature and persons. They are also inspired to give of their faith and wealth to support those who represent them in various kinds of ministries of help, healing, and compassion.

If the conference is truly a comprehensive community, the chaplain is never alone, left to his own personal resources within his or her individual relation to God. On the contrary, the chaplain is ordained and sustained by the community of faith and his or her ministry is regarded as essential to the integrity of the life of the conference and church alongside that of the local church pastor. The relation between chaplains and local church pastors is collegial and mutual, even interdependent, because neither can really exist or "serve the Lord" without the other. Positively, the annual conference structure provides a "body" in which, as Paul put it, there is one spirit but many functions (I Corinthians 12:20). Whatever else is done in other ways to keep chaplains related to the church, the imperatives of the gospel require both a unity of Spirit within God's love and a responsibility to express that love to all persons. The annual conference as a community of communities is the focal vehicle for bringing together complexity, variety, and unity. Without the conference, the individual churches are without a supportive context for participation in the holy, universal church. Without the conference, the General Conference would be an association or an assembly, not a worshiping, deliberative, and unified community as the body of Christ.

Negatively put, without the overcoming of these tensions and conflicts in the understanding of Christian ministry, the conferences would disintegrate into provincial and narcissistic organs, losing thereby their perspective on the transcendent qualities of the Kingdom and Holiness of God that prompt us to individual dignity and responsibility and bid us to temper our power and preferences by the greater good of the whole of the Church and of the human family. Paul calls us to hold to the truth in love (Ephesians 4:15). That means also to use our power and strength in love, that is, in service to the love of God for the whole of creation.

C. The Division of Chaplains and Related Ministries

The testimony of the 1236 chaplains included in this study is overwhelming (93 percent) concerning support for them and their work by the Division of Chaplains and Related Ministries. The history of the last thirty years is that of mild and sporadic support of chaplains by annual conferences and consistently strong support by the division. That general sense was reflected in a statement of an Air Force chaplain reported in a study in 1978.[5] Referring to the Division of Chaplains and Related Ministries (Commission on Chaplains), he wrote:

> "I think with the limited funds they are working with, they are doing an excellent job. However, I feel personal contact with the men and women in the field is essential. To be where our active duty chaplains are, to know what problems confront us, and to be sensitive to those problems is vital. I see the commission on chaplains in a role that surpasses that of my contact with my conference to which I am associated. I feel the Commission knows more about what I am doing . . . and cares more about what I am doing than my own bishop and members of my conference. Other than a direct reply to my annual report that I submit, I have never in fourteen years received a letter or phone call or visit from anyone representing the conference I am assigned to. Therefore, the commission for me, acts as that link to the church and I appreciate this very much."[6]

Given this strong appreciation of the Division of Chaplains and Related Ministries, what are the values and the problems in the role

---

[5]Robert L. Wilson, "Attitudes of United Methodist Chaplains Toward Division of Chaplains and Related Ministries," The J.M. Osmond Center for Research Planning and Development, The Divinity School, Duke University, 1978.

[6]Robert L. Wilson, *op. cit.*, p. 34.

of the division as the primary contact between chaplains and the church?

1. Values in a Relation through the Division of Chaplains and Related Ministries (DCRM).

The Division of Chaplains and Related Ministries has been an effective agency of the church in many ways. These may be classified as: understanding, support, advocacy, and collegiality. The duty of recruitment may also be important, but this study focuses on the ministry of persons already engaged in some form of chaplain ministry.

a) *Understanding.*

In view of the prevalence of the "outsider" status of most chaplains in relation to the annual conference, it is impossible to overestimate the importance of the division in "understanding" the chaplain and his or her ministry. That understanding functions on two different but related levels, that of affirming the integrity of the ministry of the chaplain as authentic Christian ministry, and that of recognizing the special skills that are essential in these ministries in addition to the existential qualities of compassion and commitment to Christ in sacrament, word, and order that are requisite to all Christian ministry.

The most comprehensive and all-embracing function of the Division of Chaplains and Related Ministries through the years has been affirming and defending chaplain ministry as a legitimate, viable, and valued ministry of The United Methodist Church. Chaplains have been able to continue their ministry primarily because the division has been effective in assuring them that there are many in the church who understand and appreciate what they are and what they do. The most significant work of the Division of Chaplains and Related Ministries is that of communicating an understanding to the chaplains, as well as to the institutions they serve, that the church is a steward of the initiative of God, that all of our love is a response to God.

A second aspect of "understanding" is more occupationally specific. It entails a knowledge of the peculiar kinds of stress which threaten people in the quite different kinds of settings and an appreciation of the special skills which are essential to a chaplain's effectiveness in these situations. The qualities which promise success in ministry to the mentally ill, the imprisoned, the terminally ill, or the person under military authority are quite different. Some chaplains see ministry as sharing the danger of those in one's parish, which may mean parachuting from an airplane. Some are called to be agents in a healing team among those who are acutely ill mentally and/or physically. Some make themselves open to the problems of persons again and again in counseling situations. But these are different forms of "presence" even though compassion is a primal ingredient in every Christian presence.

The DCRM carries the responsibility of more specific knowledge of these special ministries than the average bishop or Cabinet or annual conference is likely to possess. Hence there is a concrete appreciation for both the peculiar needs and the peculiar stresses of these widely different forms of ministry. It is one thing to pronounce the blessing and love of God in the conviction that these are applicable to all situations. It is another thing to make the blessing and love of God present within actual knowledge of the particular anguish people feel and in sharing that anguish. The division is charged by the church to relate the confidences of the church to persons in peculiar situations in such a way that there is no glibness in the sharing of danger or in the sharing of hope and love. The DCRM operates in two directions, toward the chaplain to provide a "context of grace" for his or her work and toward the church to keep the church aware of the brokenness and anguish of life.

b) *Support.*

Support follows from understanding and provides what the chaplain needs. In some cases support might entail something as simple and tangible as books or periodicals or a communion kit. At other times it may be complex, personal, and demanding, such as counseling a chaplain in a family crisis. Special kinds of support would also be needed in situations of acute psychological stress, burn out, and in relation to financial and other problems.

The division is a relatively small operation, and its resources are limited. Ordinarily it does not have staff or resources to respond to all calls for help or support. It certainly does not have financial resources for grants or loans to individuals in peculiar need. The more important function of the division, however, is to provide a wide-spectrum structure of support which is at the chaplain's hand in any situation of stress or need. The division exists to make this support available not as a special favor or concession but as a resource provided by the church to be constantly at the chaplain's call.

Some chaplains reflected experience with the division that was not positive. A few said they would not call on the division for anything. Others spoke of excellent support through letters, visits, and retreats, but limited effectiveness in confronting structural problems in the military, in prisons and hospitals, and other chaplain settings. But the overwhelming testimony of chaplains was high praise for the comprehensive support the division offered.

Following the break-up of a marriage, one chaplain wrote: "I praise the division for their pastoral care in those times." Support does not always mean agreement with a chaplain on an issue or approving the way a chaplain handles a problem. Yet the division is asked to support every chaplain with the widest sense of compassion and morality appropriate to Christian ministry while at the same time being expertly informed about the hazards, stresses, complications, temptations, and opportunities of every specialist ministry.

There are many structures which impact on chaplain ministries and numerous institutional problems over which the division has no power. Included would be the decisions of Congress, the pay scales and pension arrangements in religious and secular institutions, the standard operating procedures in hospitals, prisons, and other kinds of institutions, and, indeed, the appointive power of bishops within the church. It would be unfair to the division to expect it to exercise power it does not have, as it would be unfair to expect the division always to see a situation just the way the chaplain sees it. The division has limited powers, and the staff of the division as well as the chaplains are fallible persons. Neither uniform agreement nor an altogether correct solution to all problems is possible. Nevertheless, the division is empowered to provide or to help acquire whatever support is necessary to enable the chaplain to perform Christian ministry.

Even in situations over which the division has no controlling power, there is the role and responsibility of "advocate" to which we now turn.

c) *Advocacy.*

Support flows from understanding and advocacy flows both from support and from understanding. Because of its informed understanding of these special ministries, the DCRM support extends beyond upholding the individual chaplains. It embraces many church agencies and the institutions in which chaplains serve to insure that chaplains are able to provide Christian ministry. In its roles of advocacy, the division is important as an agency of the church and, at the same time is able to join with other denominations to challenge conditions and attitudes in institutions that prohibit or trivialize the function of a chaplain as clergyperson. The forms of advocacy most appropriate for the church, a secular agency, or the general culture vary considerably. This places heavy responsibility on the ingenuity of the DCRM.

The division as advocate for chaplains within the church might seem to be a case of "special pleading." Both the Methodist Commission on Chaplains and its successor, the division of Chaplains and Related Ministries, have made strong statements before the General Conferences supporting the legitimacy of chaplain ministry and requesting financial and spiritual support of that ministry by the church overall. While such appeals may have bordered on "special pleading," the church would not have created and supported the Commission (MCOC) or the division (DCRM) unless the church had been convinced that chaplain ministry was Christian ministry.

From the beginning, chaplain ministry was embraced because it was a way for the church to help society beyond the church, to serve the nation (especially in war-time), and to provide "Good Samaritan" activities for persons in severe need. These ministries were seen, however vaguely, as ways in which the church helped the world. There was little sense of the possibility that these ministries might help the church in understanding the world or in understanding Christian ministry. Recent discussion about different kinds of chaplain ministries may become more intense. For example, should a chaplain counselor in a secular institution have the same status in the annual conference as that of a chaplain counselor in a

Methodist owned or related institution? Even, so, these discussions presuppose the formal legitimacy of chaplain ministry.

The division is an advocate for chaplain ministry to the church not so much in pleading for the category, but to speak within the church for a better understanding of the significance of chaplain ministry and for more explicit ways for chaplain ministry to be visible to the annual and the General Conferences. The configuration of information, priorities, power, and momentum in the church today is such that there is little likelihood that a chaplain pastor would have a significant role on a conference committee or be elected a delegate to the General Conference. Chaplain ministry is simply tangential to the month-by-month and year-by-year activity of the conferences. To counter that disfranchisement, some would advocate special chaplain categories for conference committees and for selection of delegates to the General Conference. Whether or not that is an advisable strategy, the division has the inescapable responsibility to be an advocate of chaplain ministry within the whole church. That responsibility entails vigorous and concerted efforts to promote mindfulness about and mutual appreciation of the equal callings of the local church pastor and the chaplain pastor.

Steps have been taken in that direction. Under the initiative of the division, the 1980 General Conference voted to require meetings of the bishop, representatives of the Cabinet, and the Committee on Chaplains and Related Ministries of the Board of Ordained Ministry with clergy not appointed to local churches.

"The purpose of this meeting is to gain understanding of one another's role and function in ministry, to report to other ministers appointed beyond the local church and to discuss with them matters concerning the overall approach to ministry in the episcopal area, to interpret the role and function of extension ministries to the larger church through the offices of the bishop and his or her representatives, to nurture the development of various ministries as significant in assisting the mission of the church, and to discuss specific programs and services which the bishop and his or her representatives may initiate in which the various ministers serving in appointments beyond the local church may be qualified as consultants and supervisors." [7]

[7] *The Book of Discipline of the United Methodist Church,* 1980, p. 439, 2(b).

The 1980 General Conference also required each annual conference to elect a Board of Ordained Ministry or a Division of Ordained Ministry within a Board of Higher Education and Ministry. The legislation stipulated that at least "one member of the Board should be engaged in extension ministries and will represent these ministries with the Board" as a part of par. 723.1a, but for some reason that provision was omitted from the published *Discipline*. Both of these moves illustrate the role of "advocate" assumed by the division in relation to the church and indicate a vision of "mutual accountability" which guides the division in these actions.

The second role of the division as advocate is to the agencies that clergy serve as chaplains. The tension arising from the two roles of the chaplain as servant of the church and as servant of the agency which employs him or her has already been discussed.[8] The place of the division in relation to this issue is two-fold: as representative of the church to assure the possibility of Christian ministry within the structure of an institution, and as a representative of an individual chaplain to assist and support that chaplain in challenging a powerful manager, commander, or a large organization whose actions or policies may be unethical or demeaning. The issues involved in such a challenge are often concerns of the entire church and perhaps of all religious communities and not an isolated protest of an individual chaplain. No individual chaplain should have to carry the burden and risk of challenging an institution or a powerful person on behalf of the entire church.

In the accounts chaplains gave, we saw instances of these overarching policy questions such as a Commander ordering his subjects to worship, a chaplain's objection to the Vietnam War, and violations of informed consent in medical decisions. We noted also the statement of the Episcopal Church inviting other churches to join it "in expressing concern to the Department of Defense that the human dignity of all persons in the armed forces be scrupulously respected at all times . . . ." Churches have recently joined together in challenging abusive and degrading language to women and to minorities. There may well be action by churches

---

[8]Chapter IV above, pp. 62-63.

to challenge the way in which "no code" is decided upon in health-care settings, or the use of clergy in jails and prisons as part of the "correctional team."

In so far as the chaplain's conscience on these matters is formed by the church, the conflict with the institution should be carried primarily by the church at large and not by the individual chaplain. The division represents the church in monitoring all "chaplain positions" for their openness to Christian ministry on all these scores. That function is as important as their selecting and endorsing individual persons for the various specialist ministries.

Even under the best of conditions, conflicts and misunderstandings arise. Persons with overall responsibility for an institution may well regard a chaplain's question, protest, or complaint, as disloyalty to the institution. When the superior rates and/or sets the salary of the chaplain, a situation may develop which is quite unfair to the chaplain. The division cannot assure fairness for the chaplains in all instances, but the division carries the mandate of advocacy to use all powers at its disposal to assure fairness to the chaplain as an individual and as a representative of the church. If the issue touches on the integrity of the gospel or of Christian ministry, the division must protect the chaplain as far as possible. It may make a recomendation to the church that the institution be challenged publicly and that The United Methodist Church seek the cooperation of other churches in discontinuing endorsements of chaplains to that institution as long as structural or policy barriers to ministry continue.

The third level of advocacy for chaplain ministry engages the DCRM along with other agencies of the church in changing aspects of culture which are distinctive. It is important that the division relate what it learns from the special ministry of chaplains about what causes human brokenness, stress, danger, or suffering to the persons who have responsibility for or power to change destructive conditions that dominate our culture. There is no question that our excessive achievement orientation, overselling of sex, refusal to acknowledge limits, reliance on violence and force, persisting poverty and unemployment, and increasing cynicism about justice, opportunity, and happiness, contribute to the mess many people have made of their lives and to the general situation which many experience as overwhelming.

The division has responsibility not only to sponsor ministry to victims, but to join in challenging aspects of our culture which degrade human life and trivialize qualities of honor, compassion, trust, cooperation, community, and peace-making which are essential to the church's vision of happiness and human fulfilment. At some point the casualty-producing aspects of our culture must be reversed. The division has no small part in that battle against the powers of evil by virtue of its privileged insight through specialist ministries to the persons most at risk in our present society.

d) *Collegiality.*

Had the division succeeded in the functions of understanding, support, and advocacy, yet failed to establish a base of collegiality in Christian ministry between the local church clergy and chaplain clergy, there would be serious limits to the possibility that the church and the chaplains might "find their way back to one another." The issue which underlies all others and causes estrangement between local church pastors and chaplain pastors is the nature of relationships between clergy. Chaplains report paternalistic and patronizing behavior and attitudes from parish clergy (annual conference) towards themselves. In contrast, they speak of a collegial relationship with the representatives of the division. This contrast is due in part to a limited understanding of chaplain ministry. But what is at stake in collegiality is more pervasive and psychologically critical than the issue of understanding.

Understanding why a person engages in a chaplain ministry does not necessary foster collegiality in ministry. Collegiality in ministry may be quite strong in the absence of understanding. For example, there may be strong collegiality even if one does not understand why another is engaged in ministry among night people, "street children," homosexuals, prostitutes, or the mentally ill. There could also be understanding of such ministries without genuine collegiality with those engaged in the ministries.

There are tensions among those endorsed by the division. One friction within division constituents was explicit from the beginning of this study, tension between civilian chaplains and military chaplains. A paper on the needs of the civilian chaplaincy by Alan K. Waltz in 1974 emphasized this tension.

"The concern over the endorsement, its meaning and procedures grew out of the feeling that the civilian chaplains were and still are the step-children of the division. It may be that custom, tradition, and habit in the division have carried old procedures into settings for which they are not now applicable . . . . It would appear that some of the civilian chaplains feel that they do not have a way adequately to have their perspective presented and evaluated by the staff of members of the division. They feel that the history of the division, the background of interests, concerns and staff, and the present programming activities, are focused primarily toward the military."[9]

Suspicion of the division by civilian chaplains still continues. Two civilian chaplains returned the questionnaire for this study indicating that it seemed to be designed for military chaplains and was in no way pertinent to their ministry. There were probably many others who simply did not answer or return the questionnarie because they understood their own ministry in prisons, jails, and so on, as being too specialized to be described in broad, general terms. These reservations are quite understandable, especially in view of the preponderance of military chaplains in the earlier days of the Methodist Commission on Chaplains and the Division of Chaplains and Related Ministeries,[10] and because of the increasingly varied and specialized ministries, including industrial chaplaincies, which the division is being asked to oversee.

The first endorsement of chaplains to industry was in 1956 when three clergy were formally endorsed.

---

[9]Alan K. Waltz, "A Study of the Needs of the Civilian Chaplaincy." A Survey of Civilian Chaplains who have been Endorsed by the Division of Chaplains and Related Ministries, The Board of Higher Education and Ministry, The United Methodist Church, October 1974, pp. 63, 65.

[10]For example, in 1945, consider the number of full-time military chaplains alongside the civilian chaplains endorsed:

	Military Chaplains	Civilian Chaplains	Total
1945			
1955	445	108 + 86	639
1965	492	179	671
1975	434	229	663

However these issues might be resolved in the future, two observations are pertinent to the question of collegiality: 1) collegiality is important to keep clergy in mutual affect with one another and constantly in touch with the Christian community,[11] and 2) the overall effectiveness of the division in establishing collegiality with chaplain pastors which has kept them from being "loners." It has prevented an absolute cleavage between local church clergy and the chaplains. The division's success in this regard makes it possible for serious persons in the church to speak frankly about the estrangement and to take steps to try to avoid a complete separation.

2. Problems in a Relation Through the Division of Chaplains and Related Ministries

The chaplain story is an impressive account of a rich, courageous, and varied ministry of healing and reconciliation to many ordinary people in remote and sometimes unspectacular situations. The story of the local church is also an impressive

---

[11] A paper by Thomas W. Porter in the early 1970's anticipates many of the conclusions of the present study. The fact of estrangement and the importance of collegiality are stressed in that study also, in praise of mutual support in ministry when it is present, and a wistful if not a sadly resigned longing for it when it is absent. Porter quotes the statement of a psychiatrist which illustrates many aspects of the issue, especially the reluctance of the church to embrace experimental ministries at points of severe human stress.

> "May I inject a sad note, without seeming to complain or elicit sympathy. The very, very saddest experience of my whole life, which is my ministry, has been the repeated rejections of my ministry. Again and again I had hoped that there would be some way in which I could work with the church . . . in some capacity . . . or perhaps teach in the area of Pastoral Care . . . or as a minister of counseling in some large church that would be interested, but no. It is very strange but then again it is not so strange. The church, especially the old guard, do not trust psychiatry, which I know from experience to be closer to the heart of Christ's ministry than anything else I've done. Why cannot the church accept the fact that the extra training . . . is but an extension of the ministry of Christ? And I cannot even be identified with His ministry! That's why I have to work in a mental hospital to do his work (pp. 24, 25).

Thomas W. Porter, "Pastor-Workers and Minister-Workers: A Resource Paper on Ministers Who are Employed Outside the Institutional Church." Prepared for the Worker-Priest Task Force of the National Division of the Board of Missions, The United Methodist Church, undated (probably 1970 or 1971).

account of communal, organized, and visible embodiments of the powers of faith, hope, and love in victory over the forces of destructiveness, competitiveness, evil, and death in the present age. The impossible task given to the Division of Chaplains and Related Ministries is to relate the complex richness of chaplain ministry to that of *local church* ministry in mutual understanding and support within the comprehensive life of The United Methodist Church.

In spite of the exemplary effectiveness of the division in sustaining understanding, support, advocacy, and collegiality of chaplain ministry on behalf of the church, there are two general and three specific problems the division faces in this continuing function. The first general problem is the advanced erosion of confidence between chaplain and local church clergy. One of the effects of forces of change and challenge to the church is the necessity to focus on particular situations to help people stay afloat from day to day. This has put immense pressures on the clergy to assist persons in resolving their individual, family, economic, psychological, and spiritual problems. At the same time they must hold their own lives and families together. These pressures have almost forced a "lifeboat" or "survival" orientation within the church. This makes it more difficult to sustain the vision of the Kingdom of God with its power and grace to foster life and hope and to fortify persons by God's love to deal with these threatening events without cynicism and without despair. The tide of recent events has hit chaplain and local church clergy alike, tempting them toward a provincial sense of the meaning of their own ministry.

Within this situation of shared impoverishment, it is not reasonable to expect the division to interpret the full range of chaplain ministry to that of local church ministry or local church ministry to chaplains. It is difficult to incarnate the fullness of Christian ministry in such a way as to neutralize the accumulated effects of the estrangement and to enable the estranged parties to take steps toward finding their way back to each other. The administrative, economic, and spiritual power entrusted to the DCRM by the church is simply inadequate to accomplish what is needed. The division has been able to keep chaplains related to the church, but cannot, by itself, move in the other direction and relate the church to the chaplains.

Something only a little short of an Administrative Reformation is necessary for that.

It is hardly fair to expect the division to generate a combination of theological, ethical, organizational, and sociological power which would stimulate intensive self-critical, reforming, and renewing activity within the church at large. Administrative errors in United Methodism have contributed to the present emergency. Yet the present state of the suspicion and estrangement is such a mixture of administrative and theological/religious factors that the situation is now beyond an administrative solution. That is the case for the whole church in spite of the fact that the division is the most promising vehicle historically and logically for such a task if an administrative solution were possible.

The second general difficulty the division faces in bringing the church and the chaplains back together is directly related to the first. If the renewal of collegiality between chaplains and local church clergy is not possible through administrative reform (such as making the chaplains more accountable to their annual conferences), the problem passes into the realm of the theological/religious. What is at issue now for The United Methodist Church is the fullness of the meaning of Christian ministry. How can the administrative, financial, political, ethical, and religious power and authority of the church be most constructively focused to sustain a total and broad ministry? That issue is one for the entire church, not simply or primarily for the DCRM.

The meaning of Christian ministry in the world today is as much at issue in local church ministry as it is in chaplain ministry. The division is affected by this situation even if the solution to the problem is beyond its power and authority. The primary importance of a theological/religious vision of Christian ministry has become clear in the course of this study. But that is a problem for the whole church and will be discussed in the following chapter.

There are three concrete problems in the present operation of the division which must be faced.

a) Lack of Appointive Power.

One of the persistent complaints of chaplains is the limited value of the division in helping them move from one form of chaplaincy to another, or from a chaplain ministry to a local church ministry. There are clergy who want to enter some form of chaplain ministry but whose bishops do not concur. There are also chaplains who wish to be assigned to a local church, but, again, without the bishop's concurrence. The appointive power of the church is located in the bishops who preside over annual conferences. The division serves in an *advisory function* to monitor the need for chaplains in church or secular agencies and to endorse clergy who are competent for those special ministries. Beyond that, the division is given an advocacy role which includes constant communication with "the various professional and certifying agencies" and helping to facilitate, as an agent of the chaplains, "the transition in and out of extension ministries.[12]

There are wide differences in competencies for special ministries and there are certainly matchings which do not work. The division functions between the agencies which desire chaplains and the church, as well as between bishops and the individual chaplains. Some bishops and conferences are more positive about special ministries than others.

At the moment the division has power because it is required to endorse persons for special ministry. Beyond that, the power of the division is that of persuasion with the bishops, with religious and secular agencies, and with individual chaplains. This is probably as it should be. The lack of appointive power is a limiting factor, especially in new and difficult ventures, and it puts pressure on the competence and time of the staff of the division to engage extensively in "presuasion." This is especially true given the wide difference among bishops, agencies, and chaplains.

b) The Variety of "Related" Ministries.

A more formidable difficulty for the Division is how to relate to the various kinds of specialist ministries that are now in the inclusive category of "Appointments Beyond the Local Church," but have not traditionally entailed an endorsement from the DCRM. The more obvious persons in this category are chaplains to colleges and universities, appointees to boards and agencies of the church,

---

[12]*The Book of Discipline* 1980, par. 1610 c and f, pp. 506, 507.

district superintendents and bishops, and appointees to faculty and administrative positions in church-related or nonchurch-related educational institutions.

Even with persons previously endorsed by the division such as pastoral counselors, hospital chaplains, jail and prison chaplains, and chaplains to industry, questions have been raised as to the meaning of endorsement by the division in relation to the technical competence required in the position.

The most acute questions arise in those ministries in which professional skills are certified by professional agencies and societies, and for which ordination may not be required. In those cases, ordination by a church may be desirable and, from the perspective of the chaplain, quite important to how a person understands that work. But in various kinds of teaching, administrative work, and counseling, ordination would not be a requirement. In some instances, it might even be a drawback.

The wide range of appointments beyond the local church may constitute a problem for the division if the division were asked to extend its various functions to cover all ministries except those appointed to the local churches in the conference. The DCRM has done much to overcome the estrangement between the local church clergy and all other clergy in the church. But there would be serious problems in maintaining unity, coherence, focus, and effectiveness if the division were asked to include all appointments beyond the local church under its mandate.

c) Diversity and Unity.

As appointments other than to local churches become more specialized and require higher and more narrowly focused competence and education, the work of the division becomes even more demanding. It is obviously impossible for the division to have representatives of all specialist ministries on its staff. Even if that were possible, their unity and collegiality as ministers of the grace of God would not be assured.

It is the peculiar responsibility of the division to "understand" all specialist ministries and to interpret them to the church. At the same time, the staff of the division must understand how the ordained ministry of the church is related to these often very special situations in specific ways. The staff is asked to live between the gathered, confessing church and people caught in an environment of peculiar stress, threat, or jeopardy, without letting go of either side. There may be no more exciting a place to be! The problem of maintaining diversity and unity at the same time is not a simple one. The division must sustain a relation *to* the church and to the chaplains and *between* the church and the chaplains.

D. The Way Ahead

There probably was never a time when it was enough to seek the religious conversion of individuals and to rest assured that those persons would inevitably create a just and fair social order in this world. One sure way to miss the meaning of the Christian imperative is to emphasize simple answers to increasingly complex problems and to neglect addressing the destructive forces over which the individual has little power. The picture that emerges from the reports of chaplains is that of acute human brokenness on the one hand, and of the significance of the presence of God's love in Christ to and for all persons on the other hand. It is increasingly clear, however, that God's love must be embodied in institutions and structures if it is to be tangible and visible for large numbers of people who have no connection or relation to the church.[13]

The present study has shown convincingly that the basic problem in Christian ministry in The United Methodist Church today is theological/religious not administrative/structural. Without denying that, however, we must recognize that no theological recovery is possible apart from structural form. Although there is no administrative solution to a predominantly theological problem, an administrative, structural form may inhibit or abet the theological solution. Paul's vision of the oneness and wholeness of the church in the body of Christ, with many parts and functions, all held together by one spirit, is a model especially appropriate to the restoration of a constructive confidence among many separated parts of the

---

[13]This is in addition to those who even within the life of the church have not been able to participate in the ultimacy of God's love and Kingdom.

church. There is no life in a part separated from the body, and there is no body unless there are parts with different functions.

> God himself has put our bodies together in such a way as to give greater honor to those parts that lack it. And so there is no division in the body, but all its different parts have the same concern for one another. If one part of the body suffers, all the other parts suffer with it; if one part is praised, all the other parts share its happiness. All of you, then, are Christ's body, and each one is a part of it. (I Corinthians 12:24-27)

The model of an organic and corporate body of many parts places Christ at the center (heart) and subordinates all members (in their various functions) to the presence of Christ. Beyond that, the relation is mutual and supportive so that no member carries the whole of ministry. This means that the only way the fullness of the gospel of Christ can be carried is through upholding the ministry of others. The relation is mutual in that there is reciprocal care, listening, dependence, support, knowledge, and love. To despise any true ministry in Christ's name is to undercut one's own, because the wholeness of the gospel is carried only by the wholeness of the corporate community.

Applying this model to the estrangement between chaplain and local church clergy in The United Methodist Church, the following strategy offers promise for the future.

1. The positive functions performed by the annual conferences and by the DCRM are both important and non-interchangeable. The strengthening of these agencies and their increasing cooperation will promote the recovery of a rich vision of ministry that will temper the narcissistic tendency to regard one's own particular ministry as the totality of Christian ministry. Efforts of the annual conferences and of the division to establish a more positive relation in understanding and work are promising and must be extended.

2. Given the central place of a bishop in Methodist Church order and the limits to the numbers and kinds of ministry that one bishop can comprehend and oversee, some way must be found to relate a bishop as "pastor of pastors" to all persons in all the forms of ordained ministry in the church. The Methodist system places the center of power, understanding, and care in the person and

function of the bishop. There are ways to provide the bishop with accurate information about different forms of ministry and about individual chaplains, but there is no way to separate the functions of power, understanding, and care within the office of bishop or to delegate one or more of those powers to agencies or committees.

For example, it is not realistic to expect the division to convey understanding and care to chaplains on behalf of the church without the dimension of power. It is equally unrealistic to expect the annual conference to exercise power and/or care on behalf of the church without the dimension of understanding. That is because these functions are indivisible in the church.

The most acute problem in the present arrangement is the fragmented and limited relation between the church and the chaplains. In United Methodist order, no deputies, however good, can relate the heart of the church to the heart of the chaplain in such a way that power, understanding, and care and all other qualities of the gospel are communicated. The only way there can be institutional reconciliation is for the church to reintegrate chaplain ministry into the wholeness of its life. An expanded vision of ministry is needed that includes all ministers of the gospel and relates them to each other in mutual interdependence.

Reconciliation and reintegration may require some form of special relationship between a bishop and all persons in extension ministries. That might be done by creating three or four non-geographical conferences: a chaplain's conference, a missionary conference, a teacher's conference, and so on. It is theoretically possible to add these different categories of clergy to the jurisdictions of present Episcopal areas.

Non-geographic conferences would have the advantage of Episcopal appointments. Bishops would be present and represent the whole church. The care and nurture of pastors would be tailored to meet the needs of clergy engaged in special ministries. Such an arrangement would not interfere with the effective work of annual conferences in relation to appointees beyond the local church or of the DCRM, but could augment them. It would enable the church to address afresh the questions of clerical votes at annual conference and of the obligation of the annual conference to provide a stipend and an appointment to every member in good and full standing.[14]

This is one way in which the church and the chaplains might find their way back to one another. At the least, this arrangement would remove much of the stigma of second-class ministry and place accountability and compassion within a structure of interdependence and collegiality in the mutual effort to bring to fullness all expressions of the gospel of Christ.

---

[14]It would relieve pressures on the annual conferences if membership in these special conferences did not necessarily entail the responsibility of the church to guarantee a position and a stipend to every member. That would seem to make sense especially in the chaplains' conference and the teachers' conference where the professional requirements beyond ordination almost inevitably require individual negotiations.

VI. Theological Foundations of Christian Ministry

"Today, . . . many theologians and religious leaders are still trying to accommodate religion to the secular city, where *its only viable future appeal may be in offering a way to transcend such programmed conformity.*"[1]

"In the capitalist world in the past forty years, absolutely *nothing* new has been discovered in the political or economic sphere—neither the reorganization of society, nor the incarnation of Christian values, nor the better utilization of science, nor progess toward peace: *nothing.*"[2]

"The tasks that face us now are those of renewal and rebirth. If either dimension of the precarious balance that constitutes our country—individual freedom and variety on the one hand and communal cooperation and unity on the other—is undermined much further, the Union will exist in name only. By interpreting the broad framework of existence into which God casts our lives; by stressing man's need for and God's relation to love, justice, and freedom; and by underscoring the theme that death, evil, and negation are not the final scenes in life's drama, American theology might open renewal, promise, and national rebirth."[3]

"To affirm God is to affirm that finally, in spite of overwhelming evidence to the contrary, our struggles for personal, institutional, and historical just and loving self-transcendence in this place with these problems at this time is not in vain. For the final power with which we all must deal is in fact the hard and uncompromising reality of love."[4]

---

[1]Frederick Sontag and John K. Roth, *The American Religious Experience* (New York, 1972), p. 316.

[2]Jacques Ellul, "Lech Walesa and the Social Force of Christianity" *Katallagete,* Summer 1982, Supplement, p. 8.

[3]Sontag and Roth, *op. cit.,* p. 341.

[4]David Tracy, "On Galatians 3:28" *Criterion,* 16 (1977), No. 3, p. 11.

In earlier chapters we examined what Robert Bellah has described as the third great crisis in American history. It is the most acute crisis for the church and for Christian ministry in American history as well. The second great crisis described by Bellah occurred during the period of the Civil War. In retrospect, the struggle of the 1860's has to be seen, despite its agony, as a contained, limited, "civil," pre-modern, nontechnological war. By contrast the stakes have escalated dramatically for us today and the struggle has taken on the unlimited and total dimension of what Martin Buber called the final struggle between the *homo humanus* and the *homo contra-humanus*.[5] We need only think of a few of the issues that threaten our culture today to realize the array of "principalities and powers" with which we contend. Consider the increased numbers of teenage pregnancies and suicides, increasing cynicism about the prospect of justice, unwillingness to limit personal pleasure for the sake of the general welfare, child abuse, and the astounding evidence that fear has replaced confidence in the imaginations of many children.

Ecologically, it is a struggle between a "life-world" and a "death-world." Sociologically-economically, it is a struggle between community and a wilderness in which persons are continually isolated and threatened. Psychologically, it is a struggle between affective/compassionate inter-human bonding and defensive/aggressive self-centeredness. Ethically, it is a struggle between structures of creative justice which offer opportunity to all and structures of injustice which foment competitiveness of all against all. Religiously, it is the struggle between Gog and Magog[6] between God's Kingdom and the Kingdom of demonic powers.

The overarching nature of the contemporary crisis embraces citizenship *and* religion, patriotism *and* faith, but in a way far more complex than that conveyed by traditional understandings of the chosenness of the United States to "Manifest Destiny" under God's

---

[5]Martin Buber, in an impressive speech in Frankfurt, Germany, on the occasion of his receiving the Peace Prize of the German Book Trade, "Genuine Dialogue and the Possibilities of Peace." Buber, *Pointing the Way* (New York, 1957), pp. 232-239.

[6]Gog and Magog is the title of a Chronicle of the struggle between good and evil during the Napoleonic Wars. The title is taken from a pre-Messianic struggle discussed in Ezekiel 38 and 39.

providence which have produced various forms of American arrogance and claims to righteousness. The issue is no longer that of a nation half-free and half-slave, nor even of a nation half-prosperous and half-impoverished. Now the issue centers on true and false patriotism, true and false religion, with the contest waged in the universal human arena as to what political and religious power most fully protects and promotes human fulfillment and salvation. Strikingly new problems in human life pose critical questions for political and religious understanding today.

Our times are marked by universal and radical challenges to moral integrity and human survival that traditional Christian attitudes are either unaware of or impotent to challenge or meet. It is probably no exaggeration to say that the Holocaust, Hiroshima, the sexual revolution, and changes in religious understanding represent a crucial turning point in the history of Christendom if not in the entire history of the human family. Until the Holocaust, it was unthinkable that a human society would devote the resources of the state to destroy a cultural group simply because of race.[7] Until Hiroshima people did not even think about the possibility of a splitting of the atom with such destructive force that it would incinerate a city of 100,000 people in fifteen seconds and release radiation that would have effects on the life-world of all persons on the earth. Until the sexual revolution, only a small minority was free to acknowledge the primacy of pleasure in both male and female sexuality and to separate sexual pleasure from the responsibilities of procreation. Until the latter half of the twentieth century, it did not seem possible to Christians to be inclusive in their affections; to affirm rather than to look condescendingly upon other religions, especially Judaism; to acknowledge the role of the church in the crusades and Inquisition, slavery, the subjugation of Jews and women, and in an easy accommodation to political and economic power.

If our world is what Bonhoeffer called the "world come of age,"

---

[7]"The passing of time has made it increasingly evident that a hitherto unbreachable moral and political barrier in the history of western civilization was successfully overcome by the Nazis in World War II and that henceforth the systematic, bureaucratically administered extermination of millions of citizens or subject peoples will forever be one of the capacities and temptations of government." Rubenstein, *The Cunning of History* (New York 1975), p. 2.

the price of human adulthood is appallingly high. Richard Rubenstein estimates that a hundred million persons have been killed in the last century through war.[8] Ours is a century of unprecendented suffering and human cruelty with survivalist pressures isolating increasing numbers of persons from primal human bonding. We have cheapened the quality of life by restricting our understanding of human success to achieving wealth and power.

Most of the remedies offered for our present dilemma, including those offered by religion, are too simplistic and single-issue oriented to have any significant effect on the complex interrelation of factors in our present situation. Some exhort us to be more caring, reinstitute prayer in public schools, outlaw homosexuality, build more nuclear weapons, be harder on criminals, accept Christ as our personal savior, prohibit abortion, be less lazy, and thereby restore integrity and honor to our individual and corporate lives. Perhaps certain aspects of our lives would be improved if some of these bits of advice were followed. But the problems confronting humanity today are so systemic, structural, and general that they seem to be unaffected and unchanged by determined efforts of individuals and small groups. The pathos of even those modest gains in oneself, one's family, or one's religious group, is the denial or responsibility for and the withholding of compassion from those who are destroyed by the forces of contemporary culture: abused children, victims of injustice, those driven to violence by violence, and those humiliated by poverty and rejection. The withholding of compassion from suffering people is often accompanied by their condemnation, as if all their suffering was their own fault. These attitudes of accusation tend to encourage self-righteousness about one's own group, which is an alarming sign of religious insensitivity.[9]

The total effect of various aspects of contemporary culture upon

---

[8] "No century in human history can match the twentieth century in the sheer number of human beings slaughtered as a direct consequence of the political activity of the great states. One estimate of the humanly inflicted deaths of the twentieth century places the total at about one hundred million." Rubenstein, *The Cunning of History*, (New York, 1975), p. 7.

[9] "The Pharisee stood and prayed thus with himself, 'God, I thank thee that I am not like other men, extortioners, unjust, adulterous, or even like this tax collector" (Luke 18:11).

the church is double sided: an unprecendented challenge and an unparalleled opportunity. If the challenge is to be taken as an opportunity there must be extreme care in understanding the situation and in refounding the life of the church on the central convictions of Christian faith and their meaning within the new and complex dilemmas of life today. The recovery of the theological foundations of Christian presence and ministry is crucial not simply to avoid a complete separation of chaplain from local-church clergy and of one church or one religion from another. It is also crucial to avoid a retreat from the "world" by the church in an effort to secure salvation in the "world to come" The primary temptation of the church is to deal superficially with the present crisis of humanity—to "heal the wound of my people lightly," as Jeremiah said (Jeremiah 6:14). We are in danger of overemphasizing a parochial, denominational issue or by adopting a "lifeboat ethics" strategy of "saving" those whom we can while allowing all others to drown.

Chaplains in special ministries are helping focus on the critical aspects of a theological foundation for ministry. The primary question they put to the conventional understanding of Christian ministry is whether what is going on in the churches is related to what God is doing in the whole creation and among all people. That is an inescapable question which the church and all Christian clergy must answer today. It is incumbent upon us, then, to describe as clearly as possible what authentic Christian ministry is. That is a large issue because it defines ministry done by chaplains and local church pastors, by United Methodists and any other clergy in the Christian community.

The cumulative effect of our confidence in progress, God's favor, the superiority of white protestant Christianity, and the chosenness of America, has been to promote an understanding of the suffering of Christ which relieves us from the need to suffer with and for one another. Thus the Christian gospel has become indentified with American prosperity, progress, and law. When this happens, the gospel "saves" people from suffering and becomes the faith of the "haves," those who do not suffer. H. Richard Niebuhr pointed out the irony of this mood of confident, optimistic, evolutionary liberalism in a vivid statement: "A God without wrath brought men without sin into a kingdom without judgment through the ministration of a Christ without a cross."[10]

The tragic consequence of the loss of awareness of judgment, the cross, and suffering is an increasing isolation from the plight of persons whom God loves and for whom God suffers. Niebuhr points us toward a shift in understanding the relation between faith and suffering. Our relation to Christ, rather than exempting us from the suffering of humanity, draws us into participation in Christ's passion for the oppressed. The capacity to "feel" the plight of suffering people thus becomes a sign of genuine Christian presence. Rather than an escape from suffering, love in Christianity is understood as the motivation for the voluntary sharing of the suffering of all people until the Kingdom comes in its fullness.

Christians will not be driven from this world with all of its pain and terror, but neither will they regard the world as it is as holy and good. If it is correct to see the world as broken, and if the threats to human and Christian existence are new in quality and quantity, what may we now hold as Christian theological ground for our life and work?

A. The Central Qualities of Christian Faith

One of the permanent achievements of Biblical scholarship in the last two centuries has been to enable the Biblical writers and texts to speak for themselves against the imposition of dogmatic and cultural interpretations. The results of the more recent scholarship have shown a wider variety of perspectives in the New Testament, a significant influence of Hellenism and Gnosticism upon the New Testament, a marked Pauline influence on the de-Judaization of Christianity, widely different if not contradictory emphases among the New Testament writers, and considerably more awareness of eschatology in the New Testament than had been realized before. Many persons in the church as astute as Frances Schaeffer[11] and as simple as Jerry Falwell,[12] have feared

---

[10]H. Richard Niebuhr, *The Kingdom of God in America* (New York, 1937), p. 193.

[11] Cf. Frances Schaeffer, *Escape from Reason* (Downers Grove, Illinois, 1968) and *The God Who is There* (Downers Grove, Illinois, 1968).

[12] Jerry Falwell, *Listen America* (Garden City, 1980), *Finding Inner Peace and Strength* (Garden City, 1982).

and resisted these efforts. To them such efforts have seemed to place a human standard of scholarship above the authority of the Bible through release from the claim of verbal infallibility. To other people liberation from bondage to literal infallibility has made it possible to take the Bible seriously as a religious document for the first time.

The effect of recent Biblical scholarship has been to remove scriptural support for capital punishment, the institution of slavery, and the subordination of women to men. It has also recovered the eschatological dimension of the New Testament which provides the church with an overall foundation enabling it to assume its tasks and responsibilities in the world while freeing Christians from regarding any social, political, economic, or religious arrangement in this world as being absolute in itself.

Many of us who grew up in Christendom during the early to mid-twentieth century came to think of law, order, obedience to authority, hard work, popularity, prosperity, and personal and social success as ways in which Christ exercised lordship in the world. As a result, it was quite natural to regard agitators, reformers, and deviants from the received view of things as trouble-makers, subversives, and evil. For us the received view of the world was Christendom. Our faith was that the Christian order would prevail against all adversaries, in spite of occasional internal problems which could be solved by education, work, discipline, and punishment.

But for persons growing up in the period after 1945, the world has not been a stable Christian order but a "wilderness" of contradictory threats, pressures, enticements, and intimidations. The world is full of quite specific injustices such as racism, sexism, exploitation, brutality, and violence. More importantly, there is also a pervasive meaninglessness in the created world and in human culture. Camus correctly described the postwar situation when he spoke of the "absurd" as a separation of human expectations from the reality experienced,[13] and urged each person to create meaning

---

[13] "It is a matter of living in that state of the absurd. I know on what it is founded, this mind and this world straining against each other without being able to embrace each other." Camus, *The Myth of Sisyphus*, (New York, 1960), p. 3.

by individual effort.[14] He saw the universe "benignly indifferent" to the cause of humanity. It is no wonder that the contradictions in culture between 1945 and 1980 were overwhelmingly confusing to many, especially to the youth of the period. However, despite differences of interpretation on specific issues, there is an increasing consensus about the fundamental stance of the Christian community today. What might we say about this consensus? What constitutes the primary form and quality of Christian faith?

The discovery of the eschatological orientation of most New Testament writings has yielded a two-fold effect: a) a new emphasis on the absolute Lordship of Christ for the Christian community, liberating Christians from any absolute loyalty to nation, class, race, sex, doctrine, status, business, or denomination; b) a new sense of discipleshp to Christ through affirming the qualities of Jesus' messiahship as the norm for human life both in this world and in the world to come. These two effects merit closer examination.

1. Christ as Absolute Lord

It is always easier to see the higher loyalty to Christ than to nation (or status) in other people and other nations than in our own. From the outside, for example, it appears obvious that the church should have vigorously and consistently opposed Hitler in the name and for the sake of Christ from the beginning. Actually there was an early opposition, precisely on the basis that the Lordship of Christ stood above loyalty to the state.[15]

If we look at our own history we also find events strangely contradictory to any claim to Manifest Destiny or of Christ's Lordship. Several of those were detailed in Chapter II: violations of

---

[14] "Yet I can seize that spirit (of conqueror) only in its historical act, and that is where I make contact with it. Don't assume, however, that I take pleasure in it: opposite the essential contradiction. I establish my lucidity in the midst of what negates it. I exalt man before what crushes him, and my freedom, my revolt, and my passion come together then in that tension, that lucidity, and that vast repetition." Camus, *The Myth of Sisyphus,* (New York, 1969), p. 65.

[15] Cf. the circular letter written by Martin Niemoller on September 21, 1933 and the Bormen Declaration written largely by Karl Barth, on May 31, 1934.

human rights, required prayer in public schools, Vietnam,[16] and Watergate. Yet those, along with mistreatment of native Americans, reluctance to provide refuge for Jews being killed in Nazi Germany, and corruption in the criminal justice system that seems to favor persons of money and power, can be seen as almost righteous when placed alongside the rule of the Nazis. The important point is not whether America is a morally better or worse nation than other nations. What is of crucial importance is the assertion by the church that our highest loyalty is owed to Christ, and that the relation to Christ and his Kingdom establishes the primal qualities of love, justice, and human fulfillment which become the criteria by which a policy, action, law, or a nation are to be judged. In the religiously pluralistic situation in the United States, the propitious way to serve the state as Christians is not to attempt to baptize the law, the government, the police and military forces by rhetorically claiming a Christian nation, but rather to criticize the policies of the state on the basis of a Christian vision of righteousness and peace. Such criticism would at least remove the temptation to identify the state with the Kingdom of God. It would enable citizens to show their patriotism precisely by *not* attributing righteousness automatically to the actions of any state. Further, without destroying the influence of church and state on one another, such criticism would free the citizenry from expecting the state to be absolute or to provide the total meaning of their life and death.

However Christ is understood, as Logos (John 1:1-18), as ransom (Matthew 20:28, Mark 10:45), as Lord (Ephesians 4:5), as Messiah (John 4:26), or as God, the Christian community understands the pivotal and decisive center of all relations between God and the creation to be in and through Jesus as the Christ. The first effect of that confession is to remove all other persons, institutions, laws, traditions, and loyalties from being final or absolute in themselves. Such a removal does not mean *freedom from loyalty to persons,*

---

[16] As this is being written, experts issued a report about the Vietnam War, indicating that there still seem to be sharp differences about what was tragic about that war. There is, nevertheless, some consolation in the monument honoring those killed in Vietnam that has been dedicated in Washington.

institutions, and so on, but it does mean freedom from *the absoluteness* of those loyalties.

This conviction is foundational for clergy and lay people, whatever the source of their income and whatever framework or social structure they work within. Absolute loyalty to Christ rules out absolute loyalty to denomination or employer. The explicit religious designation and pretension of one or another employer should never be allowed to obscure this foundational fact. The treasure is the gospel, and that treasure stands over all vessels which carry it. It is hardly possible to witness to the absoluteness of the treasure and of the vessel at the same time. The treasure is always a gift of the ultimacy of God's grace and every vessel is appropriately self-effacing in witnessing to and participating in the preciousness of the treasure. Perhaps that is a part of what Emily Dickinson meant in speaking of "Moments of dominion that happen on the Soul and leave it with a Discontent too exquisite to tell."[17]

2. Christ Commands Justice and Love in This World

One of the most puzzling distortions of Christian faith is the bumper sticker: "Christians are not perfect, they are just forgiven." The dominant expectation of the New Testament that the Kingdom of God would come soon, ending the present evil age, caused those writers to emphasize salvation and the coming Kingdom rather than morality in the present age. But the new Testament never separates morality from religious faith. Christian faith is primarily religious not moral, but it does not separate faith from morality. Furthermore, there are passages which suggest either that faith and morality are the same, or that morality is the primary indication of faith. Jesus' parable of the sheep and goats is startlingly Jewish in that regard. "Come, O blessed of my Father, inherit the Kingdom prepared for you from the foundation of the world; for I was hungry and you gave me food, I was thirsty and you gave me drink, I was a stranger and you welcomed me, I was naked and you clothed me, I was in prison and you came to me" (Matthew 25:34-36). The emphasis of other passages is similar.

---

[17] "No. 627," *The Complete Poems of Emily Dickinson,* ed. Thomas H. Johnson (Boston, 1960), p. 309.

"Blessed are the pure in heart" (Matthew 5:8). "Every one then who hears these words of mine and does them will be like a wise person who built a house on the rock" (Matthew 7:24). "Let anyone who is without sin among you be the first to throw a stone at her" (John 8:7). "Finally, brothers and sisters, whatever is true, whatever is honorable, whatever is just, whatever is pure, whatever is lovely, worthy of praise, think about these things" (Philippians 4:8).

Many passages in the Epistle of James stress morality. "Religion that is pure and undefiled before God and the Father is this: to visit orphans and widows in their affliction, and to keep oneself unstained from the world" (James 1:27). "If you really fulfill the royal law, according to the scripture, 'You shall love your neighbor as yourself,' you do well" (James 2:8). "Show me your faith apart from your works, and I by my works will show you my faith" (James 2:18).

The trouble with the bumper sticker is that it separates morality from faith with the inevitable result that compassion and responsibility among human persons become separated from God's grace and forgiveness. Bonhoeffer deplored that separation labeling it "cheap grace" and a serious misunderstanding of Christian faith.[18] There simply is no legitimate way within Christianity to separate forgiveness (redemption) from compassion and responsibility. Even in our times which seem so pervasively evil as to be beyond moral reform, Stephen Tipton can explain the turn by numbers of young people to new religious movements as an effort to "make moral sense of their lives."[19] In the post World War II period, interest in the future Kingdom of God became inseparably related to the responsibility and opportunity for building a more moral society in the present age. The search focused in this period on *integrity*, integrity of both morality and faith as well as of the relation between them. Many persons have made a desperate effort to make moral sense out of life and expressed a fundamental hunger for the old values of honesty, trust, loyalty, and righteousness. Christian theology has responded by emphasizing morality as being as important as faith and the only dependable sign of a viable faith.

---

[18] Dietrich Bonhoeffer, *The Cost of Discipleship*, (New York, 1959), esp. pp. 33-91.

[19] Steven Tipton, *Getting Saved From the Sixties: Moral Meaning in Conversion and Cultural Change.*(Berkeley, 1982), p. 223.

The incredibly destructive power at our finger tips and the pervasive evil in our social and political structures impel us to a new level of moral seriousness. The admonition of the Epistle of James that one should show one's faith by works becomes freshly poignant in the necessity that persons "show their hope and belief by love."[20]

Moral responsibility for the preservation of human dignity and of the created life-world in the present age becomes inseparable from faith and love which are the characteristic signs of the kind of community one "hopes for" in the final Kingdom of God. Morality and faith have never really been separated in Christianity, in spite of different emphases in different cultural situations. Paul has put faith, hope, and love in an inseparable relation under the dominance of love in such a way as to provide part of the vocabulary of Christian literacy. "So faith, hope, love abide, these three; but the greatest of these is love" (I Corinthians 13:13).

The Christian affirms love as the primary quality of God's reign which provides a bridge between this world and the next. It limits the threat of death and gives a sustaining quality to existence in the present turbulent age as well as a unifying norm for all moral responsibility in this world. Again, Paul provides the verbal expression: "And if I deliver my body to be burned, but have not love, I gain nothing" (I Corinthians 13:3). This means that love is inseparable from Christian faith and that love is the criterion by which true faith is distinguished from false faith. Love is the quality by which we are to test the spirits, to see if they come from God (I John 4:1). Nothing can be Christian that does not reflect the gracious and generous love of God for all things and all people. Further, whatever encourages the fulfillment of persons in compassion and righteousness is resonant with God's love.

If we understand salvation as spending an eternity with God in God's Kingdom, we are asked to show the relation of that salvation to the throngs of people struggling to make meaning and moral sense out of present existence. If we understand sin to be all encompassing, corrupting all our motives and deeds, we must still distinguish between "good" sinners and "bad" sinners. If we

---

[20] James 2:18.

understand Christ to be a substitute, taking upon himself the consequences of our abuse of one another in order to satisfy God's justice, we are asked to show how being let out of jail or freed from the consequences of our evil promotes real growth in moral sensitivity, responsibility, and strength. If we understand merit and righteousness to assure the health and prosperity of persons, families, religious groups, and nations, we are asked to manifest God's love and care for all people, old and young, sick and well, good and evil, within the present world of hunger, fear, suspicion, manipulation, and violence.

Perhaps events of the past fifty years have not changed the nature of human needs and hungers so much as they have exposed a lot of sham and pretentious overclaims among self-professed Christians about fairness, love, and faith. If so, it is clear why much of human encouragement and healing are now taking place outside the churches. It is also clear why many persons within the churches are confused, discouraged, unimaginative, fearful, and at the point of burnout. Joy, compassion, and creativity are not likely to be recovered by the clergy without a reappropriation of the good news that remains good news by giving us confidence that nothing can separate us or any other person from the love of God which is in Christ Jesus our Lord, and the conviction that such love is pertinent to every aspect of every situation in which we now live in this family of troubled people.

It appears that our confidence in God and our compassionate identification with persons in distress have become limited, guarded, and protected. In the absence of a foundational and all-encompassing faith and compassion we try to shore up a program here or a few persons there. We have allowed our gratification and joy to rest on the specific and selected emphases of the region, the program, or the denomination, all of which may well be legitimate in their place. Our joy should come from a fundamental confidence in the goodness of the creation, in love as the secret to human happiness and fulfillment, and in the presence of God which gives meaning and hope to all people. Our mutual responsibility to care, to protect, and to help one another is given by the Word of God but also is written by the Creator into the fabric of our nature.

It is understandable that the betrayal of these foundational convictions has occurred. Christian faith has too easily been appropriated to serve the ends of morality, success, status, marriage, church, or nation. The result has been a compromised, if not an idolatrous understanding of God's Holiness on the one hand, and a moralized fear of affect and compassion on the other hand. Given the confusing signals that religious people send to others about what Christian faith entails, the dilemma for many persons today is that they do not see how there is a direct relation between the good news of Christ and the deepest longings of the human heart.

This does not imply that faith removes all tension, conflict, and suffering from life. On the contrary, faith engages the tension. At times faith causes the tension by setting the Christian against persons who abuse others because God's love opposes chaos and undeserved suffering.[21] That is possible because religious faith does not set the head, the heart, and the body against each other. Rather it proclaims and testifies to a love of God which embraces and fulfills human prompting toward morality (goodness), understanding (truth), compassion (love), fairness (justice), openness (hope), generosity (good will), and courage (dignity).

There are several misunderstandings of Christian faith that have become barriers and burdens upon Christian existence. Challenges and questions put by contemporary events invite the Christian community to reassess its life, faith, and work in the search for forms of Christian presence which do not insult peoples' dignity and their intellectual, ethical, and emotional search for human integrity. Within the church there has been a kind of "hardening" of doctrine, morality, and organization which betrays the mystery of God's grace. The words of Edwin Muir seem to speak particularly to our dilemma.

"How could our race betray
The Image, and the Incarnate One unmake
Who chose this form and fashion for our sake?

---

[21] "God wants *men's salvation,* and in it victory over their suffering" (E. Schillebeckx, *Christ,* New York, 1981, p. 730). Cf. the illuminating discussion of suffering, especially undeserved suffering by Schillebeckx, pp. 670-730.

"A Word made flesh is here made word again,
A word made word in flourish and arrogant crook.
See there King Calvin with his iron pen,
And God's three angry letters in a book,
And there the logical hook
Of which the Mystery is impaled and bent
Into an ideological instrument."[22]

Let us examine some of these "accepted absolutes" in the received understanding of Christian faith and seek viable alternatives within the Mystery of the Incarnate Word of which Muir speaks.

B. Changed Forms of Christian Presence

The cultural situation does not create the gospel any more than the desire for food or integrity creates them. The church squanders its peculiar moral and religious qualities if it neglects them and is content to mirror the world. Changes in culture have presented Christian faith with new challenges and forced a shift in emphasis within the Christian community. In most cases these pressures have not broken the continuity with the early church, but have evoked restatements of the meaning of Christianity. The restatement was essential to retain the liveliness and pertinence of faith to the actual lives and problems of people, yet every restatement entailed a risk of compromise or distortion.

We have suggested how the last thirty-five years in the United States have confronted Christian faith with challenges of unprecedented dimensions. In Chapter II we examined the cumulative turbulence represented by a host of movements and domestic and foreign events, and found very unclear signals to conscientious persons as to where the primary interests of morality and the Kingdom of God lay. Earlier in this chapter we looked in a more general way at the significance of events in the last half-century. The Holocaust, the nuclear threat, the sexual revolution, and the loss of shared religious/moral imperatives present humanity in general,

---

[22] Edwin Muir, "The Incarnate One," *Collected Poems* (New York, 1965), p. 228.

and Christianity in particular, with issues that traditional Christianity has never had to face.

The comprehensiveness of the shift is suggested by the fact that in all these matters humanity is now faced not so much with the inescapable judgment of God as with the inescapable and inevitable consequences of human action. In past ages persons understood their lives as finally ordered by a benevolent and providential deity, even when they were perplexed by undeserved and uncomprehended suffering. Victims destroyed in the Holocaust, persons driven to the edge of sanity in Vietnam, children killed by chemical/radiation poison, and older people kept technically alive long after any quality of humanness is present—all these tragedies make confidence in a benevolent and providential deity and in salvation in the next life seem deceptive, if not altogether empty.

Let us consider how this radically changed cultural situation calls for a reformulation of the meaning of several concrete topics: salvation, love, human fulfillment, morality, and citizenship.

1. Salvation

The spectre of possible nuclear destruction does not make the issue of salvation moot, but it certainly changes the form in which salvation is related to holiness and to any kind of human fulfillment. Salvation means "saving," "preserving," or "redeeming." It also means, as Paul Tillich stresses, health, wholeness, and healing.[23] Whichever of these terms one chooses to describe "salvation," one is affirming something that is the opposite of destruction. It would seem that nothing which destroys the creation could in any positive way be related to salvation.

There has, of course, been a strong dualistic eschatology in traditional Christianity which sees the creation as completely destroyed and replaced by a "new creation," and which marks an absolute separation in the next life between heaven and hell, the righteous and the damned.[24] Some aspects of Christian faith, however, move in quite another direction—toward a divine

---

[23] Paul Tillich, *Systematic Theology,* Vol I, pp. 215-18, 241, and Vol. III, pp. 275-282.
[24] Cf. Matthew 25:31-46.

presence to preserve, heal, and redeem the creation.[25] Yet, the dualistic interpretation continues to show remarkable tenacity in part because people fear that any alternative view will entail universal salvation and obscure the difference between good and evil. Even Karl Barth is questioned by persons otherwise strongly influenced by him because his view of the triumph of God's grace suggests that perhaps everybody will be saved.[26] The dualistic view combines contradictory elements. Salvation is seen as a gift of God's grace *and* resentment that God might choose to save all people. Such dualism also compromises the freedom and majesty of God by allowing human sin to neutralize God's presence in this history, giving the created power over the creator.[27] In such a case, salvation comes to mean being saved *from* our created nature, from everything in this existence, and being "saved" *for* an altogether new life in the next world. Thus, grace comes close to destroying what is to be saved.

There is a disturbing resonance between the dualist view and the parody of the military mind in Vietnam: "We have to destroy this village in order to save it," or the claim of parents that they must withhold love from a disobedient child in order to teach the child the difference between good and evil. The moral problem with this view is the contradiction it introduces into the word "salvation," whether one is dealing with human or divine acts. Justifying destruction on the basis of love or grace is an arrogant, if tempting, view. It confuses love with justice and nullifies the peculiar meaning of love as graciousness or benevolence.

Over against the tempting simplicity of the dualistic view, the Christian is called increasingly to feel and share the suffering of broken and abused persons in this world and to show confidence in the Kingdom of God by challenging all aspects of present culture which oppress and demean human life. The Christian affirms God's love for this world which will neither destroy it nor abandon it. Through the rainbow and the promise to Noah, God is committed

---

[25] II Corinthians 2:18, 19; II Corinthians 5:19; Romans 9-11.

[26] Cf. Barth's discussion of Michelangelo's "Last Judgment" in the Sistine Chapel. *Dogmatics in Outline* (New York, 1959), p. 134. Cf. also *The Humanity of God* (Richmond, 196), esp. pp. 60-65.

[27] Martin Buber, "The Two Foci of the Jewish Soul," *Israel and the World* (New York, 1963), pp. 34-40.

never again to destroy the world (See Genesis 8:21-22, 9:8-17). And God is committed to love the creation and all people until the end of time (Matthew 28:16-20, I John 1:7-15). The name of Christ is the name of love and that name is the way to truth and to the Almighty. To be "in Christ" is not to destroy but to participate in God's own work to preserve and to heal and to love all people as long as there is life and breath.

The Christian's rejection of dualism is not a rejection of salvation. It is rather an affirmation of salvation as participation in the qualities of God's righteousness and love that are as valid for this world as for the world to come—for this life as for the life to come. It is the affirmation of ultimate salvation through obedient service to the qualities of God's reign by denying the ultimacy of everything that poisons the creation and demeans people, and by encouraging all people in good will toward true happiness and fulfillment. In a strangely new and challenging situation, salvation becomes pertinent and timely as the assurance that God's redeeming work in Jesus will prevail against all principalities and powers in this world and the next.

2. Love

Paul's hymn to love in I Corinthians places love above faith and hope as the preeminent characteristic of Christian existence. No word in the vocabulary of the Christian is more important. It must also be recognized that no word is more misunderstood than love in present culture. Misunderstandings tend to move toward the extremes of an indulgent and non-discriminating sentimentality on the one hand and, on the other hand, toward a selective, exclusivistic, and altogether conditional understanding. Paul Lehmann has been concerned about traditional understandings of conscience in Christian ethics and has suggested the "conscience must be done over or done in."[28] Broad and contradictory understandings of love indicate a similar need: Christian love must be done over or done in. The term is nothing short of deceptive if it supports either sentimentality or only conditional care about other persons.

---

[28] Paul L. Lehmann, *Ethics in a Christian Context* (New York, 1963), especially pp. 16, 344-367.

Soren Kierkegaard wrote in his *Journal* that however much people understood or agreed with him on other things he had written, he hoped that they had understood that God is love.[29] Yet, to many persons today Christ and the cross are not signs of the presence of God's love to bless "all sorts and conditions" of persons. It was a surprise to the teaching team in a course on the Holocaust in the fall of 1982 at Emory University that Christians in the class were convinced that the cross of Christ was a clear and unambiguous sign of the love and care of God for all people. Jewish students and others in the class saw the cross as a sign of exclusion, bloodshed, holy war, and anti-Semitic contempt. The history of the cross and of the church's ambiguous manifestation of love gives evidence for both points of view. This strongly suggests that it is important for the church to be quite clear about the meaning of love.

The historical problem of the church is that a claim has been made for the unconditional love of God which embraces, sustains, and even saves us without regard to our merit. Yet the church in extreme forms of evangelism has put a clear condition upon one's receiving God's unconditional love—of believing in Jesus Christ as the only way to God's forgiveness, love, and salvation. This attitude has led inevitably to derogatory attitudes toward Judaism and other religions, and to more emphasis on converting persons to Christ than on expressing God's love for them whether or not they believe in Christ. This misplaced emphasis has resulted in three tragic consequences for the church: (a) making belief dominant over the grace of love; (b) selective and restrictive moral bonding between Christians and others; and (c) encouraging anti-Semitism which has separated Christianity from its Jewish roots and fostered unconcern about Judaism if not actual social-political-economic anti-Judaism.

(a) *Conditional and Unconditional Love*

Nothing is more important to the Christian community than honoring and incarnating both the unconditional and the

---

[29] "Only this do I have for sure, this blessed assurance that God is love. Even if I have made a mistake at this or that point: God is still love—this I believe, and he who believes this has not made a mistake." (*Journals and Papers*, X[3] A 98 n.d., 1850, entry 6623 in Hong and Hong edition (London, 1978), Volume VI, p. 318.

conditional dimensions of God's love. Without the unconditional dimension there is no real compassion, grace, and forgiveness. Without the conditional there is no difference between creating and destroying, fairness and unfairness, justice and injustice. Our task is to understand how these are both present in the love of God. Contrary to the contention of Joseph Fletcher that justice and love are the same,[30] they are held together not because they are the same, but because Christian love inevitably includes justice without being restricted to justice. The clue to the relation of love and justice is provided by the insight of David R. Walters in his work on child abuse.[31] The way people are enabled to break the cycle of child abuse is for someone to confirm the abusers, their worth and dignity as persons, without condoning their conduct. That would also seem to be true in relation to many problems such as alcohol or drug abuse, offender rehabilitation, and raising children.

The issue for Christians is not the suspension of conditional judgments about good or evil attitudes and actions, but the quality of the context in which these conditional judgments are made. The central Christian claim is that God's gracious and unconditional love sustains us, makes us responsible, disciplines us, and creates the context within which we are free and responsible for other persons. We inevitably do cowardly, ill-informed, harmful, and evil things to nature, to ourselves, and to others. These do not change the unconditional quality of God's love even though they subject us to God's "No"—God's judgment. God's love does not make everything we do right. On the contrary, God's love makes us more sensitive and caring, and more aware of our evil, in spite of our best intentions. But neither is God's love to us conditional upon our doing what is harmonious with God's will and purpose.

The liberating side of the good news we know in Christ is that God loves us and all people not because of our goodness, but in spite of our evil. The obligating, conditional side of living within this love is to remain loyal to that love in actions of justice and compassion toward all things and persons. In obedience to Christ we witness to the love of God. It makes a real difference in our lives whether we

---

[30] "Love and justice are the same, for justice is love distributed, nothing else." Joseph Fletcher, *Situation Ethics* (Philadelphia, 1966), p. 87. Cf. pp. 87-102.

[31] Cf. Chapter III, p.

accept and internalize the mercy and righteousness, the love and justice of God. This is the conditional part. But nothing we accept or refuse, affirm or deny, changes the unconditional and constant care of God manifest toward us through unchanging love. This is the unconditional and primary part of Christian love. It is the ground of both faith and hope as well as the fundamental confidence of every Christian. The tragic error the church has often made is to reverse this relation and make the gospel into a new law. This happens when we place the conditional over the unconditional, emphasize relatively minor and provincial, civic or social virtues over the crucial and life-giving qualities of unconditional love. The hunger of the heart and the "good news" proclaimed by the church would come much closer together, giving new strength and confidence to all Christian people, if we could recover the proper relation between the unconditional and the conditional dimensions of the love of God.

(b) *Human Bonding*

Martin Niemöller's comment about his conversion to the cause of the Jews under Hitler has often been cited.

> "When they came after the trade unionists I did not protest, for I was not a trade unionist. When they came after the Jews I did not protest, for I was not a Jew. When they came after the Catholics I did not protest, for I was not a Catholic. Then, when they came after me, there was no one left to protest."

The implication of Niemöller's statement extends to the farthest reaches of human isolation and community today. There is mounting evidence that people are responding to economic, social, and political difficulties by a new tribalization based on status and economic, religious, or ethnic identities. We have also seen recent doctrinaire pronouncements about the boat people the unemployed, the politically evil ones (Communists, reformers, and so on), and various racial/cultural or religious groups which function effectively to place others outside the range of human care and sympathy. It may be that we no longer "feel" the plight of the oppressed, the persecuted, the imprisoned, and the human casualties in contemporary culture. Numbers of essays on the new narcissism reinforce such an observation.[32]

A report of a survey of 1500 students contained the disturbing information that students are, in the main, motivated by self-development and survival skills rather than by social causes. One student spoke for many: "I am in the University to acquire skills which I will need in order to survive in the world, and not solve the great problems of society."[33] Another observer who was a consultant in a series of interviews of students reflected:

"In contrast, the applicants of recent years seem to care less, to do less, about the world beyond their immediate boundaries. Few express interest in international issues. Few seem to read the newspapers. And very few seem to contribute to their communities—to take a little time to meet someone else's need. Indeed, many seem to avoid any activity or endeavor that does not lead directly and surely to the next step on that greatly touted path to success. . .

"The fact is that even with all the excuses and reasons I can muster, something troubled me. It is the combination of cautiousness, precluding taking even the slightest risks where ideas and studies are concerned, and a general lack of idealism. It is the chalking up of the outstanding records that are often handed to me in the first minutes of our meeting, as though what is on paper matters more than the person."[34]

But perhaps the most ominous evidence of the evasion of human bonding is the Milgram experiment at Yale University in 1960-1963.[35] This was an experiment on obedience. The purpose of the experiment was to find out how much pain people would inflict on others in obedience to authority before their own feeling and conscience would cause them to revolt against the "authority" and refuse to inflict further pain on other persons.

The experiment was simple. The participant given the role of

---

[32] Cf. especially Christoper Lasch, *The Culture of Narcissism* (New York, 1978), David Bakan, *The Duality of Human Existence* (Boston, 1966), and Peter L. Berger, *Facing Up to Modernity* (New York, 1977), particularly pp. 70-80.

[33] *Chronicle of Higher Education*, Vol. XXIV, No. 6, April 7, 1982, p. 16.

[34] Rhonda M. Gilinsky, "How will We Find the Philosophers in the World of Lawyers and Doctors?" *Chronicle of Higher Education*, Vol. XXIV, No. 24, February 24, 1982, p. 25.

[35] G. Stanley Milgram, *Obedience to Authority* (New York, 1969).

"teacher" would ask the learner the proper pairing of certain words. When the learner answered wrongly the teacher would inflict an electric shock. The shocks gradually increased from 15 up to 450 volts. Although the teacher was subjected to a modest shock of 45 volts before the experiment began, and although screams of pain issued from the learner who was in the next room, a surprising number of "teachers" went all the way up to 450 volts of electric shock on persons who gave wrong answers to questions. They did so simply because an "authority" in a white coat told them they must continue if the experiment was to succeed. Psychiatrists predicted that only one person in a thousand would go to the point of administering 450 volts to another person. Actually twenty-five out of forty of those acting as teachers "went the limit," even though they we told the learner had a heart condition and could hear his agonizing screams until he became silent at around 300 volts.

Many questions can be raised about different aspects of this experiment, but they do not alter the astounding findings that most people allow social and political "roles" to override any bonding they feel with other human beings. This is an acute problem not only because of the individualism in our culture generally, but because much of the doctrinal content of Christianity is received mainly through an intellectual conversion which requires making a distinction between the "saved" and the "unsaved." Often there is no moral and humane bonding with non-Christians. In some cases an intellectual conversion to Christianity is limited by status consideration and never accomplishes a conversion of the affections into a sense of inter-human dependence and solidarity.

Given our present situation it should be impossible to become fully Christian without moving into a relation of mutual dependence characterized by compassion and care for all persons. That kind of participation in God's love is an elemental prerequisite to acknowledging Christ as Lord. But traditionally the procedure has been reversed and an intellectual confession of Christ has been emphasized first. Such was true even for Kierkegaard who made the love of others a *duty*. It is all too clear that mere confession of Christ has not removed the various kinds of "insider-outsider" categorizations of persons. A critical quality of Christian love in our technological, success-oriented culture should be the decisiveness of moral and compassionate bonding with all persons which affirms that what happens to people is the "bottom-line" of all considerations. This human criterion stands in sharp contrast to "status" and "money" as the final measure of the worth of persons. Whoever nurtures moral bonding serves the will of God. Naming Christ as the manifestation of love in the gathered community is important in the life and worship of the church. However, care for others should not be limited to that community and must at times be manifestly partial to those in special affliction or need.

(c) *Anti-Judaism*

It is increasingly apparent that one of the most disastrous faults of Christian history has been the radical separation of Christianity from Judaism and the resulting anti-Semitism and anti-Judaism that Hitler and lesser demonic persons have been able to use for their own purposes. There is no group of people whom Christians have categorized, cursed, and separated from their love in a comparable way. Over the last twenty years, the "crucifixion of the Jews"[36] has begun to move Christians to think about the relation between the earlier crucifixion of Jesus and the modern crucifixion of Jesus' people. Popular thought still moves on the basis of ethnic stereotypes or on an Enlightenment assumption that ethnic identifications are incidental. In either case traditional Christianity has belittled Jews and Judaism. But a group of Christian scholars who know both the latent and manifest anti-Judaism in Christian history has been growing and their efforts to expose and reverse this scandal are beginning to bear fruit.[37]

During the Hitler period there were courageous, self-sacrificial acts of many individual Christians in Europe which saved the lives of many Jews. In Denmark nearly all of the 7000 Danish Jews were saved. But in the rest of Europe and in America the Christian church as an institution was extremely slow to speak for and to defend the Jews. Hitler's caustic remark to Bishop Berning that he was only doing to the Jews what the church had said about them for two centuries has a ring of truth, even though Hitler embraced a hard

---

[36] Franklin G. Littell, *The Crucifixion of the Jews* (New York, 1975).

[37] The work of Franklin G. Littell, Paul van Buren, Roy and Alice Eckardt, Krister Stendahl, Harry James Cargas, Robert McAfee Brown, and John T. Pawlikowski is especially important.

racist definition of the Jew which went far beyond a religious rejection.

An important and urgent agenda for Christians in our day is to make every effort possible to understand and to remove the breach between Jews and Christians within the house of God's people. Such an initiative must be taken by Christians, for Christians can hardly offer hope for reconciliation to humankind generally until the long story of "fratricide" within the family is brought to an end. The recovery by Christians of a Jewish sense of the goodness of the whole creation along with the acceptance of responsibilty to "prepare the way of the Lord" are critically important to the concreteness of the responsibility of the church to be loyal to the love of God for all people.

3. Human Fulfillment

The peculiar value proclaimed by religious faith is holiness or salvation. As we have suggested, that value has traditionally been expressed far too much in terms of an eternal bliss in another world. The emphasis on another world entailed a way of personal morality that assured future salvation but it hardly led to taking seriously the conflicts, contradictions, and structural trivialization of human life in the here and now. As a result, the manifold technical accomplishments of civilization have been accepted with little attention to the way these accomplishments also brought a general demeaning of human life in modern culture. Too often the failures in the realization of human happiness and fulfillment in this world are attributed to sin and little effort is made to raise the level of dignity and opportunity for all persons. What does this have to do with Christian presence in today's world?

There are two kinds of overreaching oppression of people in the world today. One form is imposed on people by a totalitarian system of economic, social, political, and religious control. The other form imposes a leveling conformity to which people submit although they have the freedom and power to reject such a life. In this latter case the failure to use freedom critically and constructively tends to reduce awareness and nurtures insensitivity to evil. It was the righteous conformity of many Americans who could not see the evils of the culture that led many to protest and demonstrate after World War II for human rights, for the self-government of peoples and nations, for genuine relationships of friendship and love, for equal opportunity, and for peace.

These movements have continued in different ways with varying degrees of success. Each focused on particular flaws within the system but stopped short of facing the crisis of confidence in ourselves, our institutions, and in the rightness of our cause. The present crisis of confidence in our culture is pervasive and indicated by a general dullness, boredom, lonesomeness, and unhappiness as much as by the number of suicides, murders, divorces, abortions and addictions to alcohol, drugs, and TV. The one age group whose death-rate has increased in recent years is that of the eighteen to twenty-five-year-old youth. A startling increase in teenage suicides, automobile accidents, and homicide seem to be the main causes of that increase.

Something new is happening in American culture which goes beyond the contradictions and conclusions of the decades immediately after the end of World War II. When the war ended there were no serious doubts about America. On the contrary, as we saw in Chapter I, there was exuberant self-confidence. Even when conflicts arose about prayer in schools, human rights, Vietnam, and Watergate, there was never any fundamental doubt about the future of the United States. I remember a conversation in 1980 with Norman Cousins, long-time editor of the *Saturday Review,* about the stability and strength of the United States. I expressed concern about a new and extremely self-centered mood, a loss of care for the general welfare which seemed to be growing since Watergate. Cousins rebuked me firmly, saying that the strength and future of the American system were assured precisely because of the way in which that crisis in government was handled without a minute's loss in authority and continuity. Cousins was an incisive and steadying voice of conscience for America during a difficult time, and I do not challenge him without pause. But I kept thinking of what might have happened if the tapes, the so-called "smoking gun," had not been made and introduced as testimony against President Nixon's firm claim of executive privilege.

Beyond the issue of Watergate there is mounting evidence of a radically new problem in American culture that affects the task of the Christian church in a dramatic way. Special Prosecutor Leon Jaworski indicated that problem on July 24, 1974:

> " 'What happened this morning,' said the tired old man, 'proved what we teach in schools, it proved what we teach in college, it proved everything we've been trying to get across—that no man is above the Law. . . .'" This case, said Jaworski, would shape what the young of America would think or say or do in this system for all of the next generation. Unless the young people believed, really believed in our institutions, the system simply would not work." [38]

Today a generalized uneasiness in American culture places us in the critical situation of losing confidence in the integrity of our entire enterprise. Our achievements in the recent past include the ability to resist an oppressor (Hitler), to clarify the relation between church and state, to eliminate some violations of human rights, and to come to terms with the national tragedies of Vietnam and Watergate. We have also made progress in strengthening our institutions of government, law, medicine, education, and religion. We have made some headway in cleaning up the air, lakes, and rivers. But while we spent much time and money on these specific projects, we have not noticed how the world has changed. We have expended massive amounts of moral capital on issues of relatively less importance. The priority problems we now face concern the universal quest for human happiness. Despite all of our accomplishments, we are not a confident, joyful, and peaceful people.

Why? What has happened? Basically we have misused most of the opportunities of the post World War II world because we have continued to work for specific goals as if the world had not changed. The euphoria of *pax Americana* after World War II produced an exaggeration of qualities that may be virtuous in moderation but which in the extreme have become bizarre, strident, and unfulfilling vices. Making one's family secure and sparing children some of the struggles of our youth is virtuous, but when the effort leaves no time for conversation, play, and

---

[38] Theodore White, *Breach of Faith* (New York, 1975), p. 6.

communal activites in the family, the result is enslavement to an economic definition of human success that often brings alienation between spouses and between parents and children.

Max Horkheimer refers to this as the "withering away of the human."[39] Emphasizing diligence and achievement, even "dreaming the impossible dream" is virtuous, but if the effort is utopian and without regard for persons who are hurt by our rise to importance and wealth, there is a loss of human affect which cannot be compensated by power and wealth. Caring about one's country and protecting it is a virtue, but devotion to one's country which obscures flaws and prohibits an active effort for the happiness of persons in all nations limits the possibilities of friendship and mutual relationship across national boundaries. Maintaining an adequate police and defense force is important, but basing our relation with one another and with other nations on fear and force is a betrayal of our faith, our history and ourselves. Maintenance of national honor is a virtue, but if that obscures the interdependence of peoples and nations in preserving a life-world of human happiness and peace, then honor becomes dishonor and destroys what it sets out to preserve.

The most important resource for national security is the justice, opportunity, and happiness that the United States offers its citizens. The most important export item we might send other countries may well not be economic or military assistance or threats, but the sharing of our hope for freedom, justice, opportunity, self-determination, and happiness with other people. The inevitable result of loss of confidence among the people of the United States is fear, and fear manifests itself in reliance on weapons, both in international affairs, and by vigilante groups at home. Human happiness cannot rest on fear. Nor can it be equated with economic gain. The number of people who have "made it" but are not happy is evidence of that truth. The gospel entails a claim about trust, compassion, and love as essential to human fulfillment. Christians are not the only ones who know this, but Christians "know" it is such a way that they do not "fear" that it may not be so. Moreover, Christians know the imperative of love in such a way

---

[39] Max Horkheimer, *Critique of Instrumental Reason* (New York, 1974), p. 33.

that no efforts to deny that fact can change the inevitable connection between personal happiness and communal efforts to protect other persons and to provide opportunities for their fulfillment.

Hope for human fulfillment is not utopian, but neither is it unrealistic. Indeed, it is a self-fulfilling disposition in that it offers to others a possibility that they have denied to themselves. Yet the hope is real. In glorifying our nation, in boasting of our achievements, in cultivating our ability to dominate people, and in celebrating our wealth and power, we have surely sought happiness and fulfillment in limited and even in wrong ways. Happiness should instead come from our success as human persons, from relations of mutual respect, trust, and helpfulness with others, from movements toward peace and encouragement to all. Christian presence promotes human fulfillment. That presence challenges all aspects of national life and culture which compromise human fulfillment and demean life.

The challenge and opportunity of the church today may be the same as for Father Delp who wrote from prison before he was executed by the Nazis: "To restore divine order and proclaim God's presence—these have been my vocation, the task to which my life is dedicated."[40]

4. Morality

In contemporary American society, a certain moral confusion has resulted from what Steve Tipson calls the "delegitimation of utilitarian culture," the revelation of serious flaws in all of the institutions of the United States. People of the religious/political Right correctly sense the crisis and the danger to the future of America if this crisis is not met. But the issues on which these groups choose to spend their moral efforts and the tactics they employ obscure the real nature of the crisis in morality. Therefore, the efforts and tactics of the Right betray the forms of morality that are most characteristically Christian and most needful at the moment. In the issues of sexuality, weapons and armaments, and prayer in public schools, these groups take definite and clear-cut positions. They see the

---

[40] *The Prison Meditations of Father Alfred Delp* (New York, 1963), p. 50.

complex issues of sexuality as focusing on the reversal of the 1973 decision of the Supreme Court legalizing abortions. They focus the issue of armaments on the importance of American superiority in nuclear weapons while the issue of the relation of church and state is reduced to the reinstitution of prayer in public schools.

As important as these projects of the Right may be in themselves, they represent an oversimplification of the Christian investment in these matters. Collectively, even if successful, they would not necessarily represent a reversal of the most crucial dimensions of the "demoralization" of American culture today. Abortion is an important moral question, but it should be faced within the context of the stake Christians have in reducing the number of unwanted pregnancies; in providing every child with an environment which encourages the child's health, self-worth, and growth; and providing the woman with an environment supportive of her mental, emotional, and physical health. There are obviously two contexts for abortion-related issues, the public one and the Christian one. That abortion may be allowed in the public domain does not mean that it is a viable moral choice for a Christian or for persons within the Christian community. Abortion is seldom a moral choice within the Christian community, and it is never a "good" choice for anyone. The justification for its availability in the public domain is two-fold: abortion may be the least "bad" choice and no public or private community is willing to take responsibility for a child born from an unwanted pregnancy.

Christian concern about sexuality is much more complex and comprehensive than making abortion illegal, although it certainly includes alarm about the number of abortions and, especially, the number of teenage pregnancies (about one out of seven girls is pregnant by the age of eighteen in the United States). The problem is so acute and so important that it deserves the mature moral wisdom of the Christian community. That wisdom would include a number of things: 1) emphasis upon the naturalness of sexuality within the goodness of creation; 2) frank and open education about the place of sexuality in the meaningful life of the person; 3) seriousness about the decision for coital sexual activity before marriage and the responsibilty to avoid an unwanted pregnancy;

4) appreciation of sexuality for procreation and for human pleasure, tenderness, and mutual affection; 5) a positive orientation toward the future of the human family through the desire for children with the intention to provide them a nurturing environment; and 6) the explicit intention of Christian people to be the kinds of persons they ought to be by living in a community which is faithful to the Lordship of Jesus Christ both within and over against a secular culture and a secular world. It is a strange and confusing over-simplifiation of the Christian's involvement in human sexuality to expend large amounts of moral energy trying to get people to refrain from sexual activity and trying to reverse the Supreme Court decision legalizing abortions. That moral energy could be much more wisely used in providing people an option to secular culture through the life of a Christian community fashioning itself after the breadth and depth of the righteousness and the love of God.[41]

A radically complex issue of compelling importance is that of nuclear armaments. Again, the religious Right wants to be sure of American superiority in nuclear weapons and delivery systems and comes almost to the point of asking God's blessing on our weapons to deliver us from and, if necessary, destroy our enemies (presumed naturally to be God's enemies as well). In spite of serious errors on our part, World War II is probably the last war that can be understood in terms of the forces of light against the forces of darkness. Indeed, the worst horrors of the Nazi program were not actually known to most of us until after the war was over. The real issues of the war probably eluded us because of our limited information and our daily involvement in quite specific tasks.

Winston Churchill suggested the overall significance of the struggle when he said we were engaged in a battle for human civilization. General Eisenhower issued an order after his first visit to a liberated death-camp in Germany requiring all troops to visit the camp. He said: "After seeing this, even if they do not know what we

---

[41] "It also helps us ask the right question for giving direction to our future. For the issue is not whether x or y form of sexual activity is right or wrong, as if such activity could be separated from a whole way of life. Rather such questions are but shorthand ways of asking what kind of people we should be to be capable of supporting the mission of the church." Stanley Hauerwas, *A Community of Character* (Notre Dame, 1981), p. 194.

are fighting for, they will surely know what we have been fighting against."[42]

Our temptation is to continue to think of all warfare between nations in terms of World War II as if we could now fight a limited war with limited weapons and with only local or limited damage to the life world.

All that has changed with the production and use of nuclear weapons. After Hiroshima moral concern has to relate the justification of the use of force to the effects of that force not only on an "enemy," but upon "neutrals," upon ourselves, and upon persons not yet born as well. Now the issue is not how to prevail over an enemy, but how to preserve the whole of creation while, at the same time, maintaining the protection of our citizens against all enemies, foreign and domestic.

In this regard, Christian moral presence does not completely reject the use of police force which may be necessary to protect people from abuse and destruction by others. But the primary concern of the Christian community is to seek to reduce misunderstanding and tensions among people and nations, to reduce on all sides the number of nuclear weapons, to educate all people to understand our common interhuman stake in the preservation of the life-world. We are called to "use the time" to develop direct human contacts across national boundaries that will increase our mutual advantage in avoiding war and, perhaps, discover new positive ground for understanding and peace. Blessing weapons is a bizarre and crude misrepresentation of Christian morality in relation to national security, to solving conflicts between nations, and to living in the Kingdom of God.

Christians know that war only ends war, it does not make peace.

---

[42] Compare the words of Colonel William W. Quinn (7th U.S. Army), introducing a booklet on the Dachau Concentration Camp. "Dachau, 1933-1945 will stand for all time as one of history's most gruesome symbols of inhumanity. There our troops found sights, sounds and stenches horrible beyond belief, cruelties so enormous as to be incomprehensible to the normal mind. DACHAU and death were synonymous. No words or pictures can carry the full impact of these unbelievable scenes but this report presents some of the outstanding facts and photographs in order to emphasize the type of crime which elements of the SS committed thousands of times a day, to remind us of the ghastly capabilities of certain classes of men, to strengthen our determination that they and their work shall vanish from the earth." *DACHAU*, republished by the Center for Research in Social Change, Emory University (Atlanta, Georgia, July 4, 1979), p. 2.

Hence, without eschewing all use of force, the Christian moral presence is realistic about the possibility of the destruction of the life-world and concerned to provide a positive option to the finality of fear, force, and national sovereignty. The Lordship of Christ entails a hope for all people and all nations. Christians are called to create and to cultivate the options of understanding, trust, and peace within and among nations. In spite of excessive preoccupation in many nations with nuclear over-kill, Christians are convinced that salvation involves primarily the understanding and reconciliation of persons *with* others, not the forceful victory of some *over* others.

Several groups of people, including Physicians for Social Responsibility, have become increasingly active in alerting all persons to the threat of nuclear weapons to the human life-world.[43] Debates about the possibility of a "winnable nuclear war" become more abstract as people sense the absolute horror of such a possibility and invest their moral energies to do everything in their power to make that kind of destructiveness unnecessary. In a post-Hiroshima world the Christian community looks beyond national boundaries more than ever as the priority of new efforts at understanding and persuasion is made clearer on the negative side by the threat of nuclear war, and on the positive side by the clear and positive implication of God's love for all people. Christian ministry in our time is inevitably against the absoluteness of the nation state and the *primary dependence* on military power to maintain peace. As the possibility of nuclear destruction comes closer, the importance of a preserving, firm, realistic, persuasive, and mutually beneficial option offered by Christian courage and love becomes more urgent.

The issue of prayer in the public schools is similarly oversimplified by the religious Right except that people seem to be less thoughtful about the matter and more subject to escalated rhetoric such as the claim that the Supreme Court has "taken God out of the schools and put secular humanism in." The complex issue of how eduation

---

[43] See especially "The Churches and the Nuclear Debate," *Anticipation*, November 1977, No. 24, and the continuing debate among American Catholic Bishops on the question reported in an article, "God and the Bomb" in *TIME*, November 29, 1982, Vol. 120, No. 22, pp. 68 ff. Cf. also a statement by United Methodist Bishops in *The Interpreter*, February 1982, p. 21.

can include ethical and religious values while respecting the religious heterogeneity of the American people is obscured by the oversimplified plea for prayer in schools—a plea voiced by people who have not generally taken advantage of the invitation from the Supreme Court in 1962 and 1963 to introduce the study of religion into the curricula of the public schools. Should the study of religion be competently presented, it would at least be possible for a student to reason about religion in relation to his or her reasoning about history, science, and ethics. Prescribed prayer in public schools is fraught with possibility for misunderstanding, denominational abuse, or reduction of prayer to glib generalizations which ultimately reduce all religious faith to insignificance.

The resources of religious faith are certainly important to the morality and values of the American people. That has been particularly vivid in relation to the modern forms of individualism in America that tend more and more to lack altruism, perspective and resources to warrant limiting individual desires for the sake of the common good. From the beginning the vision of America entailed an obligation to God's righteousness as well as a petition for God's favor. Prayer in public schools may all too easily neutralize the depth and character-forming power of religious faith by including only the request for God's favor. And the request for God's favor upon the nation becomes a bland expression of patriotism rather than the demands of God's righteousness and love. Ironically, the introduction of prayer in public schools would actually diminish the possibility of genuine religion by confusing a nondiscriminating patriotism with a relation to God.

Again, the crisis in American morality and education tempts people to seek a quick, clear, and direct solution. The issues of morality and education are too complex and too important than the single focus on the issue of prayer. Religion has a stake in public morality, embracing justice and fairness for all. Religion also has a stake in education, insisting on students' non-prejudicial introduction to all kinds of knowledge and on their freedom to respond to truth. But religion is neither morality nor learning. On the other hand, the intimacy and ultimacy of prayer involves the most fundamental and life-orienting qualities of ones life. Those qualities are best nurtured in voluntary communities that cultivate and transmit foundational meanings of faith, hope, and love. From these communities arise the stability and self-worth of an individual that morality and education presuppose but cannot supply.

Even in a time of increasing numbers of "unchurched" people the temptation to use prayer for the purpose of morality and education should be resisted. The greater interest of Christian faith is to eschew force in the teaching and practice of faith and to nurture a relation with God which will both stimulate and provide a norm for morality and education. Using prayer in such a way as to adulterate the ultimacy of the God relation encourages the acceptance of the prevailing morality and education in a culture as being absolute. When that happens the power of religion to illuminate and enrich morality and education is lost. It is better to persist with ambiguity and lack of unanimity while retaining all of the dimensions of faith, than to achieve a temporary gain and long-term loss by distorting Christian faith by "using" religion to shore up morality and education.

We have seen a similar pattern in the moral issues of sexuality, nuclear warfare, and prayer in public schools. In each case a claim was made for Christian presence that shifted the focus from an almost exclusive emphasis on what is the specifically Christian behavior to a recognition of the complexity of the problems and the overriding responsibility to preserve the life-world and the dignity of all persons in it. While individual Christians may find different answers to these major issues, the radically new situation is bringing all Christians as well as many non-Christians together in a unified recognition of general social/human problems. There is a growing unified insistence upon a morality to keep the life-world healthy, to establish opportunity, justice, and fairness for all persons, and to encourage inter-human cooperation and compassion.

5. Citizenship in the State

Robert Bellah has led a lively discussion of civil religion in the United States. He believes that a revival of civil religion is essential to the success of the American experiment.[44] Many would agree in that the institutions of freedom are not likely to survive unless there is freedom for all; unless there is a sense of right and wrong that informs the consciences of the people quite apart from statute law; and unless there is a positive care for the citizenship of all persons in spite of ethnic, religious, moral, and cultural differences. There is no chance for America if people use the system to get the maximum gain for themselves without regard for others. Perhaps it is not correct to label these qualities of respect for others, citizenship for all, and care for the general welfare as "civil religion." But if that is what "civil religion" entails, the concept of "civil religion" is pressed to the extreme and becomes a form of worship of the state. The idolizing of the state is always a danger. We have seen that the confusion of religion with the success of the nation has often taken place in the main-line churches. Will Herberg's thesis that the "American way of life" had become the religion of America under the labels of Protestant, Catholic, and Jew is a case in point.[45] In Chapter II we saw how the worship services in the White House during Nixon's presidency also encouraged the full identification of religion and nation.

The greater danger in the loss of civil religious values is that there will be no continuing commitment to the general welfare, that religious people will withdraw energy from public concern and center that concern in their own housing, schools, business associations, and social life. The delegitimation of our public

---

[44] "As a first step, I would argue, we must reaffirm the outward or external covenant and that includes the civil religion in its most classical form. The Declaration of Independence, the Bill of Rights, and the Fourteenth Amendment to the Constitution have never been fully implemented. Certainly the words 'with liberty and justice for all' in the Pledge of Allegiance are not factually descriptive. But while I can understand the feeling of a Garrison that such hypocritically employed documents should be rejected, I would follow the course of Weld and insist that they be fulfilled." Robert Bellah, *The Broken Covenant* (New York, 1975), p. 151. Bellah is referring to William Lloyd Garrison and Theodore Dwight Weld, leaders in the antislavery movement in the middle of the 19th Century.

[45] "American religion and American society would seem to be so closely interrelated as to make it virtually impossible to understand either without reference to the other. . . . Americanness today entails religious identification as Protestant, Catholic, or Jew in a way and to a degree quite unprecedented in our history. To be a Protestant, a Catholic, or a Jew are today the alternative ways of being an American." Will Herberg, *Protestant-Catholic-Jew* (Garden City, 1955), pp. 15, 2274.

institutions and federal insistence on non-discrimination in employment, school admissions, and selective service registration have
caused some religious groups to refuse to support the public
institutions of the United States. That trend has now reached
alarming proportions. The Christian community has an obligation to
challenge it.

The absolute separation of religion from the state by religious
enthusiasts is as much a danger as the unification of religion with
the state by political zealots. Without compromising the separation
of church and state the Christian community should recognize the
necessity of a political order for the security and peace of people,
and support and criticize that order *as a political order.* But the
church should not expect the state to be the church. Church and
state are two different kinds of institutions. One functions on
persuasion, conscience, and assent; the other functions on force,
law, and duty. Even so, there is no church that is not beholden to the
state for public order. It is a part of the church's life to exercise
citizenship in the state and to instruct its members in the obligations
of citizenship. While teaching the duties of citizenship, the church
claims a higher law and a higher loyalty than that of the state.

If there is a conflict between the law of the state and Christian
morality, be it about racial segregation, registration for the draft, or
fighting in Vietnam, the Christian is to show the higher loyalty by
submitting to the law of the state and at the same time insisting that
the state is not the highest law. The state can only tell one what one's
duty is and impose punishment for disobedience. But the state
cannot determine what is right either for its subjects or for itself.

In the "Birmingham Jail" episode, Martin Luther King, Jr.
demonstrated the proper relation between the church and the
state. He accepted arrest at the hands of the state because he
violated its law. But he committed that violation in the light of a
higher law. From the perspective of the higher law, the law of the
state was unjust and had to be challenged and changed. King
challenged the justice of the law by submitting to the punishment
imposed by the state. Similarly, all citizens owe the state both
obedience and criticism. In nurturing its constituency in both
obedience and criticism the church is an effective force in
protecting itself from political manipulation and in protecting the

state from religious subversion. Peter Berger states the case well: "I do know that one must not permit the John Birch Society and its ilk to preempt American patriotism. Indeed, there is a political mandate of preventing such preemption."[46] I would only add there is also a *religious* mandate for preventing such preemption.

As moral issues increasingly deal with public and social-economic issues, public law and citizenship become increasingly important. Hitler's success in co-opting the systems of government, justice, economics, and religion in Germany in the 1930's, and the difficulty the Nuremberg Tribunal had in finding a basis in law for the trial of those who brutalized and killed millions of people are of too recent memory to allow indifference to these questions. In our day, Winthrop's vision of a "city upon a hill," a light to all people of the earth, is dimmed by our failures to achieve the promise of America. Dimmed as it may be, the American experiment is still a bright light among the systems of government that prevail in the world today. That light will be more illuminating if persons of religious faith within the United States insist that the state be the state, not a church, and will invest much of their evangelistic energy in moving the state toward securing the freedom and rights of all people.

If America is a "nation with the soul of a church" as Sidney Mead claimed, then some form of commitment to justice and the general welfare is incumbent upon us as a people. Should that affection and commitment be lost, the "American dream" and the "American Spirit" will die. The transition from an assumption of perfection and infallibility to a recognition of pluralism, fallibility, and serious mistakes is troubling and confusing. It is still possible through courage, devotion, political realism, and humility to sustain the dream and thereby to renew hope for the citizens of this nation and of the world. The church is extremely important to that task for it is the vocation of the church to insist that the final criterion of all political forms is the rights, dignity, and quality of life they provide for the people. If political and economic power can be kept in relation to the rights and dignity of the citizen, there is a possibility

---

[46] "On Being an American," in Peter Berger, and Richard J. Newhouse, *Movement and Revolution* (Garden City, 1970), p. 83.

that the plight of "throw-away people" can be changed and that a new kind of national consensus and unity might be found. Robert Bellah appeals wistfully for the realization of such a possibility:

> "The recognition of the broken covenant does not mean to me the rejection of the American past. We are not innocent, we are not the saviors of mankind, and it is well for us to grow up enough to know that. But there have been Americans at every point in our history who have tried to pick up the broken pieces, tried to start again, tried once more to build an ethical society in the light of a transcendent ethical vision. That too is part of our tradition. . . ."[47]

C. The Absolute and the Relative

An indelible impression was made on me during my student days in the late thirties and early forties. I was singing in the choir at a university church where a popular clergyman was guest preacher at a union Thanksgiving service. The minister had listed a number of things for which he was thankful: that he lived in America, was healthy, was happily married, that God had graciously forgiven him and called him into the ministry of The Methodist Church, and so on. Then I was startled as if by a sudden crack of thunder to hear him say: "And I am thankful today that I was born white." Although I knew the cultural significance of that statement and was aware that being white rather than black in the south at that time entailed many privileges, I was deeply disturbed that a revered minister entrusted with the "good news of the gospel" could say such a thing in a sermon.

The preacher was absolutely sincere, but he was also sounding a sour note on the trumpet of the Lord! For years that event has puzzled me. Gradually the realization has come that the preacher had tragically confused a relative cultural difference with an absolute truth. He confused a condition within humanness with humanness itself. Like the Pharisee in Jesus' parable who said "God, I thank thee that I am not like other men. . ." (Luke 18:11), the preacher from my past focused on cultural differences that obscure the more profound sense in which one is thankful that one is

---

[47] Robert Bellah, *The Broken Covenant* (New York, 1975), pp. 141-141.

like other persons in bearing the *imago dei,* in being created to care and trust and love, and in being hurt by the same abuses and healed by the same powers.

During what Bellah calls the second and third great crises in the United States, the church gave ambiguous signals about the dominant interests of the Kingdom of God.[48] Perhaps such ambiguity is inevitable as the religious community seeks to relate the absolute truth of the gospel to the relative events and situations of history. Chaplains as well as parish clergy are always "troubled" because the fit is never tight and precise between the will of God and the problems of justice, violence, meaninglessness, and estrangement in human society. It is easier for us to see now that the interests of the Kingdom of God were carried more clearly by Martin Luther King, Jr., in Birmingham in 1963 than by the clergy who wrote him before he was arrested and jailed.[49] But that does not mean that the clergy's interest in public order was not legitimate, nor that the discerning of God's purpose in that encounter was plain and simple. Difficult decisions about the meaning of Christ's presence within the complexity and ambiguity of life will continue. One can only hope a greater unity will develop to enable us to avoid catastrophic destruction as we deal with compelling social, economic, and political issues.

At the end of the discussion of the crises in America between 1945 and 1980 in Chapter II, we quoted the plaintive reflection of Robert Bellah.

> "But for the last fifteen years or so my attitude toward America has embodied a tension—*odi et amo*—of affirmation and rejection. Of all earthly societies I know that this one is mine and I do not regret it. But I also know through objective observation and personal tragedy that this society is a cruel and bitter one, very far, in fact, from its highest aspirations." [50]

Many clergy and members of the church would say a similar thing about Christian faith. They, too, have a lover's quarrel with the

---

[48] Cf. Chapter II, pp.
[49] Cf. Chapter II, pp.   and Appendix A.
[50] Cf. Chapter II, pp.

church that embodies affirmation and rejection. In May, 1981, some faculty of the Candler School of Theology at Emory University planned a "Pilgrimage Project" to bring several recent graduates back to the campus for a few days reflection on their first years of ministry. Included in the group was Susan Henry-Crowe who had been pastor of rural churches for two years and "textile" churches in South Carolina for three years. She described her ministry as follows:

> "The vision is a vision of the fulfillment of God's creation, in God's time. A vision of what is to be—a just world, a righteous place, a community that seeks to do justice and love kindness (Micah 6:8), a people who turn their swords to plowshares to feed the hungry of the earth, a place, a time in which the meek inherit the earth, the peacemakers and the poor are blessed. And yet we can only see glimpses of the New Age—the fulfillment of creation. Our task is to keep the vision, the dream alive. Our task is to be faithful.

> "Faithfulness is our willingness (even though angry, despairing, and tempted to let go) to wait for the vision. As the writer of Hebrews reminds us, "Faith is the assurance of things hoped for, the conviction of things not seen" (Hebrews 11:1). Laying hold of what I understand to be the vision of God's whole creation helps to keep the dream alive and gives my being in ministry integrity. I am not called to save or redeem the world (that has been done for us). I am called to manifest God's love in me and bear witness to that in a hostile, cruel, unjust, and broken world. This sense of purposefulness has been central in my ability to live, and work, and survive in the parish." [51]

The secret to faithfulness to the vision is to live the difference between the absolute and the relative yet to keep these related. The absolute conviction of the Christian centers on the love of God in Christ present to all that God has made; protecting, coaxing, persuading persons to ground their lives in that love. The relative side of that faith is the expression of God's unconditional love to and within all persons and circumstances. The unconditional love of God in Christ is what supports patience, faithfulness, persistence, courage, praise, joy, and compassion among Christians. That unchangeable love of God (James 1:17-21) is not and cannot be

---

[51] *Ministry and Mission*, Candler School of Theology, Emory University, Volume 6, Number 2, Spring 1981, p. 2.

shaken by any condition in history. In the power of that love the Christian is enabled to identify with the poor and the oppressed whether in Nazi Germany with Dietrich Bonhoeffer or in segregated America with Martin Luther King, Jr. That love enables us to challenge and to change the structures of oppression which stand for a time against God's love but do not finally prevail in the Kingdom of God.

When Jesus appoints the seventy to go to Chorazin and Bethsaida and Capernaum, he tells them: "He who hears you hears me, and he who rejects you rejects him who sent me." When they return from their mission, they are happy to the point of boasting of their success.

> " 'Lord, even the demons are subject to us in your name.' And he said to them, 'I saw Satan fall like lightning from heaven. Behold, I have given you authority to tread upon serpents and scorpions, and over all the power of the enemy; and nothing shall hurt you. Nevertheless do not rejoice in this, that the spirits are subject to you; but rejoice that your names are written in heaven' " (Luke 10:18-20).

In spite of the fact that the Kingdom has not come in fullness and that many faithful ones have indeed been hurt, this passage is a triumphant confirmation of the finality of the power and love of God. The author of Revelation puts it differently: "The kingdom of the world has become the kingdom of our Lord and of his Christ, and he shall reign forever and ever" (Revelation 11:15b). Perhaps, because of the radical dimensions of anguish, suffering, and pain in the world today, one must sing that with less *fortissimo* than Handel suggests for the text in *The Messiah*. But the central conviction holds for the Christian community that nothing can separate us or any others from the love of God in Christ Jesus our Lord (Romans 8:38-40). This is the absolute truth which grounds our lives, which exposes our emptiness and meaninglessness when we substitue something else for that truth. The inescapable love of God in Christ gives us the vocation not only to show this love to the casualties of the culture but to challenge the "principalities and powers" that seek to remove the sacral dimension from human life.

Dame Barbara Ward has described the situation with characteristic clarity, disavowing all kinds of utilitarian manipulation of religion, yet emphasizing the interrelation of religion and citizenship in our time.

> "It is, however, one thing to argue that a recovery of faith in God is necessary as a safeguard of western freedom. It is quite another, to put forward sociological and political and historical facts as the basis for a revival of faith. Such a procedure runs the risk of resembling the hypocrisy of eighteenth-century cynics who argued that religion was good for the poor because it kept them contented. Faith is not a matter of convenience nor even—save indirectly—a matter of sociology. It is a question of conviction and dedication and both spring from one source only—from the belief in God as a fact, as the supreme fact of existence. Faith will not be restored in the west because people believe it to be useful. It will return only when they find it to be true." [52]

For us in the church, in western culture, in the United States, it is the truth of faith that makes it in any way really "useful." It is the truth of faith that opens people and the created world to the grace, freedom, and power, to the ultimacy and absoluteness, of the creating and redeeming God. That is the hard certainty on which all Christian ministry rests. In the general confusion created by the loss of legitimacy by all institutions in our culture, including the church, the truth of faith in the fundamental legitimating reality. That is what Sontag and Roth indicate in their statements introducing this chapter, that "by stressing man's need for and God's relation to love, justice, and freedom; and by underscoring the theme that death, evil, and negation are not the final scenes in life's drama, American theology might open renewal, promise, and national rebirth."[53] Should that renewal penetrate the church as well, the lament of Jacques Ellul might be changed to a rejoicing that, finally, the Christian community has discovered a way to order society toward human community and peace.[54]

---

[52] Barbara Ward, *Faith and Freedom* (Garden City, 1958), p. 267.

[53] Frederick Sontag and John K. Roth, *op. cit.*, p. 341. Cf. p. above.

[54] Cf. Ellul's statement on p. 219 above.

Conclusion

What may we now say about the chaplain story and why it is significant for the church and for American culture?

It is a story of thousands of persons who at considerable risk have affirmed with their lives a commitment to persons in difficult situations, to the United States and to the power of Christian faith.

It is a story of persons who know the flaws and evil in us all but who invite us in our various situations to accept the love of God for us, a love which holds us accountable for our evil but affirms a worth in us that is given by God in spite of our evil.

It is a story of compassion for many who have not shared in the joys of health and prosperity, a compassion expressed not in theoretical detachment but in "being with" those who suffer in such a way as to take their pain seriously and, in spite of that, to confirm the meaning of their lives within the mystery of the love of God.

It is a story of "Christian presence" to both staff and residents in jails and prisons, witnessing to qualities of humaneness, justice, and forgiveness, encouraging those who are incarcerated "for righteousness sake" and offering the possibility of new life to those who are there because of their wrongdoing.

It is the story of clergy who, beyond the rescue of casualties, have challenged "principalities and powers" to make more fair and considerate the laws and institutions that structure our common life.

It is the story of generous care for people with problems and pains, people of different religious orientations as well as those with no religious interest at all. At times chaplains do not understand why they are drawn toward persons in all kinds of compromised and difficult situations, why they are drawn toward the abused, the exposed, the afflicted, the oppressed, and the dying. They sense their work as related to the love of Jesus for all people, but they do not have clear theological and institutional support which sustains them in the name of the church, in the name of Jesus, and in the name of God.

It is a story, especially with military chaplains, of exposure to danger, loneliness, separation from family and friends, and seeming abandonment by the church, in order to share hope, love and faith with those who are ordered to protect the security of the United States in faraway places, whether or not they agree that the mission is important to America.

This is not the only story around, but it is an impressive and important one, with significant implications for the Christian church and for citizenship in the United States.

Implications for the Church

The most significant challenge of the chaplain story to the church is to renew her identity as a Christian community. Without agreeing with everything the chaplains say, the church must consider seriously and deeply how faithfully the church enfleshes the wideness of God's love for all persons in all situations, and empowers this community to spend itself in expressing God's holy righteousness and care that not a single person live and die alone, that not a single person be lost.

This would entail changes for most churches in doctrine, worship, organization and education. In doctrine, the decisive emphasis would be a recovery of an understanding of Christ as among us not to judge the world but to save the world through an inclusive love for all people. The unconditional love of God, the graciousness of God towards all, must dominate the conditional, judgmental and exclusive aspects of love. Hence, justice and righteousness would be both reinforced and transcended but never suspended, by God's holy love for all the creation. The joy of Christian ministry arises from the foundational confidence that God's love for us is not based on our response to that love. That means that all clergy are especially commissioned to keep open new possibilities for persons precisely because God's love is not changed by our acceptance or rejection of it and because God's love is pertinent to every human situation.

In worship, chaplains challenge the church to keep the suffering, the afflicted and the oppressed in mind as they sing hymns of thanksgiving and praise. Even in the sacrament of communion, chaplains ask the church to remember Jesus' prayer, "thy kingdom come," and to keep aware that the kingdom of love and peace has not yet come.

In organization, the church is asked to reassess all of its structures and procedures, insisting that they be subordinated to the presence of Christ to preserve the creation, to establish justice and righteousness, and to promote reconciliation and peace. In particular, chaplains are calling the United Methodist Church to consider whether present church organization is adequate to serve the interests of the Gospel in the world today and to seek new dimensions of collegiality in Christian ministry among all clergy, local church pastors and chaplain pastors.

In education, chaplains are asking the church to relate knowledge of the Bible and central theological convictions to the complex and somewhat insulting pressures of contemporary life. It is essential that persons who call themselves Christian know both what they are and what they are striving to be, and to know how and why that is Christian. It is increasingly important as the culture becomes more secular that education in and by the church nurture Christian affections, dispositions, hopes, and character. That nurture will embrace compassion and conviction, the mark of Christ on one's whole being and the manifestation of the characteristics of that identity in life and work. Numbers of members of the church, sizes of budgets, and organizational efficiency are as "sounding brass and tinkling cymbals" unless membership, resources and organization promote loyalty to the Gospel.

Implications for Citizenship

Reflecting on the earlier crises in American history, the Revolutionary and Civil War periods, we found both ground for hope and cause for concern in facing the post World War II crisis in America. The ground for hope is the relation between religious faith and political action throughout our history, a relation suggested by the revised form of the Pldge of Allegiance, ". . . one nation, under God, with liberty and justice for all." The cause for concern is that this sacral sense of American destiny has so often been interpreted in a self-serving rather than a God-serving way, as justification for dominating other nations and peoples rather than as vocation to lift a light to serve the cause of human rights and dignity among all people.

Two changes in America's self-understanding and two changes in the total life-world affect that concern and that hope. Between 1945 and 1980 the dominant mood of optimism and self-confidence changed almost completely to a mood of uncertainty if not self-doubt. That radical shift was inevitable because of the superficiality of the optimism, the presumption that America had the answer to the problems of all nations. Such unrealistic optimism was bound to be shattered by exposures of flaws within American people and institutions, with citizens pitted against citizens for rights, justice, and honor. The realization of a lost innocence and a lost righteousness left America demoralized, searching for firm ground for confidence in the future of America.

As the loss of innocence began to take its toll, a new individualism, predominantly hedonistic, began to develop. Robert Coles described that as a loss of "shared imperatives" which had previously informed the citizenry, providing a framework holding together the "common good" and individual pursuit of happiness. As long as there are "shared imperatives" which sustain a care for the general welfare, people voluntarily restrain their desires for pleasure and profit for the sake of the greater good of the whole. The erosion of "shared imperatives" is related to the considerable loss of confidence in American institutions and is a change of great importance to the future of the United States.

These two changes have occurred at the same time external events began to present unprecedented challenges to our political, social, and military arrangements. Whether we like it or not, we now live in the nuclear age and the Holocaust age. Together, these two changes place all humanity in a shared life-world which either sustains us all or destroys us all. The Holocaust requires us to use our cultural differences to strengthen our mutual dependence upon respect for all. The nuclear thrust dissolves the finality of national boundaries and national self-interest, requiring people of all nations to find ways of resolving differences through mutual cooperation. The alternative of mutual destruction is absolutely ruled out.

The future of American citizenship is more secure if we as a people do two things. We must recover and nurture a care for the general welfare, a care for liberty, justice, and opportunity for all.

Our institutions will cease to preserve freedom if the sense of the "inalienable rights" of all drops out of the consciousness of the people. That consciousness is both a fundamental premise and a goal which underlies the institutions of freedom. It is that premise which keeps us from being a totalitarian, police state.

If America is to have a future, we must also affirm our institutions and improve them, acknowledging flaws where they exist and seeking to remove them. It is unrealistic to expect the state to be perfect or to be the final authority on what is right or wrong. There is no perfect state, here or elsewhere. All states are imperfect instruments to control violence and assure social arrangements for human happiness. In spite of the serious flaws discussed in Chapter II, there have been impressive strides in America to combine freedom and dignity for all in education, the right to vote, health care, economic opportunity, religion, and cultural enrichment. The task now is to avoid undercutting the American experiment by cynicism and unqualified condemnation. The challenge now is to work in and with our institutions to increase their effectiveness in serving the welfare of all.

Faith and Citizenship

The chaplain story has shown that there are political, social and economic as well as religious aspects to the crisis in the search for meaning among us today. On both the political and religious sides the answer is not to abandon confidence in America or in religious faith, but to raise both to a higher level of maturity. On that level we can be quite frank in the loss of innocence but fundamentally confident that our institutions serve values that are valid and can be changed to serve those values even more fully. Confidence is based not on perfection but on the truth of the ideals and a commitment to improve the instruments through which they are implemented without expecting the instruments to be infallible.

This study has brought us to acknowledge the critical importance to the future of America of a shared commitment to the rights and dignity of all. The irony of that discovery is that the state cannot generate devotion to the ideals upon which that future depends. On the other side, the study has brought us to acknowledge the importance of social, political and economic arrangements to the church if the church's devotion to God's love for all is to be tangible in the realities of daily life. The irony for the church is that the church cannot "govern" the institutions of the total society upon which the expression of God's love and care for all people depends.

It is precisely at this point that the positive relation between church and state is most clear. The state as an institution with the power of force depends on the church (religion) to foster through persuasion a commitment to the liberty, rights, justice and welfare of all persons. The church as an institution of moral power depends on the state to guarantee through government what is implied by ideals which are kept alive by faith.

Benne and Hefner have expressed this relation in an impressive way.

> For Westerners there is no tradition that describes our point better than the Hebrew-Christian strand . . . . The tradition asserts, "I will lift up my life in the quest for achievement and personal fulfillment, but in so doing, I know that I exist for the sake of my whole world, for my land and for all my brothers and sisters. My achievement is nothing if it is not theirs as well. My personhood is nothing if it is not an increase of their wholeness." [1]

On behalf of all the chaplains whose story is in and between these lines, I offer this account of Christian ministry with the hope that it will stimulate the kind of spiritual and political regeneration that is desperately needed in America today. The passage Jesus quoted from Isaiah has poignant meaning for all of us—lay persons, local church pastors, and chaplain pastors alike—who are devoted to Christ and Christ's presence among us.

> The Spirit of the Lord is upon me,
>   because he has anointed me to preach
>   good news to the poor.
> He has sent me to proclaim release to the captives
>   and recovery of sight to the blind,
>   to set at liberty those who are oppressed,
>   to proclaim the acceptable year of the Lord.[2]

---

[1]Robert Benne and Philip Hefner *Defining America* (Philadelphia, 1974), p. 148.
[2]Luke 4:18-19, Revised Standard Version.

Appendix A

The following is a verbatim copy of the public statement addressed to Martin Luther King, Jr., by eight Alabama clergymen, which was answered by the well known "Letter from Birmingham City Jail."

April 12, 1963

We the undersigned clergymen are among those who, in January, issued "An Appeal for Law and Order and Common Sense," in dealing with racial problems in Alabama. We expressed understanding that honest convictions in racial matters could properly be pursued in the courts, but urged that decisions of those courts should in the meantime be peacefully obeyed.

Since that time there has been some evidence of increased forbearance and a willingness to face facts. Responsible citizens have undertaken to work on various problems which cause racial friction and unrest. In Birmingham, recent public events have given indication that we all have opportunity for a new constructive and realistic approach to racial problems.

However, we are now confronted by a series of demonstrations by some of our Negro citizens, directed and led in part by outsiders. We recognize the natural impatience of people who feel that their hopes are slow in being realized. But we are convinced that these demonstrations are unwise and untimely.

We agree rather with certain local Negro leadership which has called for honest and open negotiation of racial issues in our area. And we believe this kind of facing of issues can best be accomplished by citizens of our own metropolitan area, white and Negro, meeting with their knowldge and experience of the local situation. All of us need to face that responsibility and find proper channels for its accomplishment.

Just as we formerly pointed out that "hatred and violence have no sanction in our religious and political traditions," we also point

268

out that such actions that incite to hatred and violence, however technically peaceful those actions may be, have not contributed to the resolution of our local problems. We do not believe that these days of new hope are days when extreme measures are justified in Birmingham.

We commend the community as a whole, and the local news media and law enforcement officials in particular, on the calm manner in which these demonstrations have been handled. We urge the public to continue to show restraint should the demonstrations continue, and the law enforcement officials to remain calm and continue to protect our city from violence.

We further strongly urge our own Negro community to withdraw support from these demonstrations, and to unite locally in working peacefully for a better Birmingham. When rights are consistently denied, a cause should be pressed in the courts and in negotiations among local leaders, and not in the streets. We appeal to both our white and Negro citizenry to observe the principles of law and order and common sense.

Signed by:

C.C.J. Carpenter, D.D., LL.D., Bishop of Alabama

Joseph A. Durick, D.D., Auxiliary Bishop, Diocese of Mobile-Birmingham

Rabbi Milton L. Grafman, Temple Emanu-El, Birmingham, Alabama

Paul Hardin, Bishop of the Alabama-West Florida Conference, United Methodist Church

Nolan B. Harmon, Bishop of the North Alabama Conference, United Methodist Church

George M. Murray, D.D., LL.D., Bishop Coadjutor, Episcopal Diocese of Alabama

Edward V. Ramage, Moderator, Synod of the Alabama Presbyterian Church in the U.S.

Earl Stallings, Pastor, First Baptist Church, Birmingham, Alabama

Appendix B

QUESTIONNAIRE FOR UNITED METHODIST CHAPLAINS SINCE 1945

Name _____ Age _____ Conference _____ Telephone _____

Type of Chaplaincy: Military: Army _____ Navy _____ Air Force _____ Coast Guard _____

Civilian: VA Hospital _____ General Hospital _____ Specialized Hospital _____

Institutional _____ Industrial _____ Other (specify) _____

Full-time Chaplain: From _____ to _____
(Please indicate separate dates if you have served in different types of Chaplaincy.)

Present Status: Active Chaplaincy _____ Retired (if military) _____ Other _____
(If you are not active in the Chaplaincy now, what form of ministry or vocation did you enter immediately after leaving the Chaplaincy?)

	Strong YES	Moderate YES	No Opinion	Moderate NO	Strong NO
1. Were there important changes and developments in the Chaplaincy which you were active?					

If yes what was the nature of those changes?

2. Has the United Methodist Church supported you in your ministry as a Chaplain?

A. Was this support through the Division on Chaplains?

    Was the nature of this support pastoral?

    Was the nature of this support logistical?

    Was the nature of this support educational?

    Was the nature of this support collegial?

B. Was this support through your Annual Conference?

    Was the nature of this support pastoral?

    Was the nature of this support logistical?

    Was the nature of this support educational?

    Was the nature of this support collegial?

3. Did you desire or need support which the United Methodist Church failed to give you?

4. Did the Chaplaincy offer you opportunities for significant Christian ministry?
If yes, indicate the most significant opportunities.

271

	Strong YES	Moderate YES	No Opinion	Moderate NO	Strong NO
5. Are there aspects of the Chaplaincy which you think should be changed? If yes, describe these briefly.	___	___	___	___	___
6. Were there aspects of the Chaplaincy which were compromising or frustrating to your Christian ministry? If yes, indicate briefly what these were.	___	___	___	___	___
7. Was there conflict between your role as minister and your role as representative of your employer (command or management)?	___	___	___	___	___
8. During your active Chaplaincy, did the persons under your pastoral care have personal conflicts or conflicts of conscience? If yes, what were these conflicts about?	___	___	___	___	___
a) Love, sex and marriage	___	___	___	___	___
b) Alcohol and/or drugs	___	___	___	___	___

272

c) Failure to do one's duty, letting others down _____

d) Moral questions about what one is expected to do _____

e) Misrepresenting records, hours, scores, etc. _____

f) Loneliness, abandonment, loss of self-worth _____

g) Problems regarding friendship and respect for others _____

h) Loss of meaning in life and work _____

i) Other: _____ _____

9. During your career as a Chaplain, did you have conflicts of conscience? _____
If yes, indicate briefly the nature of these conflicts.

10. In your judgment, have United Methodist Chaplains overall performed significant Christian ministry since 1945? _____
If yes, indicate outstanding aspects of ministry.

	Strong YES	Moderate YES	No Opinion	Moderate NO	Strong NO
11. Have United Methodist Chaplains overall missed important opportunities for Christian ministry since 1945? If yes, please comment.	—	—	—	—	—
12. Do Chaplains know something about Christian ministry which the United Methodist Church overall should take into account? Is yes, describe briefly.	—	—	—	—	—
13. Would you encourage a talented and promising young clergyperson to consider the Chaplaincy as a form of ministry? If yes, why?	—	—	—	—	—

274

14. If you have written or published articles, logs, journals, sermons, or other papers within or about your ministry as a Chaplain, please list them below.
(We would welcome copies of anything you regard as indicative.)

275